Reconsidering Drugs

Reconsidering Drugs

Mapping Victorian and Modern Drug Discourses

Lawrence Driscoll

palgrave

First published 2000 by
PALGRAVE™
175 Fifth Avenue, New York, N.Y. 10010 and
Houndmills, Basingstoke, Hampshire, England RG21 6XS.
Companies and representatives throughout the world.

PALGRAVE™ is the new global publishing imprint of St. Martin's
Press LLC Scholarly and Reference Division and Palgrave
Publishers Ltd (formerly Macmillan Press Ltd).

ISBN 0-312-22272-6

Library of Congress Cataloging-in-Publication Data
Driscoll, Lawrence Victor.
    Reconsidering drugs : mapping Victorian and modern drug
discourses / Lawrence Driscoll.
        p.   cm.
    Includes bibliographical references and index.
    ISBN 0-312-22272-6
    1. Drug abuse.   2. Drug abuse—History.   3. Drug abuse in
literature.   4. Drugs of abuse.   I. Title.

HV5801.D554   2001
362.29'09—dc21   00–059142

A catalogue record for this book is available from the British Library.

Design by Letra Libre, Inc.

First edition: October 2000
10 9 8 7 6 5 4 3 2 1

Printed in the United States of America.

We must love truth for itself, to such an extent that we do not love it for ourselves but against ourselves. We must ever contradict ourselves; we must always welcome the opposite of our thought and scrutinize what worth this opposite may have.

—*Nietzsche*

Although the most clear-sighted judges of witches and even the witches themselves were convinced the witches were guilty of witchcraft, no guilt in fact existed. So it is with all guilt.

—*Nietzsche*

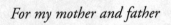

For my mother and father

Contents

Preface

Walter Benjamin has written that "The reader, the thinker . . . are types of illuminati just as much as the opium eater, the dreamer, the ecstatic. And more profane."[1] Accordingly, I would hope that this text will stimulate a process of profane illumination in the reader. Benjamin suggests that *thinking* is "eminently narcotic" and I hope my readers will be prompted to think in such a way as to slip themselves past the guards that usually patrol the borders of our thought.

My hope is that this book will be of use to anyone whose theory or practice comes into contact with drugs. I imagine that it would be of interest to clinicians and psychologists, as well as to sociologists and policymakers in health and government. I would hope that my analyses will open a space for them to reevaluate our accepted theories and practices, and hopefully encourage them to locate new ways of approaching drugs at a time when it is becoming more and more clear that current practices are stagnating. My intention throughout this book is to open up some discursive space for ourselves so that we can construct other discourses about drugs that will not produce the damaging consequences that we are currently experiencing.

I also hope that this book will offer readers of cultural theory, media, and literature a chance to focus on the subject of drugs in such a way as to open up a range of possible readings in other areas of cultural studies. Due to their proximity to drug discourses I hope that the book can provide readers of class, gender, and race with a way to rethink how these frameworks are related to established drug discourses. I believe that the real difficulty with "the drug problem" is that it is not a field of knowledge in motion but is an accepted body of truth around which other discourses simply orbit. It is the unquestioned centrality of this truth that I think needs to be disrupted if we are going to move beyond the current borders of our thought. While this book is by no means exhaustive, I hope that the fissures that I will open can continue to be explored.

Although there are bound to be gaps and omissions in my selection of texts, I have tried to focus on what I see as the discursive foundations of how we shape our knowledge of drugs and their users. I have tried to focus on the discourses that we generate about drugs rather than any particular authors. I have therefore chosen to open up the discussion by working with authors who I felt raise some of the central discursive concerns. Here you will find chapters that orbit around Wilkie Collins, Robert Louis Stevenson, Sigmund Freud, Anna Kavan, William Burroughs, and Ray Shell. I have also drawn on the work of Conan Doyle, Jean Cocteau, Charles Baudelaire, Jean-Jacques Moreau, as well as looking briefly at Aleister Crowley, Kim Wozencraft, Irvine Welsh, and Fitz Hugh Ludlow. Discussions of literary texts are placed alongside analyses of discourses from medical history, sociology, counseling, and psychology, as well as looking at narratives that we use in popular culture, ranging from English antidrug advertising to Hollywood cinema. Finding different ways of talking about drugs is not an easy task, and I have had to choose an eclectic range of texts and discourses because the roots of our drug discourses are far from localized. Discourses that appear in an official psychological report one day will show up in popular culture the next. I have tried to follow the discourse wherever it seemed to lead rather than limit myself or the reader to a restricted area.

In many ways drug discourses seem to have a very good free trade agreement and cross borders and time zones with impunity. Therefore, you will find a discussion of both English and American drug discourses and it may seem that I am conflating the two countries. However, while it was true in the 1960s that English drug policy was radically different from that of the United States, since former president Ronald Reagan and prime minister Margaret Thatcher redrew much of the political map in the 1980s, the drug discourses of both countries have become almost indistinguishable. For example, Avril Taylor's discussion of Scottish women heroin users in chapter six is not meant to be seen as a regional exception, but is meant to stand as an example of how heroin addiction could be read in any Western country. Similarly, I think that readers in England will find that the discussion of William Burroughs will reverberate throughout British culture and is far from restricted to the United States. The trans-Atlantic success of the film *Trainspotting* is proof that when it comes to drugs, the English and the Americans are speaking the same language. Obviously there are local differences, such as the legalization of marijuana in Holland and various policies in Switzerland, and Sweden, but I have tried to examine the roots that hold the bulk of Western antidrug discourses together, rather than looking at the surface variations.

Objections could also be raised by a literary historian that I have moved too quickly across literary time zones. Again, the focus of the book is the construction of our own current drug discourses; for example, I am more interested in what Burroughs can tell *us* about how we treat the concept of control, rather than trying to place Burroughs's comments in relation to the

1950s and the Beat writers of his generation. I have done this with all the literary works in the hope of liberating the voices of the texts from the restrictions of a strict historicism. Similarly, the discussion of Anna Kavan in chapter six is intended to open a discussion of how we could rewrite the structure of our own drug narratives, rather than trying to explain her work in relation to British experimental fiction in the 1940s.

My other omission is any extended discussion of legal drugs. While narratives surrounding alcohol deploy the same logic as our drug narratives, for the sake of space I have had to exclude this discussion, which really deserves a book in itself. Other omissions include extended discussions of LSD, mushrooms, or legal drugs or medicine such as Prozac, simply because these subjects would require more space than is currently possible. The discussion that follows will deal primarily with illegal drugs such as cocaine, crack, heroin, and marijuana. Obviously, the field of drugs is almost beyond the scope of any one writer's areas of expertise, but I hope that I have pointed to several of the core concepts that need to be further dealt with.

Acknowledgments

B y the time this book was going into press I realized that so many people had nudged, prodded, and guided me that without their assistance this book would still be lingering in the backwaters of my mind rather than being in your hands. With that consideration it behooves me to offer my sincerest thanks to those who have given me a whole range of opportunities in which I could complete this book.

I would first like to tip my hat to the University of Southern California, which provided me with generous financial support that gave me the space to focus on my research. This support was obviously the responsibility of people who had faith in my abilities even at moments when I did not. For a large bulk of the support, I would like to hold Dr. Betty Bamberg personally responsible for giving me the wherewithal to keep a roof over my head for many a long summer. Thanks are also due to Penny Von Helmot for continuing to offer me a supportive and encouraging environment and for making my time with Thematic Option a thoroughly memorable experience. I am also indebted to USC for granting me an Oakley Fellowship, which allowed a substantial portion of this manuscript to be completed. I would also like to thank the English Department at USC for supporting me from the very beginning to the end.

I offer my deepest thanks to James Kincaid for providing me with the chance to see my ideas through to completion in a form that has hopefully allowed them to have the effectiveness they deserve. Without his continually refreshing smiles and liberating encouragement, this book would have languished uncontrollably. I would also like to thank Maura Burnett and Amy Reading at Palgrave for having faith in this project from the very start. I must also thank Kristi Long, Donna Cherry, and Rick Delaney for their very perceptive commentary on my work, as well as for taking such painstaking care over the details of the manuscript. A writer is only as strong as his or her editor, and in this case Kristi, Donna, and Rick have shone lights into the murkiest corners of my manuscript, enabling me to move forward even when I thought my way was blocked. For their skills and perceptive comments I remain humbly indebted. The strengths of what you are about to read are due to their skills while the weaknesses are all my own.

I would like to thank many people from USC who helped me along, but particular attention must be drawn to Ronald Gottesman, who provided me with many hours out of his busy schedule to offer priceless guidance and friendship, even in the darkest hours. Much of Ron's assistance went outrageously beyond the call of duty, and for such help I will be ever thankful. Similar genuflecting needs to be carried out in the presence of Tania Modleski, Peter Manning, Jean-Jacques Courtine, and Ross Winterowd for their constant encouragement.

Since 1996 I have had the good fortune to work with a wonderful group of people at Santa Monica College, and it is my pleasure to thank Nina Theiss for giving me a whole range of opportunities. I would also like to thank Joanne Laurence, Gary Todd, David Zehr, Karin Costello, Dianne Englemann, Mario and Ernest Padilla, Hari Vishwanandha, Don Doten, Susan and Gaya Sterr, Gordon Dossett, and Charles Donaldson for creating an unparalleled educational environment that is also warm, supportive, and stimulating. I would also like to thank my students at Santa Monica College for showing me how important it is that we challenge ourselves to think beyond what the culture permits.

A project like this needs not just supporters but also fellow travelers, and I must thank my immediate colleagues who often found themselves in the same boat as myself. I can only hope that I offered as much kindness as I received. Chris Lippard will know what I am talking about, as he has been riding our profession since the beginning, and his love of literature and politics always served to remind me of the responsibilities that we have, not only as scholars and teachers, but also as social beings. His comments on my written work were stellar and he could always be relied upon to tighten up a dangling modifier or two. I would also like to thank Hema Chari for pushing me at a crucial moment in my career, providing me with an opportunity that in my own foolish blindness I did not think was within my reach. A heartfelt thank-you also needs to be extended to Young-Ok An not only for helping me to unravel some of the theoretical knots that I got tied up in, but also for providing me with a sense of perspective when I could no longer see the forest for the trees. My warmest thanks also go out to Danielle Muller for offering herself as an intellectual guinea-pig for my ideas, and also for taking the time to read rough drafts and offer much needed commentary and guidance. I would also be remiss if I did not thank Helen Franks for keeping her eyes and ears open, enabling me to cover a wider field of research than would be possible for one person alone. For his constant friendship and encouragement, thanks are also due to Simon James. Jane Lilienfeld also deserves a special mention for coming out of the blue and pushing me to a level that I could never have attained alone. The opportunities that Jane provided represented a crucial landmark in the course of this project.

Finally, I must thank my mother, my father, and my sister for offering their guidance and support. Without their love this book would never have been started. I would also like to thank Caroline Kenyon at the Metropolitan Police (UK) and Jeff Kirsch at the Ad Council for permission to reproduce some of their anti-drug advertisements.

Introduction

> What is "familiarly known" is not properly known, just for the reason that it is "familiar." When engaged in the process of knowing, it is the commonest form of self-deception, and a deception of other people as well, to assume something to be familiar, and to let it pass on that very account. Knowledge of that sort, with all its talking around it never gets from the spot, but has no idea that this is the case. . . .
>
> —Hegel

The Drug Maze

This book aims to resurrect a number of voices within nineteenth- and twentieth-century culture that have experienced drugs in ways substantially at odds with our own constructions.

We continually keep ourselves out of the equation when we investigate the problem of drugs, assuming that only *they* use drugs, and that *we* have the cure, and are somehow in control. Unfortunately for everyone, drug programs are paid thousands of dollars to ensure the survival of this current discourse. Researchers give publication space to sensible approaches to the problem, the media only reports the success stories, and novels and films that tell this kind of truth about drugs are hailed as honest, powerful, and true images of drug use. All avenues of the discourse are designed only to restate what drugs are, not to rethink the boundaries that produce the concepts in the first place.

When it comes to drugs there is always room for discussion, so long as you agree to talk in a way that is acceptable. However, when we attempt to find alternative positions on the question of drugs it is often very hard to (re)articulate these (admittedly) odd voices so that they can be heard as clearly as the antidrug, or even the prodrug, rhetoric. What you will find in this book is a strange grouping of voices whose comments on drugs will deliberately try to unsettle what it is that we think drugs can and cannot mean in our culture. More importantly, I hope that these voices will open a series of new windows, letting in some fresh air on the subject, which may enable us to configure new ways of thinking about drugs and addiction in the future.

The discursive roundabout of pro- and antidrug logic has been spinning for so long that we no longer realize, as Nietzsche points out, that our "truths are illusions of which one has forgotten that they are illusions."[1] The alternative, and it is the line of inquiry that I will pursue in this book, is suggested by Gilles Deleuze: "You should not try to find whether an idea is just or correct. You should look for a completely different idea, elsewhere, in another area, so that something passes between the two which is neither in one nor the other."[2] It sounds like an overwhelming task, but I think that we can move beyond a whole host of "problems"—from murders in Columbia to crack babies in Chicago—by allowing ourselves to move what drugs can and cannot mean into this other area that Deleuze is suggesting.

How can such a thing be done? I would argue that one way is to change the narratives that we like to tell ourselves about drugs. If drugs are "powerful" and we must "resist" them, why do we not create a narrative in which drugs have no power? We insist on giving drugs all the power in this play, letting it take the central role, allowing it to hog the limelight, as it plays the demonic villain. Instead, why not make it shift scenery, or sweep up the dressing room, or, better yet, keep it on stage but give it a heroic role, or a comic part, or even make drugs into the good guy? This way, the story would not have the same old ending. New endings could be written, and maybe we could even have a new beginning. At the same time, we should turn the spotlight on ourselves for a change. What role do we play? At what moments in the narrative do we cheer? When do we boo, and why? What is driving the perpetuation of this narrative? How does our role in this scenario affect what drugs can and cannot mean? Another strategy would be to refuse to play the game that (we assume) drugs want to play. If they insist on being important, we could call their bluff, ignore them, give them nothing to do, make drugs boring and uninteresting, and while we are at it, shift some of the power that we give drugs onto ourselves.

David Joselit points out that "[i]t is the material unconscious, a set of social conditions that determine what can and cannot be said or what can and cannot be believed at a particular historical moment."[3] I would agree that there are parameters that make certain voices and positions possible in our culture while silencing others. The mistake that we make, however, is in thinking that the range of possible/impossible positions constitutes a field of truths that permits us to operate as we wish and reach our desired goals. Perhaps this network of "truths" actually creates a maze in which we lose ourselves. This would explain why so many well-intentioned ideas about drugs end up unraveling into repressive "lock them up" scenarios, or why we see government after government finding themselves unable to handle drugs effectively. It is too easy to think that we "really" do not wish to see an end to the drug problem; I think we do, but the parameters that we have made available to ourselves are not permitting us to find ways to move forward. Such a position also clarifies why many intelligent and caring people have written books on how to solve the drug problem, only to find in the last instance that they are unable to think through drugs in ways that do not repeat the wrong turns and dead ends that we have traveled before.

Moreover, it becomes apparent that if we proceed with trying to unravel "the drug problem" while the structure of the maze is still in place, we shall (and this is presently the case), get nowhere. By stepping outside the maze to see how it is constructed we shall get a better sense of how to move around inside it. More productively, having stepped outside it and having realized that the maze, in the shape that we have inherited it, does not have a center where we can rest or an exit, we may decide that we do not wish to go back inside. With so many penalties and so little rewards for anyone, the game is no longer worth playing. Having left behind a mode of thinking and speaking about drugs that was failing to do what we wanted (i.e., to stop drugs from being or causing a problem) would mean that future attempts at thinking about drugs would actually stand a chance of being effective. Having reached such a point, as Foucault notes, "it becomes worthwhile to think."[4] If it seems a daunting task to rewrite the landscape of drug discourses, we can be encouraged by the realization that this landscape is already a field in motion. Maybe it does not always move in a direction that is helpful to everyone concerned; nevertheless, the terrain is already wonderfully unstable, which makes our job of moving it so much easier. To paraphrase Foucault, he reminds us not to forget that "[t]here have been, and will be, other distributions of [drug discourses]."[5] For example, one need only compare the map of the Reagan era with the current landscape regarding the legalization of medical marijuana to appreciate how easy the discourses can shift to accommodate positions that were previously, quite literally, unthinkable. Obviously, this remapping of our discourses will create a dilemma for all of us.

Let us begin by assuming that all political viewpoints agree that there is room for improvement when it comes to the drug problem. The more conservative side of the debate tends to want to hold onto the maze of discourses as it currently stands. So, for example, we have the widely held belief that drugs need to be "resisted" and that we must "struggle against" them. If we are to dig new channels for our discourse to flow into, we have to let go of the assumption that this idea of resisting drugs is "natural" and unquestionable. So, if from a conservative position we wish to improve the safety of our children, we will have to abandon the very beliefs that we feel protect them.

We will have to agree that it is our "knowledge" of the situation that prevents us from being really effective, and in order to really be helpful we will have to let go of the beliefs that we cherish about "resisting" drugs in order to make any improvement.

Now, this is not to assume that the Left side of the political spectrum has all the answers and can just sit back while the Right learns its lesson and change how it thinks. The Left is no different in this game than the Right. In part, this is because we have allowed ourselves to construct a discourse about drugs that seems to go beyond political divisions, so that Left and Right agree on what drugs mean, but because the Left also has a strong desire to hold on to their axioms about drugs. For example, Gary Webb's recent critique of CIA involvement in the flooding of South Central Los Angeles with crack cocaine in his book *Dark Alliance,* may attack government corruption but does nothing to move us away from what cocaine may or may not mean. In fact, Webb's narrative requires that crack remain an "evil" pharmaceutical so that those who allowed it to be marketed in Los Angeles can also be scripted as evil. Such a discourse is not an alternative voice outside of the maze that we have constructed—it is part of it. In the generic drug scenario we have black powerful villains doing harm to white neighborhoods who wish to be drug free. In Webb's narrative (which Willowbrook/Watts Congresswoman Maxine Waters refers to as "the truth"), we simply have white powerful villains (the CIA) doing harm to black neighborhoods who wish to be drug free.[6] The unquestioned assumption in both narratives is the meaning of the drugs themselves. In both stories, drugs are assumed to be the real villain, and whoever gets closest to them automatically gets to play the bad guys. As long as the meaning of the drug itself is not questioned, then both stories can run on indefinitely.

Having considered the framework of the antidrug discourses, then surely the prodrug groups would have a different story to tell about drugs. Yet it seems that the prodrug camp also agrees to play by the same rules and validates the "sickness" side of the equation by simply adopting it as an emblem of their rebellion. Drug use then comes to signify a "healthy" active rejection of a "sick" bureaucratic society: prodrug and antidrug slogans simply become interchangeable anagrams of the same logic. An example can be seen in the debate over the role of needle exchange programs, which give clean needles to addicts in return for their old ones. Running the risk of being seen as prodrug, these programs must position themselves not as being interested in drugs *qua* drugs and pleasure, but as operating in the interests of health. Safely positioned on the health/antidrug side of the binary gives them the discursive space that allows them to operate without the suspicion that they might be prodrug. The current framework of drugs thus ensures that we are forced into being suspicious of something like a needle exchange if we feel, like the government, that it is validating the drug user, or worse, if we feel that it occupies a position that is condoning the use of drugs. The legal objection to government funding of needle programs, for example, is that government money cannot be used to buy syringes, that will then be used to inject "illegal" substances. The same rhetorical cul-de-sac emerges in the debate over medical marijuana. The drug can only be permitted into the space of "health" once it has been declassified as a "drug" and reclassified as a "medicine."

What kinds of stories about drugs do we like to tell ourselves? What other stories might be available to us? What other stories could we tell about drugs? What stories seem to fit while others are left silent?

What I wish to do in this book is go back down some of the pathways that have led to where we are now and try to see if there were any turnoffs that we overlooked in our rush to solidify our knowledge. This will entail examining the ways in which we have come to know what is "sensible" and "true" on the subject of drugs, and conversely, how we have come to know what is "unacceptable" and "wrong." In order to do this I need to disturb and disrupt our conventional lines of thought on the subject of drugs. Again, my hope is that this will open up new terrain in which to think through a field of human behavior, which—at the moment—we can only perceive as the "problem" of drugs. In this book, I wish to disturb our "knowledge" by listening closely to those voices on drugs that we find hard to hear while feigning deafness in the face of voices that usually hold center stage in the drug debate.

A recent advertisement campaign in Los Angeles (paid for by the Coalition for a Drug-Free America) showed a huge cannabis leaf and a caption that read: "It makes you respond ten seconds slower to 'Hey Stupid!'" From commonsense logic like this, to DARE programs (Drug Awareness Resistance Education), Narcotics Anonymous, and professional psychology journals and books, the understanding uniformly across the board is that taking drugs constitutes a "stupid" activity, and that avoiding drugs is the "smart" thing for anyone (especially "kids") to do. What we will listen to in this book, though, is a series of voices and texts, which reveal that drugs resist such easy formulations. Jean Cocteau felt that drugs could be utilized in intelligent ways, and tells us that he "remain[s] convinced, despite [his] failures, that opium can be good and that it is entirely up to us to make it well-disposed."[7] This comment seems to point to a central concern of this book, which is that what drugs mean is entirely up to us, and if we wish to move away from the "problem" of drugs, then we should rewrite our scripts in order to "make" them mean something else. As Aleister Crowley points out, "dope itself doesn't really mean anything vital," and he suggests that we "have got to learn to make use of drugs" in the same way that "[our] ancestors made use of lightning."[8]

Drug Positions

By now this is also probably starting to sound like a prodrug argument: however, I can assure you it is something far more perverted than that. Outlining whether I have an anti- or prodrug "stance" is really only an answer to the question "where do I stand on drugs *within the limits of the discourse as it exists.*" I am not arguing that we step outside the discourse (even if that were possible), or that if we simply stop talking about drugs the problem will go away. My position is that we should recreate for ourselves a discourse of drugs in which it would no longer be of any use to ask the question if one is either *for* or *against* them. We need to stop thinking of drugs as being good or evil, but find a discursive space for them in our culture, which places them, in Nietzsche's terms, *beyond* good and evil.

The question that follows from the "what's-your-stand-on-drugs" routine is the question that several colleagues asked me in the course of writing this book, which concerns my (supposed) desire to "empower" and "legitimate" drugs and/or the drug user. The inquirer normally asks this question while pointing to the "grim realities" of inner-city crime, gang activity, crack babies, and the "spread" of AIDS. The suggestion is that my legitimation of drug users would involve releasing some kind of crucial cultural brake, resulting in a massive rise in death and disease. One could, if they wish, assume that I *am* attempting to legitimate the drug user, as a way of opposing the "illegitimate" status that they already have. Yet, there would be very little point in my doing such a thing because to legitimate the drug user could only mean legitimating the discourses that already produce the drug user in our culture. Since drugs are already a fully operational field in our culture, they do not seem to be in any need of legitimation. If William Bennett during his term of office as drug-czar can call for the "beheading of drug dealers," and Daryl Gates can suggest that "casual drug users should be taken out and shot," drugs must already be surrounded and written through with legitimate and functional fields of knowledge.[9] To "legitimate" the drug user, whether through antidrug or prodrug rhetoric would finally amount to me pulling harder on the brake, as opposed to releasing it. My aim instead is to offer an analysis, not so as to prove or "legitimate" any side of the debate, but instead to ask us to consider how we got to the point that only allows us to hold two positions about drugs: pro and con. Once we have surveyed the parameters of our knowledge we may then be eager to extend ourselves into new regions. My point then, to extend the hill metaphor, is that we are not on a hill, and consequently there is no need for any kind of brake. Even if our cultural vehicle does move a little, it cannot hurt to see the landscape from a different viewpoint; at least we would get another perspective on our location.[10] Maybe we can then get off the beaten track and explore what other ways of speaking about drugs are available to us.

It is hopefully clear by now that I am suggesting that the language of drugs is not something that we articulate and speak, but something that speaks *us*. This language that we speak and have come to believe in certainly operates as an ideology, and as an ideology, the discourses of drugs constantly remains fluid and undefinable. As Marc Redfield points out, "the term ideology names a representation that is fictional or rhetorical, on the one hand, and politically and referentially efficacious, on the other."[11] This would explain why, in spite of over 100 years of medical and legal expertise, the concept of "drug addiction" remains unresolved and elusive. A recent article in the *Journal of Drug Issues* is openly entitled "Addiction: The Troublesome Concept" and outlines how drug addiction "is a troublesome concept not only in the public arena, but also in the research and theoretical literature in drug studies."[12] While even professionals are not sure what kind of "concept" addiction is, we apparently "know" that it is "troublesome." Ronald Akers outlines how addiction is really a meaningless concept suggesting that "The label of addiction is attached to the behavior because the person is assumed to have lost control of the substance use; when asked why the person has lost control, the answer is that he is addicted. In other words addiction causes addiction."[13] In short, suggests Akers, "so many different definitions and diffuse meanings have become attached to it that addiction is a muddy term [that] . . . has passed into that group of terms that elude precise definition."[14] Akers' focus on addiction's elusiveness, is in itself deceptive because now the elusiveness has expanded to the point where it is the concept of drug addiction itself that is deceptive and elusive. Like Stevenson's Hyde, drug addiction is constantly appearing in one place only to disappear and reappear in a different location with a new disguise, having sneaked back into the laboratory while we were not looking. Eve Sedgwick has suggested that we live in a culture of "addiction attribution," in which even activities like exercise can be addicting. But this stems from our own rhetoric yet again. Having decided that drug addiction is going to be elusive, we end up having to say that everything is addictive in the hope of perhaps hitting our target. We end up then with a kind of "addiction continuum," in which all addictive behaviors are, at root, linked. Such a narrative, while not very helpful for actual drug users, does provide a space in which books such as *From Chocolate to Crack* can be written, read, and generally accepted as offering us the "truth" about what addiction means.

Having outlined the blurred boundaries of the term "addiction," Akers finds himself returning to a position of rational scientific objectivity in order to come up with a satisfactory definition of addiction. For Akers, "*Freed from the ideological and emotional connotations, the term addiction is simply* a label *objectively* applied to a category of behavior that can be studied as a dependent and independent variable in social and behavioral research."[15] Unfortunately, such a stance, far from assisting the emergence of new ways of structuring addiction, simply returns it to the place of medicine and science by reinforcing the sense that "addiction" represents an unassailable truth that is somehow beyond or separate from ideology and power. Only by miraculously removing "addiction" from ideology can Akers see it clearly.

If that is what the terrain looks like in the sciences, drugs also emerge as a slippery and elusive concept in the humanities. A recent issue of the critical theory journal *diacritics* (Fall 1997) was devoted solely to the study of "addictions." Note that the plural already denotes some kind of excess baggage, some loose slippage as drug use metamorphoses into "addictions." A recent edition of *differences* (Spring 1993), "On Addiction," also suffered from the same slippage in that the collection of essays ranged from essays on Elvis and Carmen to serial killers and kleptomania. Some of this slippage can be put down to the current state of critical studies in the United States, which as Angela McRobbie has outlined, is little more than "a messy amalgam of sociology, social history, and literature, rewritten as it were into the language of contemporary culture."[16] For the editors of the *Cultural Studies* anthology, the methodology of the field "could best be seen as bricolage."[17] When we then turn to *diacritics,* we are offered the same looseness as we saw in Akers. For example, the table of contents lists essays with titles such as "Heidegger's Craving: Being on Schelling" "Drinking Rules: Byron and Baudelaire," "Trauma, Addiction and Temporal Bulimia in Madame Bovary," along with an essay on addiction and beating in Woolf, and two essays on virtual reality. The range is certainly stunning, but only in the sense that we are silenced by the size of a concept so unwieldy that it has to be cut into separate areas in order to be digested safely. This expansion of the concept of drugs to include everything from writing to computers makes it nearly impossible for us to see what it is we are dealing with. The editor of *diacritics,* Marc Redfield, acknowledges that in recent years "the concept of addiction has come to operate as one of those rhetorical switching points through which practically any discourse or practice or experience can be compelled to pass."[18] That would be fine, but Redfield concludes by suggesting that the collection of essays draws attention to "the necessity of dwelling with the possibility that the figure of addiction is *unreadable.*"[19] Once again we have come full circle, and we are back to Akers and the idea that the figure and the reality of "drugs" is at once everywhere, and yet impossible to pin down.

This notion that drugs are "slippery" and elusive also crops up, not surprisingly, in self-help literature. One pamphlet on PCP from the University of Southern California student health center contains a "Name Game." The diagram is a series of concentric circles with the different names that PCP has had over the recent years, from "dust" to "goon," and "crystal joints" to "gorilla biscuits." The "game" is not really a game; all you can do is turn your head a bit and read the names, but the text underneath the diagram tells us the point of the game: "Tracking all the things that PCP's been called over the years is impossible. But even a partial list shows how tricky it is to pin down something as slippery as PCP."[20] Somehow it would seem that the range of labels for a substance automatically confers upon it some kind of terrorist identity that "means" that it is actively resisting being tracked down.

My aim in this study is thus to offer, through readings ranging from the Victorians to the present, a means by which to neutralize the power of the discourses that we use for drugs so that they no longer appear as "natural" and "rational" medico-legal solutions. I will be suggesting that it is not drugs, but the discourses of drugs as we have currently formulated them that is the drug "problem."

Another objection to this study would suggest that I am conflating so many different kinds of experience and boiling it all down to the convenient label "drugs" that I can then use willy-nilly, to say whatever it is I want to say about "drugs." Yet my use of "drugs" has actually been stolen from the culture. For example, when we see DARE stickers saying "DARE to keep kids off drugs," we automatically know what the referent is. It is those "drugs" that is the subject of discussion here. Similarly, one could also object that I am blurring "drugs" into "addiction," yet the prohibitions against "drugs" are not separate from the fear of addiction: the culture makes the leap from "drugs" to "addiction" magically instantaneous. For us drugs *mean* addiction, and vice versa. I have attempted to open up the inquiry into this troubled and troubling arena by offering what philosopher Jacques Derrida asked for, which was "a thoughtful reflection on the axioms of this problematic and on all those discourses which inform it."[21]

This book thus aims to write a history of the present, that is simultaneously, a counter-memory, a history which deliberately "forgets" conventional ways of thinking. As Foucault points out:

> History becomes "effective" to the degree that it introduces discontinuity into our very being—as it divides our emotions, dramatizes our instincts, multiplies our body and sets it against itself. "Effective" history deprives the self of the reassuring stability of life and nature, and it will not permit itself to be transported by a voiceless obstinacy toward a millennial ending. It will uproot its traditional foundations and relentlessly disrupt its pretended continuity.[22]

In Nietzsche's phrase, the only truths about drugs that we currently possess are merely "an army of metaphors" that come together to constitute our understanding of drugs, but is little more than "deception through meaning."[23] For Nietzsche:

> ... to be truthful, that is, to use the usual metaphors, therefore expressed morally: we have heard only about the obligation to lie according to a fixed convention, to lie gregariously in a style binding for all. Now man of course forgets that matters are going thus with him ... by this very forgetting, he arrives at a sense for truth.[24]

If we have forgotten that our truths are illusions, then what is needed is an act of re-remembering, not a passive forgetfulness, but an active forgetting of all that we *think* is most true. This is why re-thinking drugs in a way that would be worthwhile will always feel awkward, wrong, and stupid. However, as Gayatri Chakravorty Spivak reminds us, this is the only way out: "active forgetfulness is the cure for the fever of history."[25] For Nietzsche, "[t]he historical sense makes its servant's passive and retrospective. Only in moments of forgetfulness, when that sense is intermittent, does the man who is sick of the historical fever ever act."[26] For Nietzsche, what we need is an "act of choosing forgetfulness."[27] This book will try to encourage such acts of willful forgetting.

Re-positioning our drug discourses is made easier by the fact that the way we currently understand drugs offers us a mime of the actions that we need to be undertaking in the task that confronts us. For Jean Cocteau, the advantage of opium is that it "first takes away our memory."[28] To take drugs is not only unhistorical, it is also an active willing of differance, it is active forgetfulness. As Nietzsche states, "the antidotes of history are the "unhistorical" ... By the word "unhistorical" I mean the power, the art of forgetting. ..."[29] What we still need is Nietzsche's "gay science" (which is still very queer to us): "The will to ignorance, the joyful wisdom, must also be prepared to rejoice in uncertainty, to rejoice in and even to will the reversal of all values that might have come to seem tenable."[30] Moreover, as Gayatri Spivak points out, it is this gay science that is "the greatest threat to the chain of self-preservative interpretations that accepts its own activity as 'true' and 'good.'"[31] Surely our own rhetoric of drug use is little more than a highly effective chain of self-preservative interpretations, which should be forgotten if we wish to liberate *differance* and move to a space where we do not have to frame drug use only as a problem.

Foucault asks us to imagine how thinking could be freed from the categories of truth and falsehood: "Drugs—if we can talk of them generally—have nothing at all to do with truth or falsity. ... In fact, they displace the relative positions of stupidity and thought. ..."[32] The difficulty in writing about drugs in ways that deconstruct accepted positions, however, is that once you start speaking of a space outside of the ideological maze the likelihood is that you are not going to be heard or taken seriously. I would like to suggest that if we are to unravel the problem of drug addiction, we are going to have to think in ways that will seem "stupid" to us, and we will have to speak in ways that will cause us to worry about what people will think of us.

Drugs are very versatile. We use them all the time and for many things: they explain domestic violence, the breakup of the family, welfare problems, vandalism, crime, AIDS, issues of race and gender, economics, personal freedom and its limits, as well as the need for surveillance and DARE programs. They are very useful to us, which I presume explains the strong resistance to rewriting them or moving them to a rhetorical space whereby they would not be so useful. If drugs were not a problem, how would we explain all of these other categories? They may mean a lot of things but we radically restrict the ways in which drugs can be meaningful. People who then make suggestions that they could be rewritten are usually dismissed as insane/dangerous and/or stupid.

As regards the partial thought that drugs (may) provide, Derrida feels that "the recourse to dangerous experimentation with what we call "drugs" may be guided by a desire to consider this alleged boundary from both sides at once, to think this boundary as such. . . ."[33] This book will therefore use drug literature as a way of allowing us to temporarily enter into the phantasm, to undo the endless struggle of thought/stupidity, and hopefully come out on the other side holding in our hands, if not an Asphodel, then at least a partial thought. Jean Cocteau tells us in *Opium: Diary of his Cure* how "Everything one achieves in life, even love, occurs in an express train racing toward death. To smoke opium is to get out of the train while it is still moving. It is to concern oneself with something other than life or death."[34] Similarly, if we are to move outside of the limits of the pro and con drug binary that presently entraps both us and our addicts, we must also get out of the train of our knowledge while it is still moving. As William Burroughs says: "The Cure is always: Let Go! Jump."[35]

Making Drugs Mean

The nineteenth century saw the emergence of a process whereby many aspects of modern human behavior came under medical and moral scrutiny. Driven by a confidence in the ability of empirical analysis, many cultural behaviors were, for the very first time, classified, measured, and labeled. As the century progressed, public and private activities of the nation were to be made available to an expanding army of accountants, planners, politicians, and doctors. Concern was expressed that disease represented a threat to the health of the body politic and that the nation's productivity and growth could only be guaranteed if illness and disease were brought under strict control and surveillance. While many bodily maladies were classified as diseases, many other bodily conditions came to receive the same label. Berridge and Edwards point out that while "[d]isease entities were being established in definitely recognizable physical conditions such as typhoid and cholera . . . the belief in scientific progress encouraged medical intervention in less definable conditions."[36] The result, as they state, is that "[t]he post-Darwinian revolution in scientific thinking encouraged the re-classification of conditions with a large social or economic element in them on strictly biological lines."[37]

While we tend to think that our understanding of drug addiction is located in some timeless psychological fact, or chemical certainty, the ways in which drugs have come to be understood in their current form is the result of a fairly recent set of historical and social factors. However, while this medicalization of drug behavior is meant to be above morality, sanctioned by science and medical fact, it cannot avoid redeploying a whole host of values and morals. As Berridge and Edwards point out, the medical discourses of addiction that we are still utilizing with such damaging effects were never "scientifically autonomous. Their putative objectivity disguised class and moral concerns."[38] Many Victorian doctors believed that drug addiction was a "disease" that you could be "cured" of, and they often administered chemical "cures." Alongside this model grew a belief that what was needed was a focus on the patient's "will," something that was often attempted "by the inculcation of family and community values."[39] The Victorian doctor Oscar Jennings believed that alongside medicine, restoring the patient's willpower would restore them to health. For Jennings, the patient's willpower—like some lucky survivor who is found in the collapsed building of the self—is "buried under a heap of collapsed intentions and broken purposes, [and] must be dug out."[40] Treatments were thus very often social, rather than scientific, and, as one would expect, activities that "reflected acceptable social values were recommended" as an aid to full recovery.

Today, we continue to operate under this double approach of medicine and the moral imperatives to strengthen the will, for they provide us with our "understanding" of what drugs and addiction "really" are. While it is easy for us to laugh at the foolishness of Victorian theories that claimed that masturbation could lead to mental and/or physical illnesses, we will not allow our own formulations on drugs to be questioned in the same way.[41]

In the area of drug behaviors, the result was that activities that had previously been categorized under abstract moral positions were now classified as medical and physiological facts. This shift was made possible by the development of "disease theories" that, when applied, transformed a person's behavior into a "disease." As Berridge and Edwards suggest, "disease theories were part of late Victorian 'progress,' a step forward from the moral con-demnation of opium eating to the scientific elaboration of disease views."[42] The results can be seen in the work of Edward Levenstein, for example, in whose words we like to recognize an echo of our own views on drug addicts and their "illness."[43]

In his 1878 work *Morbid Craving for Morphia,* Levenstein describes the precautions that must be followed when dealing with the drug user. We are informed that "the patient" (who, it is assumed, is suicidal) must be placed in a separate room, which, "for the sake of control, is to have only the most necessary furniture." In an adjoining room for the "medical attendant" the following drugs are to be kept "under lock and key:—a solution of morphia of 2 per cent., chloroform, aether, ammonia, liq. ammon. anis.; mustard, an ice bag, and an electric induction apparatus." Having made the patient take a warm bath "a confidential person has to search all his things for morphia, which, notwithstanding the patient's assurances to the contrary, is some-times concealed in the most ingenious manner. . . ." Levenstein feels that these precautions are necessary and that "[o]nly after we have done this can we commence the treatment with the assurance of not being deluded."[44] Levenstein's medical advice offers a condensation of the ways in which the addict is still perceived today. Like Levenstein, we "know" that addicts are untrustworthy, deceitful, suicidal, with no "real" interest in being cured, "in-genious" and above all, suited to incarceration. The addict has the ability to generate a fear in the medical establishment that they will somehow be de-luded: only with the most highly efficient surveillance can the addict be con-tained. Levenstein goes on to tell us how "Educated, intelligent, and hitherto respectable ladies and gentlemen will so far forget themselves as to lie willfully," warning us that "the patients are not to be trusted." His advice is to treat them "like people under age" and to "protect them from tempta-tions by keeping a watch on them."[45]

While this seems natural to us, Berridge and Edwards point out that in the early half of the nineteenth century, the treatment of drug behaviors was largely dictated not by the medical establishment but by the patient. A doc-tor would be called only to relieve any troubling *symptoms* caused *by* the drug (usually opium), but the doctor never felt the need to rid the patient of the drug itself. However, by the second half of the century doctors were moving into the center of the equation and "drug addiction," now heavily discussed and debated, became a "medical growth area" as medical textbooks emerged containing sections on this new disease of "morphinism."[46] Berridge and Edwards suggest that "[a]ddiction was a new medical specialism; and there were plenty of doctors willing to acquire and demonstrate the expertise."[47]

Although he was outlining a framework for sexuality, Michel Foucault's analysis of homosexuality serves as a useful screen through which to view the status of the drug user. For a moment allow me to insert the addict into Foucault's formulation and you will see what I mean. Following Foucault, our rhetoric of drug addiction is an "endeavor to expel from reality the forms of [behavior] that [are] not amenable to the strict economy of reproduction: to say no to unproductive activities, to banish casual pleasures. . . ."[48] The result is that we can look back and forward to a time when

> [Drug users circulate] through the pores of society; they [are] always hounded, but not always by laws; [are] often locked up, but not always in prisons; [are] sick perhaps, but [are also] scandalous, dangerous victims, prey to a strange evil that also [bears] the name of vice and sometimes crime.[49]

The smoothness with which one can insert the position of drug addicts into the history of sexuality thus attests to a distinct sense that the cultural perception of the two fields is contiguous. In our culture the fear of drugs is energetically operative and is "endowed with the greatest instrumentality" and is "useful for the greatest number of maneuvers and is capable of serving as a point of support, as a linchpin, for the most varied strategies."[50] It is this "instrumentality" that I believe is holding the current rhetoric of drugs in place, preventing it from being unraveled. The outcome of this Victorian scenario was that "[a] hybrid disease theory emerged in which the old moral view of opium eating was re-formulated in 'scientific' form, where social factors were ignored in favor of explanations in terms of individual personality and biological determinism."[51]

Alongside attempts at making addiction into a disease remained the question of the individual's will. Addiction, while being treated as a medical disease, was also understood as a vice, and one in which the addict indulged. Addiction was thus understood as "a disease of the Will," which meant that the individual was also responsible for their "disease."[52] As Berridge and Edwards point out, this left the addict in a double bind: "[t]his strong moral component ensured a disease theory which was individually oriented, where the addict was responsible for a condition which was somehow also the proper province for medical intervention. Opium eating was medicalized; but failure to achieve cure was a failure of personal responsibility, not medical science."[53] Discourses like this serve only to trap the drug user. The result, as we well know today, is that "[h]ealth [became] equated with self-discipline."[54] In the nineteenth century, addicts were thus seen as being abnormal and deviant from accepted patterns of social thought and behavior, and, as now, it was thought that the rise of drug addiction represented a risk to the efficiency of the economy and presaged "national decline."[55] Today, alongside seeing addiction as a physical behavior, it is now packaged alongside questions of sexuality, race, and class. This strange mixture of drugs and "political" issues was again standardized in the Victorian period. As Berridge and Edwards show, addiction was not the only "behavior" that was brought under the rubric of a medicalizing gaze: "Criminality, insanity, homosexuality and poverty were among the conditions re-classified in this biologically determined way."[56] An example of the ways in which these discourses supported each other (and continue to do so) can be seen in the cases of "drug addiction" and "poverty." The nineteenth century divided morphine takers into two categories: morphinists and morphinomaniacs. It was believed that morphinists *wanted* to be cured, and therefore were morally superior to the morphinomaniacs who had no desire to be cured and therefore could be classified as literal lunatics. This classification spills over into the Victorian understanding of poverty. A distinction was made between those individuals that constituted the "deserving" poor, and were worthy of charitable help, and the "undeserving" poor who, by being unwilling to help themselves, were beyond help and could be treated on a par with criminals. Again, while we laugh at the supposed folly of some Victorian ideas, the logic of this framework feels far from alien to our current way of thinking. Similarly, we need feel no mercy for the addict, nor any guilt, because the discourse informs us that they are the architects of their own doom. A brief glance at any current self-help books on drug addiction and the current professional journals and books in the field will show the reader how this medical/moral framework from the Victorian period has been unquestioningly adopted and deployed.

So long as we try to pull away from drugs, and remain far enough away from their borders we are ensuring that the binary of "addiction/ freewill" stays in place. The story of the endless struggle against drugs, and the (never-quite-free-enough) will, can then continue to be told. We want to see drugs as a form of escape, especially as an escape from work. After all, is not the drug addict, languishing in a pleasant daze, our emblem for the epitome of laziness (and pleasure)? In figure 1, the school child is seen as being at risk from drugs with the notion that drugs are opposed to work, which automatically equals health. We then teach children that work is healthy, while implying that play is unhealthy. As in the rhetoric of AIDS, "knowledge is power" and here the student's failure to arm himself with knowledge (whether of drugs/AIDS or history/calculus) has led to a weakened condition that made him "vulnerable" to drugs. The story that we tell of the child being offered drugs by an older student while in the school playground would appear to reinforce this sense that "play time" is always a potentially dangerous activity. This rhetoric of drugs is then seen to "make sense" when it dovetails with the rhetoric of AIDS, in which youngsters (and adults) are urged to "play safe" when it comes to sex. It would seem that we feel that play (by having no concern for will) is somehow inherently dangerous and unhealthy. Perhaps, as Sedgwick suggests, giving up the notion of a free will may present a way of sidestepping the pitfalls and problems that our current discourses always manage to generate.

Antidrug leaflets published by the Do It Now Foundation also outline how getting off drugs requires willpower. They suggest that if we get depressed once we stop taking drugs, we will have to find a way to "keep on staying straight."[57] The body and mind will be somehow "scarred" from the drug use so we will have to allow ourselves time to "heal." The body and mind can do this alone, but it is better if you "help them along." If we do not feel that we can go through this healing process alone, we should "visit a treatment program" or "exercise [our] options" by doing exercise. Whatever we do to help ourselves, the ex-user is advised to "do it—and keep it done," this way we will eventually re-assemble the scattered parts of our body and mind and will then be able to "pull yourself back together." Another leaflet offers us a "Theme Song for Recovery" that allows us to recognize how we are dealing with chemically dependent loved ones and what we can do to help them. The mainstay of this leaflet takes us right back into the heart of Victorian discourses in that our first step is to recognize that the person "has an illness." By singing the "Theme Song of Recovery" (which is nonaddictive and "can be used again and again"): "It confronts the disease as the culprit, and helps you to separate the person and his or her behavior from the disease." It is almost like the logic of any of the *Alien* movies where the creature must first be isolated and prevented from being able to reach anyone prior to being destroyed. Once the "person" is safely back in our arms, the "culprit" can be destroyed. There is a feeling here as well that drugs are *like* a "parasite" (or demonic possession) that desperately and actively wants to stay in the body and damage its "host." The straight ones who care for the drug user will then have to make the drug "let go" of the person. This metaphor is backed up by the truth of science, which now "reveals" that the brain has receptor sites that opiates and crack "switch on" and tenaciously cling to.

The argument that runs throughout this book is concerned with locating various ways by which we could begin to embrace drugs in meaningful and less damaging ways. My position is that resisting and excluding drugs is never going to be an effective strategy. Only by moving closer to drugs and finding a position in our culture that *includes* them will we start to see the "problem" of drugs begin to evaporate. I am suggesting that we shall have to go *toward* drugs in order to go through them and to understand them: not keep away from them. Again, this is a simple lesson to learn if only we would listen to Jean Cocteau: "Drive opium off the ship; it will hide in the engine-room."[58] Clearly, if we keep driving drugs away, they will (and do) hide in the dark and cause trouble, so let us try to be to accommodating and find a

The head of the class.

There are two kinds of heads.
The ones that wind up excelling in school.
And the ones that smoke pot and do drugs.
Which head you turn out to be is up to you.
You can resist an offer of drugs.
Just say no.
You'd be surprised how well it works.

Send for a free booklet, *Peer Pressure: It's Okay To Say No.* Write: Say No To Drugs. P.O. Box 1635, Rockville, Maryland 20850.

Figure 1. The sleep of reason (reproduced with permission of the Ad Council).

place for drugs. Instead of driving them off the ship (or, rather, out of our communities), we should welcome them aboard and invite them to join us. It is my belief that with a courageous effort on our part we will be able change drugs from an "enemy" into a "friend." An example of this trend can be seen in the opinions of the Scottish drug police chief Tom Wood (Deputy Chief Constable of Lothian and Borders). Wood "appeared to say that politicians were not prepared to face the challenge of cannabis," while Pat

Chalmers of the Joint Grampian Police Board said that the "blunderbuss an-
tidrugs message" was not working. Speaking after the conference, Mr. Wood
said that he had been "trying to contribute to the discussion and move the
debate along." None of the political parties had taken up the issue of de-
criminalizing cannabis, he said because "none of them had the stomach to
take this matter on." Annabel Goldie, who is the conservative Tory Party
drugs spokeswoman, reflects the reaction to these kinds of suggestions by
telling us that people would be "horrified" to read of the Liberal Mr. Jim
Wallace's "open minded" approach.[59]

The voices that we shall explore in this book suggest therefore that our
cultural fear of drugs as some sort of pharmacological black hole are unfounded, and that only by *embracing* drugs and re-fashioning and re-writing
them can we hope to make peace with drugs and with ourselves. Of course,
"common sense" tells us that for a culture to even consider such a policy
would be "horrifying" and "suicidal." However, it may well be that it is the
cultural *resistance* to this idea that is horrifying and suicidal, while new directions may offer welcoming solutions that remain as yet unexplored.

Unsettling Approaches

This book is concerned primarily with the discourses that we have generated
around drugs. When faced with such a large task, it was necessary for me to
limit the choice of texts in order to be able to present a sense of focus. Thus,
I have begun with the late Victorians because we have inherited their construction of drugs, and therefore have been unable to include extensive discussions of De Quincey or Coleridge.[60] I have also been unable to include
any detailed treatment of alcohol. The text focuses primarily on cocaine and
the opiates, and this choice is simply a matter of space. I also feel that, given
my own position, it would not make sense to place all available drugs under
the easy rubric of "drugs." Other people have covered the hallucinogens and
marijuana with more skill and knowledge, and I leave those areas of analysis to them.[61]

Not all of the texts you will come across in this book would be classed as
literature. Given that the focus is on discourses about drugs, I selected my
texts on the basis of the best examples of the discourses that I was concerned
with. The book is thus a mixture of literary and nonliterary texts. A sensible
objection would involve asking why I have chosen, generally but not exclusively, to unravel the discourses of drugs through readings of literature and
various forms of cultural narratives rather than by using more "scientific"
methods of inquiry. One answer is that literature can help us to re-think
drugs in the same way that it can be used to unravel positivistic notions of
history and knowledge.[62] For Michel Foucault, literature allows us to meet

language at its limits, pushing language to the point where it breaks down, and it is at this point that I hope to be able to see our current discourses of drugs unravel. Foucault suggests that, "[l]iterature is not language approaching itself until it reaches the point of its fiery manifestation; it is rather language getting as far away from itself as possible. . . ."[63] Literature can thereby offer us a space in which to see ourselves, or as Marcel Proust suggests, literature "expresses for others and renders visible to ourselves that life of ours which cannot effectively observe itself and of which the observable manifestations need to be translated and, often, to be read backwards and deciphered."[64] Moreover, literature, in helping us to move beyond the maze of discourse presents us with a challenge which requires courage to confront. For Proust, this "[includes] the courage of one's emotions. For above all it [means] the abrogation of one's dearest illusions, it [means] giving up one's belief in the objectivity of what one had oneself elaborated" (x).[65]

The nonliterary texts will hopefully speak for themselves. I wanted to see how the discourses of drugs are played out when they are utilized in the culture. To that end, I have again chosen discourses and cultural moments that can maximize our knowledge of the truths that we keep telling ourselves about drugs.

The first three chapters center around the late Victorian period, for I feel that this period was the crucible in which so many of our current discourses can be traced. My analysis begins with the introduction of the Pharmacy Act in 1868, a year that also saw the publication of Wilkie Collins's novel *The Moonstone*. In the opening chapter I explore the major perameters that my discussion of drugs will constantly confront throughout this text: the place of the family, the questions of race, gender, and class, and the authority of the medical profession. In addition, this chapter deals with emergent constructions of the drug user as well as the omniscient desires of the Law and the police. I would argue that Collins placed himself in direct opposition to the discourses of his moment by constructing a text that attempts to unravel the limits of late Victorian thinking about the meaning of drugs. Given that the period was on the verge of moving drugs from a medical to a criminal category, Collins's text exposes the folly of such a measure. The novel articulates how such binary thinking will not solve what are perceived as problems but instead will exacerbate them.

Chapter 2 takes the discourses surrounding the drugged self as its focus. Drawing on Doyle's presentation of Holmes's cocaine use, and Baudelaire's reading of the hashish eater, the chapter opens up our constructions of the drug user as someone (or rather some thing) which is no longer in possession of a Self. In focusing on Stevenson's *The Strange Case of Dr. Jekyll and Mr. Hyde,* I am interested in locating how Hyde sees his drugged self as natural, while it is only Jekyll who feels that the drugged self must be destroyed.

I will examine how, as we continue to work with Jekyll's perception of the drug user, we leave ourselves with no solutions to the drug problem other than destroying ourselves in order to obtain the phyrric victory of establishing a drug free society.

Chapter 3 focuses on Freud's writings on cocaine. While drug counseling and addiction therapy is held together by a Freudian framework, this chapter explores the paradox that Freud's beliefs about cocaine continue to fly in the face of these accepted and unquestioned truths about the meaning of drugs. Whereas we operate as if we know what cocaine means and simply try to deploy our discourses around this meaning, Freud asks us to reconsider whether we know what cocaine can mean. Even though Freud found himself accused of irresponsibility, he insisted that cocaine need not be dangerous. Held in the shadows of the Freudian canon, these troublesome writings on cocaine do not say want we want to hear about drugs, and so they continue to question the constructions that we have created for ourselves.

Chapter 4 takes the idea of control as its focus. From the Mexican border patrols to body searches in schools, the issue of drugs is primarily a question of control. The surveillance and control of our bodies, racial groups, welfare recipients, or drugs themselves represents the target for the bulk of any drug discourse. This chapter will use the work of William Burroughs to raise the possibility that control cannot be a solution to the drug problem at any level. For Burroughs, it is our faith in control that holds us back from creating new discourses for drugs. In Burroughs's terms, our real sickness as a culture is not from drug use, but from our addiction to thinking that we have to rid ourselves of all drug use.

Chapter 5 examines the work of Marsha Rosenbaum, Elizabeth Ettore, and Carter Heyward to see how this question of control is currently constructed and understood in relation to women's drug use.[66] I am interested in exploring how the solutions that these three writers generate for women's drug use results in a discursive framework that has control as its central goal. I will suggest that these solutions are actually inhibiting us from seeing women and their drug use in ways that would liberate us and them from discourses and practices that in the end can only produce more harm than good. Through the work of the sociologist Avril Taylor, fiction writer Anna Kavan, and the clinician Dr. John Marks, I will introduce some European perspectives as a way of highlighting ways of providing women drug users, and ourselves, with ways of talking about drugs and gender that resist the dictates of control, and in turn provide us with new ways of negotiating our relationship to women's drug use.

The most visible aspect of contemporary drug use centers around the issue of race. In Chapter 6 I want to examine how our current antidrug position remains racist in theory and in practice, and how our discourses are disempowering everyone. My analysis will reveal that only by adopting an *anti*-antidrug position can we give ourselves the space in which to rewrite our relationship to drugs *and* race. It will become clear that our racial discourses are not independent of our drug discourses. If we wish to change either of these discursive fields, then both our truths about drugs and race are going to have to be erased and replaced with discourses that we will probably feel are unacceptable to us from our current limited disadvantage point. I would suggest that our current ideas about drugs and race are neither empowering nor enlightened, and that no new approaches to drugs and/or race can appear in our culture until we actively forget the truth of these discourses.

Chapter 1 🏵

"Unpopular Everywhere," or Forgetting the Self, Remembering Drugs.

... opium sometimes hurts, but also, sometimes, it helps.

—Wilkie Collins[1]

My reason for beginning with Wilkie Collins's novel *The Moonstone* is that it presents us with a discourse on drugs that is at odds with our current constructions. While presenting a model of drugs that we find unimaginable from our current moment, the novel also raises all of the topics that we continue to struggle with on the question of drugs: the role of the family, the place of race, gender, and class, the role of the medical profession, cultural perceptions of the drug user, and the function of the Law and the police. Collins's text raises all of the pertinent questions that I will try to sustain throughout this book. At a time when the culture was moving inexorably toward the simple demarcation of the drug field into the normal and the pathological, Collins's text asks us to reconsider the validity of such a strategy. It is my contention that the novel clearly demonstrates that such binary thinking cannot hope to solve our own "drug problem" effectively, and rather than being healthy and helpful, Collins exposes the fact that our current positions are actually damaging and unhelpful.

While we are unable to let a case of drug use go unnoticed, Terry Parsinnen has pointed out that in the nineteenth century, "Opium habituation cases rarely appeared in the medical press because, for the most part, neither habitués nor medical men considered the condition worthy of mention."[2] In contrast to our own knowledge of opium as a poison, for the first half of the nineteenth century, it constituted "a familiar and frequently used remedy."[3] As Dolores Peters points out, "opium appears to have been called upon as a specific remedy, especially in cases of diabetes, consumption, syphilis, cholera, and rheumatism [as well as] smallpox, dysentery, whooping cough, dropsy and gout [and] chest disease, fever and delirium tremens."[4] In this milieu, however, there was, according to Peters, a certain "lack of consensus" regarding the medical significance of opium.[5] Frederick Fluckiger asserted in 1868 that "science is far from having an exact idea of the nature of opium."[6] However, in May 1857 a bill was introduced to Parliament aimed at reclassifying opium as a poison. Interestingly enough, this bill, which finally came into force as the Pharmacy Act of 1868, had very little to do with addiction. As Peters tells us, "the medical and pharmaceutical professions were guided by the logic of common usage; the desire to restrict the sale of opium because of its potential for habituation was not a major factor in their consideration. Only in retrospect does the Act appear to have represented the first important step in establishing the principle of legislative regulation of narcotics so familiar in the twentieth century."[7] Many objections to the Pharmacy Act were voiced by the medical profession and pharmacists. According to Peters, "some pharmacists wished to exclude opium from the schedule of poisons altogether." One contemporary commentator proposed that opium should be seen "as being a substance coming under the same category as tobacco [and therefore it] is a medical question whether persons ought to be permitted to take opium or not. . . ."[8] *The Pharmaceutical Journal* declined to openly support the bill, arguing that the inclusion of opium as a poison was "a most unfortunate addition."[9] This ambivalence on the part of the culture toward opium reflects, I feel, a degree of openness toward the drug and its definition that we have since lost. As Peters points out, "no reliable distinction could be drawn between the quasi-medical use of opiates and habitual use."[10] The aim of the Pharmacy Act of 1868 was to eliminate this blurred boundary and establish the modern guidelines that we continue to deploy. It is in the context of this uncertainty over the role of opium that we can turn to Wilkie Collins's *The Moonstone.* What we shall see is that Collins was writing against the current of the Pharmacy Act and its line of thought and was striving to maintain the place of opium as a substance that can help the community, rather than as a dangerous poison that it must expel.

Very often, what looks like the truth about drugs may actually be very unhelpful. Unlike the recent film adaptation of Irvine Welsh's novel *Trainspotting,* Collins's novel has no interest in reinforcing our current truths about drugs. A range of writers reviewing *Trainspotting* all agree that what we are seeing is a "gritty" and "realistic" portrait of drug addiction.[11] Yet for all of this assertion that we are getting the truth about drugs, the film seems to be content to repeat, verbatim, various accepted "truths" about addiction. For example, a baby dies while everyone is busy getting high, Tommy is killed by toxic plasmosis due to the general squalor into which his life "collapses" as a result of his addiction. Another character loses an opportunity for a job by being high on speed. Similarly, the notion that "the family" offers the protagonist his only hope for a cure is restaged via Renton's detox in his teenage bedroom. These vignettes, rather than being the truth about drugs, are only *a* truth, one that we have come to accept as *the* truth. Rather than being a fresh honest approach to drugs, Renton's role in *Trainspotting* repeats the same truths that have remained static since Frank Sinatra performed them in *The Man with the Golden Arm.*

The other truth about addiction that is played for us in *Trainspotting* is the suggestion that "independent" thinking and a "strong will" lead to health and direction in life. Above all, drugs are shown as horrifying, and the self that they produce even more so. For example, we are shown how Renton is so lost to his "true" self that he is prepared to fish around in a filthy toilet in which he has just defecated, in order to retrieve two opium suppositories that he has lost. By the end of the movie, the protagonist is seen as justified for cheating on his friends and running off to London with the money that they made from a drug deal, and quitting heroin. In part, this surely explains the film's success in ideological terms: it is comfortably antidrug.[12] While *Trainspotting* was praised for giving us a realistic portrait of drug addiction by "telling it how it is" and pulling no punches in order to give us the "hard truth" about drugs, it slavishly rehearses the major elements of twentieth-century representations of drugs.

However, if we take a look at Wilkie Collins's novel *The Moonstone,* we shall be presented with a very different "truth" about drugs. In contrast to the success of *Trainspotting, The Moonstone* was not at all favorably received. When it was published in 1868, reviewers thought that the novel should not be seen as literature at all, but like the "hocus-pocus" of the inscrutable Indians that appear in the novel, was no more than a mere piece of "magic." *The Pall Mall Gazette* offered the following comment:

> Mr. Collins is in the habit of prefixing prefaces to his stories which might also lead one to think he looks upon himself as an artist. Whether this is mere self-delusion or a trick for deluding the public, who can tell? . . . A conjuror at a county fair has as much right to prate about his art. . . . True . . . in sliding panels, trap doors, and artificial beards, Mr. Collins is nearly as clever as any one who ever fried a pancake in a hat. . . . But is this, then, what fiction has come to?[13]

Critics such as D. A. Miller have accepted T. S. Eliot's notion that *The Moonstone* is the "first detective novel." Yet Nuel Davis relates how "[in] July and August [of 1868] other newspapers concluded more regretfully that as a detective novel *The Moonstone* could not be literature" while the *Daily Telegraph* significantly "condemned the laudanum passages."[14] Obviously, unlike the highly acceptable solution offered in *Trainspotting*, Collins's contemporaries knew quite well that *The Moonstone* was proposing something that was most definitely an *unacceptable* solution. The novel is clearly working in opposition to the "logic" of the Pharmacy Act. Collins is trying to keep the meaning of opium open to a range of possibilities, rather than allowing it to be restricted to only one label, as the Pharmacy Act was aiming for.

In her biography of Collins, Catherine Peters opens her chapter on *The Moonstone* by telling us that while writing the novel, Collins was going through a very difficult time in his life. Suffering from severe pain in his eyes, and taking large doses of laudanum, (opium mixed with wine) he dictated the novel to an amanuensis.[15] Peters suggests that Collins was "grateful to laudanum for helping to carry him through."[16] Unlike in *Trainspotting*, where the drugs can only abduct you into addiction, in Collins we see him expressing his gratitude toward opium. This anecdote is also related by Kenneth Robinson, who points out that "[Collins] confessed to Mary Anderson that the last part of *The Moonstone* was written largely under the effects of opium. 'When it was finished,' he told her, 'I was not only pleased and astonished at the finale, but did not recognize it as my own.'"[17]

In *Trainspotting* the protagonist becomes Other through his drug use. The difference is that while in *Trainspotting*, this drugged self is seen with disgust (there is really no separating Renton from the faeces and urine that he is soaked in), in Collins, the drugged self produces a sense of pleasure and astonishment and is openly accepted and acknowledged. In *Trainspotting*, we are made to loathe and/or fear (or laugh at) the drugged self; in Collins, and as we shall see in *The Moonstone*, we shall need to be "grateful" toward it. Moreover, Collins seems to be suggesting that drugs, rather than being a quicksand toward death, as *Trainspotting* proposes, can actually assist us: as he says, " . . . opium sometimes hurts, but also, sometimes, it helps."[18]

Familiar Drugs

This anecdote of Collins regarding his creation of the later sections of the novel opens up a series of possibilities that may offer us a way of rethinking our own understanding of the relationship between the "Self" and the drugged "Self." If, as we believe, drugs undermine our ability to control ourselves and what we say or do, then they also open up a question regarding the ownership of the drugged self. Moreover, as Collins suggests, what kind of gap between Self and non-Self can be opened up, or maybe closed, by drugs?

Jean Cocteau has said that the first thing that opium does is "take away our memory," and that in this state "the body thinks."[19] Similarly, Catherine Peters tells us that "opium may have wiped out [Collins's] memory of the original planning" of the novel, and it would seem that memory is, in part, a memory of the Self and its desires.[20] On being presented with a text that he felt someone else had written, Collins is not frightened or disappointed by this split between agency and creation (as we see in *Trainspotting*), but instead is "pleased and astonished."

The sense that drugs are connected to the emergence of a separate Self surfaces in our own ways of talking about and "understanding" drugs. In a recent advertisement entitled "Facing Reality," put out by the Partnership for a Drug-Free America (see figures 1.1 and 1.2) the narrative of AIDS infection is seen through metaphors that come close to condensing the narrative structure that Collins uses for *The Moonstone*. The heading says "Get High. Get Stupid. Get AIDS." In this discursive structure drugs produce a separate Self, one that has no Will, a Self that by default one must be ashamed of, and it is this other irresponsible self that inevitably leads to AIDS. The difference is that "the night before" here produces the threat of disease, not a text, and that those involved are far from "pleased" with the result. The cure for this situation is to "Get Information." The strip provides the reader with a vicarious second chance, parallel to the way in which Jeanine and Barry—the cartoon characters in this scenario—are magically reprieved through accurate memory: they recall that their worries are unfounded because they are not real. The cartoon characters are immune to the virus by not being real, and yet we are supposed, as the title states, to "face reality."

For Collins, we would say that the other Self was produced through laudanum, by passing into a zone where Self-knowledge was not allowed to go, permitting the emergence of a different Self, one that was no longer recognizable as the Self. For Jeanine and Barry, the heterosexual one-night stand provides the basis for the link between drugs and the non-Self through the medium of stupidity. Drugs are here being made to lead to stupidity, and "stupidity," being a supposedly will-free zone, produces unsafe, "senseless" sexual behavior.[21]

The anaphoric, syllogistic structure of "Get High. Get Stupid. Get AIDS" almost functions as a form of drug control. Whatever it is that we say drugs can or cannot do, here they are being made to produce a specific effect: AIDS. By policing the boundaries of the Self/non-Self divide in order to keep separate the two realms, drugs are made into a conduit joining both in such a way that drugs can lead *only* to AIDS as the outcome of the narrative. Drugs are not being allowed to tell any other narrative, only that they

Figure 1.1. Terrifying narratives of the self (reproduced with permission of the Ad Council).

Figure 1.2. Drawing out our senseless behavior (reproduced with permission of the Ad Council).

join hands with AIDS. By stopping drugs from being free to signify differ-ently, the narrative ensures that AIDS *will* be the result of drug use. In short, the advertisement requires that this be the case; otherwise the story that en-ables us to "understand" the "reality" of drugs and AIDS could not be told.

For Jeanine and Barry, as for Collins, drugs appear to erase the Will so that something strange is produced, whether it be a text that at first is disowned or unrecognizable, or a series of acts that when you were "in your right mind," you would not normally have done. In the words of Barry and Jeanine: "Oh I must be really stupid. I must be really dumb. What did I do? How did I get myself into this mess?" The sensible answer to their questions is that the "I" did not do anything; drugs produced a "non-I," and it was the non-I that got my "Self" into the whole mess. The cure for AIDS-related behavior is thus to prevent the non-Self from emerging, which means saying "no" to stupidity by saying "no" to "drugs."

In contrast, *The Moonstone* allows a very different series of relationships between these factors to come into play so that drugs and the non-Self undergo a substantial revision from the kind of meanings that we currently attach to them. The protagonist, Franklin Blake, is given without his knowledge a dose of laudanum; that night, as a result of the drug, he wanders off into his fiancee's (Rachel Verinder) bedroom, steals her priceless Indian diamond, and hides it in the house. In the morning he has no recollection of his activity. The diamond is reported stolen and the whole family is in turmoil, with suspicion falling upon everyone in the household. With the help of the opium addict Ezra Jennings, Blake spends the rest of the novel tracking down the guilty party, who, he is finally "pleased and astonished" to discover, is none other than himself. In Collins's novel, the same double move is at play as in "Facing Reality." As with Jeanine and Barry, Blake is not really guilty: momentarily without a will, Blake enters into the status of the one dimensional cartoon characters, or an automaton, and so his Self cannot be said to have "committed" a crime. Similarly, the diamond is not really stolen, it has just been misplaced. The mystery therefore emerges out of the gap that the drug produces between the Self and the non-Self. Peter Thoms suggests that *The Moonstone* is about the success of "consciousness as order and control," and the elimination of falseness and surface, which finally produces "maturity" and "community" out of "non-meaning and mystery."[22] However, I would like to suggest that the narrative ends and the mystery is solved, not by saying no to drugs and stupidity/unreason as Thoms and T. S. Eliot are suggesting, but paradoxically by "saying yes" to them.

Under the advice of his doctor's assistant, the much feared and despised addict Ezra Jennings, Blake takes the opium again, with the result that the non-Self is collapsed back into the Self, and the Will, like the diamond, is restored to its rightful place. The important difference between "Facing Reality" and *The Moonstone* is that whereas our cultural moment fears the non-Self (that it will drag us into the horrifying clutches of the unwilled), for Collins, the non-Self is quite comfortably seen as part of the Self, and actually belongs to it. Moreover, it is only by reentering into the space of the non-Self that the problem is removed.

In *The Moonstone,* Collins uses Blake to show us that the non-Self is inextricably linked to the Self and it cannot be policed against, or held outside, or eliminated altogether, without also throwing out the part we want to keep: the Self. Collins's way of talking about drugs suggests that by overcoming the need to repress the non-Self in turn mitigates the need to repress those substances that can produce this non-Self: drugs. If the unwilled Self can be accommodated as being a necessary and indigenous part of the Self, then it would no longer need to be eradicated and repressed. The control of the Will, and of drugs, would no longer be needed or effective, and so in the case of our own understanding, drugs would no longer have to lead straight to crime, disease, homelessness, or AIDS.

In the section of *The Moonstone* named "The Discovery of the Truth," Franklin Blake goes to the Shivering Sands, an area of quicksand on the beach not far from the Verinder household. It is here that Rosanna Spearman, one of the servants of the Verinder household, has hidden a major clue to the mystery of the misplaced diamond by hiding a nightgown worn by the "thief" on the night of the crime. Blake pulls on a chain that lifts a metal box to the surface and inside is the gown. Blake looks at the name tag on the gown and finds the name of the criminal:

> There were the familiar letters which told me that the nightgown was mine. I looked up from them. There was the sun; there were the glittering waters of the bay; there was old Betteredge advancing nearer and nearer to me. I looked back again at the letters. My own name. Plainly confronting me—my own name . . . I had discovered Myself as the Thief.[23]

When the gap between Self and non-Self is collapsed into one, Blake finds it hard to speak, and he becomes momentarily speechless:

> I have not a word to say about my own sensations.
>
> My impression is, that the shock inflicted on me completely suspended my thinking and feeling power. I certainly could not have known what I was about, when Betteredge joined me—for I have it on his authority that I laughed, when he asked what the matter was, and putting the nightgown into his hands, told him to read the riddle for himself.
>
> Of what was said between us on the beach, I have not the faintest recollection. The first place in which I can now see myself again plainly is the plantation of firs.[24]

This knowledge that there is really no Other, no criminal except himself, produces in Blake a state of "complete bodily and mental prostration."[25] It has also produced a situation parallel to the effects of the drug on Collins in our opening anecdote, in which Collins was pleasantly "amazed and astonished" by encountering his non-Self. This realization that there really is no Other when it comes to drugs is something that we too need to acknowledge. The gap between Self and non-Self, willed and unwilled, needs to be collapsed into one, and as with Franklin Blake, only then can the problem that the drug created also be removed. It is not insignificant that Collins chooses to locate the question of Blake's self/knowledge in a quicksand. We still desire to see addiction as a quicksand, which only an exertion of will power can save us from. Yet quicksand, as a psychological landscape, operates in the opposite way: the more you struggle to extricate yourself, the deeper you sink. Instead of struggling to extricate ourselves from the rhetoric of addiction, it seems that Collins is suggesting that we should learn to float on it, which paradoxically deprives the rhetoric of its strength.

(Dis)trusting drugs

After the death of Lady Verinder we hear how her Will must fall into the hands of the Law as "Mr. Bruff folded up the Will" for safe keeping.[26] In his reading of the novel, D. A. Miller argues that Sergeant Cuff is unable to solve the mystery, suggesting instead that it is solved by the more Foucauldian apparatus of the family. However, the text makes it clear that the family are anxious because they have to reach *beyond* the borders of the family, to the addict Jennings, in order to solve their "domestic" mystery. As our drug policy failures clearly reveal, *this* mystery cannot be "solved" either by the law of the state, *or* the law of the domestic family. As much as we may want to believe it in our own historical moment, Collins's text makes clear that "the family" is *not* an antidote to drugs. The one person who can bring about the solution to the mystery, the addict Jennings, is perceived as foreign/poisonous, and the Verinders balk at the idea of thinking of him as "one of the family." As the addict Jennings knowingly remarks, "distrust of me was at the bottom of all this."[27] Despite their initial resistance, it will be the person whom the family thinks is most dangerous that will hold the solution to their problem.

We first hear of Jennings when a housemaid of Lady Verinder, Rosanna Spearman, due to her knowledge of the mystery, begins behaving "not like [her]self." The main housekeeper, Betteredge, decides that since she has decided to "forget herself" that "This is a matter for the doctor to look into . . . It's beyond me."[28] They try to contact Dr. Candy for help, but are told that he has a "fever" so they turn to his addicted assistant: "a certain Mr. Ezra Jennings—was at our disposal, to be sure. . . ."[29] However, it appears that "nobody knew much about him . . . He had been engaged by Mr. Candy, under rather peculiar circumstances; and right or wrong, we none of us liked him or trusted him."[30] We discover from Betteredge that Jennings is carrying out Candy's work but there is "Not much of it now, except among the poor. *They* can't help themselves, you know. *They* must put up with [him]—or they would get no doctoring at all."[31] The local poor, while being perceived as lacking in will power (their poverty makes them dependent upon Jennings's medical care), *also* dislike him. Jennings manages to articulate an irrational fear in the minds of the local working class, as well as the bourgeois Verinder family: as we know, a hatred of drugs is not limited to class. Betteredge is thrown into confusion by Jennings and cannot make up his mind whether it would be a good thing to allow someone like Jennings into the house, but at the same time he wants to put an end to Rosanna's strange behavior.

Blake visits Jennings but is disturbed by his attraction to him and decides to leave, but finds himself unable to do so: "While my knowledge of the world warned me to answer the question which he had put . . . and then to proceed on my way out of the house—my interest in Ezra Jennings held me rooted to the place. . . ."[32] Jennings and Blake realize that they are walking in the same direction and leave the house together. As they do so, Blake again reminds us that the addict/doctor's assistant "[Jennings] was evidently no favourite in the house. Out of the house, [he] had Betteredge's word for it that he was unpopular everywhere."[33] Surprisingly, in spite of our own cultural "advances" the addict, unlike other marginal groups is alone in still being "unpopular everywhere." Luckily for the Verinder family, Blake decides not to take "the popular view" of the addict and confesses that "it is not to be denied that Ezra Jennings made some inscrutable appeal to my sympathies, which I found it impossible to resist."[34]

Betteredge, who offers us our first impression of Jennings, feels strongly—although he is not sure why—that Jennings represents a danger to the household. The following interchange between Blake and Betteredge details these fears without substantiating or locating them:

> "You don't seem to like him, Betteredge?"
> "Nobody likes him, sir."
> "Why is he so unpopular?"
> "Well, Mr. Franklin, his appearance is against him, to begin with. And then there's a story that Mr. Candy took him with a very doubtful character. Nobody knows who he is—and he hasn't a friend in the place. How can you expect one to like him, after that?"
> "Quite impossible, of course!"[35]

The reasons for fearing Jennings thus bear no relation to his actual behavior. The first reason is his "appearance" and the second is "a story." While this man has "produced too strong an impression on [Blake] to be immediately dismissed from [his] thoughts," the following chapter opens with another dismissal of Jennings by Betteredge: "Having told me the name of Mr. Candy's assistant, Betteredge appeared to think that we had wasted enough of our time on an insignificant subject."[36] The impression that he makes upon Blake is "perfectly unaccountable," but it does weaken; and as the "effect" of Jennings begins to fade (like a drug wearing off), so "[Blake's] thoughts flowed back into their former channel."[37]

What is it about this addict that affects Blake so forcibly and yet is "perfectly unaccountable"? When we first encounter Jennings, Blake says that he was "the most remarkable man that [he] had ever seen," yet the contradictions that he embodies make it impossible to place him accurately:

> Judging him by his figure and his movements, he was still young. Judging him by his face, and comparing him with Betteredge, he looked the elder of the two. . . . His complexion was of a gypsy darkness. . . . His nose presented the fine shape and modeling so often found among the ancient people of the East, so seldom visible among the newer races of the West. . . . His marks and wrinkles were innumerable. From this strange face, eyes, stranger still, of the softest brown—eyes dreamy and mournful and deeply sunk in their orbits—looked at you, and (in my case at least) took your attention captive at their will."[38]

The addicts' marginality operates at nearly every conceivable level in this description: his appearance allows his age to remain undefinable, his mixed blood makes it difficult to ascertain his nationality, and his feminine constitution postpones any decisions concerning gender. His affection for Blake defers judgment on his sexuality, while his drug habits confuse his class status by turning him from a respectable middle-class doctor into a social outcast. By flickering constantly on the edge of our field of vision, Jennings, like our own category of the addict, may be "insignificant," yet simultaneously we find that we cannot keep ourselves from being drawn to them.

Jennings is finally allowed to administer a second opium dose to Blake, which reveals how he had innocently stolen the diamond while under the influence of opium. The feared drug user has thus been able to cure the stain on the family name. Jennings also brings about the reunion and marriage of Rachel Verinder and Franklin Blake. Betteredge, typically, celebrates this union as a victory for the domestic realm, yet what is overlooked by the family is that it has been brought about by that "insignificant subject" and drug addict, Ezra Jennings. It now becomes clearer why the *Daily Telegraph* felt it necessary to "condemn the laudanum passages" of the novel.[39]

Drugging the Law

Toward the end of the novel there is a direct encounter between the effects of the opium and Mr. Bruff, the family solicitor for the Verinder family. He embodies not the police, but the Law. Bruff's responsibility is to see that Colonel Verinder's will is carried out properly. There are six main narrators in the novel and Bruff is given an entire narrative. Prior to the second and final opium experiment Jennings receives a letter in which "Mr. Bruff expressed the strongest disapproval" of the course that Blake was about to embark upon. Looking out for Rachel Verinders' interests, the solicitor feels that "[The opium experiment] was quite unintelligible to his mind, except that it looked like a piece of trickery, akin to the trickery of mesmerism, clairvoyance. . . ."[40] On the evening of the experiment that will prove Blake's innocence, and restore the missing diamond to its rightful owner, Bruff outlines his continued resistance to the use of the opium. Jennings sees Bruff "with his papers in his hand—immersed in Law; impenetrable to Medicine." However, he does manage to pull himself away from his legal papers when Jennings administers the dose to Blake.[41] When Blake begins talking "to himself," Jennings knows that the drug has taken effect, and the result is that something very strange happens to the power of the Law:

> Mr. Bruff resumed his papers, with every appearance of being as deeply interested in them as ever. But looking towards him now, [Jennings] saw certain signs and tokens which told [him] that the Law was beginning to lose its hold on him at last. The suspended interest of the situation in which we were now placed was slowly asserting its influence even on his unimaginative mind.[42]

Jennings realizes that the effect of the situation meant that he had "utterly forgotten" his two companions, while also causing Betteredge to become "oblivious of all respect for social distinctions."[43] Jennings also "saw the Law (as represented by Mr. Bruff's papers) lying unheeded on the floor."[44] Blake's drugged circular mumblings, which go nowhere except back into himself, are potent enough to drug the law, making it forget itself. We place value on the ability the rationality and logic of the law to solve our drug problems yet for Collins it is evident that only once the law has been disabled and shut down by the effects of the opium can the mystery be finally solved: as long as the law holds sway, the problem caused by drugs will remain in place.

During this second opium experiment Blake tries to hold out against the effects of the drug and Jennings realizes that "the more he fidgeted and wondered, the longer he would delay the result for which [they] were now waiting. . . ."[45] Betteredge, on the other hand, as a result of cooperating with the social "effect" of the situation, becomes no stranger to the loss of free will and by doing so becomes familiar: "Betteredge dropped to the lowest depth of familiarity with [Jennings], without a struggle to save himself."[46] Whereas we feel that struggling against drugs is what must be done, here the struggling against drugs keeps the mystery alive by preventing it from being uncovered, and also keeps people, groups, and categories separate. Giving into drugs, far from destroying the family, paradoxically produces closeness and "familiarity," as well as bringing about the end of the mystery. Collins's lesson for us is clear: only by allowing drugs *in,* can the family be saved.

While we are currently very busy striving to ensure that our Will is free, Collins is pointing out that any attempt to separate the inside from the outside, the "pure" from the "poisonous," or "free will" from "addiction" is doomed to fail: they are always wrapped up in one another. Only by working *with* drugs on the margin where they intersect with the family can the mystery be lifted. If the Verinder family had insisted on our "healthy" Just Say No position, the stain on the family name would never have been removed.[47]

Given Collins's framework, it would seem that any attempt to produce what Sedgwick calls "a pure space of voluntary," or a space in which the Will is totally free can never be located, and will continue to result in the *production,* and not the elimination, of a drug problem. Only by giving up our belief in what John Dent calls the "fairy tale" of free will can we unravel what we now perceive as the nightmare of addiction.[48] The paradox of our own logic is that it is through the addict (unwilled/un-Self) that our "knowledge" of free will is kept in circulation, while our "knowledge" of free will sustains our "knowledge" of the drug addict. As Hegel points out, such knowing knows nothing at all, but does not know that it knows nothing.

While Jennings has no trouble with letting go of the Will and all that it holds onto, we insist that it be preserved at all costs. The flaw in our argument, though, is that this "natural" and supposedly "sensible" response to drugs always has to be articulated in the form of a threat: "you *must* stop your will from weakening."

Hearing the Drug User

In conversation with Jennings, Blake raises the subject of Mr. Candy's memory and asks Jennings if the doctor could perhaps explain the events following Rachel's dinner party on the evening that the diamond went missing. Jennings has a manuscript of Candy's incoherent mumblings during his fever, and so replies that it may be possible to reconstruct the events without recourse to Candy himself. Confused, Blake asks Jennings how such a thing is possible. Jennings's response points to the silence to which the addict is still exiled: "My only difficulty in answering your question is the difficulty in explaining myself."[49] The drug addict is in a discursive position whereby his statements are either unheard or considered invalid, and Jennings fears that he will have difficulty in convincing Blake of the truth of what he says. The same barrier to understanding what the addict "means" reappears when Jennings tries to persuade the Verinder family that the use, and not the exclusion of opium, will be the key to the family mystery.

Jennings suggests that Blake was acting under the influence of laudanum on the night of the dinner party, which provides the solution to the mystery, but one which would be unacceptable to the family, insofar as it means the criminal is "one of the family." While the family are intent on more detective work and more assertion of autonomous will, Blake agrees to the solution to the mystery but is aware that it is going to be very difficult to convince the Verinder family of the need for his strategy. As Jennings points out, "how are we to carry our conviction to the minds of the people?"[50] Blake responds by pointing to Mr. Candy's manuscripts containing the fragmented narrative relating how Candy performed the drug experiment on Blake on the night of the dinner: "Useless, Mr. Blake! Quite useless . . . those notes are of my making; there is nothing but my assertion to the contrary, to guarantee that they are not fabrications. Remember what I told you on the moor—and ask yourself what my assertion is worth."[51] Jennings does suggest one possible source of validation which he feels could have the weight of an "independent testimony" with Blake and the family: De Quincey's *Confessions of an English Opium Eater.*[52] It would appear that Jennings can only validate his position as an addict by reference to another addict.

This distrust of the addict returns when Jennings tries to convince the Verinder family to accept that his "experiment" can solve the mystery. Reverberating down into our own moment, Rachel points out to Jennings that "[The family] seem to be in a conspiracy to persecute you."[53] The difficulty of accepting his kind of solution is still quite plain to us, who see "the family" as a bulwark of free will holding out against an ever rising tide of drugs. Collins seems to be suggesting the opposite: it is the family's resistance to the solution provided by drugs that is causing the problem. Obviously it is not easy to convince people that Jennings's solution is right, just as it would be hard to convince people now that the only way to bring an end to the "problem" of drugs would be to *stop* struggling against them.

At one point in the novel, Jennings tries to speak openly about his situation in society, but can only indicate that he is an absence, stating that he is "a man whose life is a wreck, and whose character is gone." Blake "attempted to speak" but Jennings stops him, and continues: "I have mentioned an accusation which has rested on me for years. There are circumstances in connection with it that tell against me. I cannot bring myself to acknowledge what the accusation is. And I am incapable, perfectly incapable, of proving my innocence."[54] Having gone to such lengths, Jennings is still unable to speak: "[Blake] looked round at him. . . . His whole being seemed to be absorbed in the agony of recollecting, and in the effort to speak." Unable to speak of his past activities, Jennings and his story are destined to stay ill, because they are beyond "recovery": "'There is much that I might say . . . about the merciless treatment of me by my own family, and the merciless enmity to which I have fallen victim. But the harm is done; the wrong is beyond all remedy.'"[55] By not being allowed to speak of his own innocence, the disruptive potential that the addict embodies is kept silent, (which keeps the mysterious space that he represents excluded and threatening). By being kept Other, by being kept outside, the addict is also forced to remain poisonous yet perfumed; hated yet desired. Collins seems to be suggesting that one way to unravel the "problem" of drugs would be to unravel the mysterious (and attractive) narratives that surround "the addict." Our current (and damaging) construction of drugs would then no longer be available to us. However, such a move can only be made by allowing the drug addict to enter into the space of health/family and make them part of it, instead of excluding them: for the moment it seems that this is a step that our culture cannot yet make.

Recovering Drugs

As with the mystery of the diamond, in which the story can continue as long as things stay hidden and covered up, so we privilege "recovery" (as opposed to "uncovery") in the field of addiction. Yet such an emphasis only ensures that the drugged Self is recovered in a veil of mystery. Hidden from view, drug users are pushed back from whence they came, set up as a space of illness and obscurity. The "re-covery" of the addict, which is the goal of the propaganda of free will, ensures that the non-Self is re-covered, buried once again, hidden from view, so that it can then begin, again, to exert its "addictive" power. We place recovery in the same category as health and cure, yet for Blake, real recovery occurs when he un-covers, which entails not separating himself from his drugged Self but realizing that it is part of his Self. As long as the metal box with the clue to the thief's identity lies buried in the sand, Blake and the family are destined never to solve the mystery and Blake will always be guilty. Keeping a firm distance between the pull of addiction and your Self is what we call "recovery," but for the Verinder family such a position, which they are reluctant to let go of, is what constitutes their domestic "sickness." For Blake, the end of the mystery comes when he closes the gap between himself and the metal box, curing himself by discovering that he is his Other, and cannot hope, nor would he wish to be, separated from himself. It would seem then that if we are to cure ourselves of the "problem" of drug addiction, we should do the same and bring drugs nearer, closing, rather than keeping open, the gap between the Self and the supposed "non" Self.

The novel closes with three statements. One is from Sergeant Cuff's assistant; the second from the captain of *The Bewley Castle,* and the third is a statement by Mr. Murthwaite. In the first two narratives the men relate the story of the diamond's final disappearance, while the third and final narrative from Mr. Murthwaite in India, relates the story of the restoration of the moonstone to its "proper" place in India. These narrators attempt to give the impression that the problem has been finally brought to an end by showing how the thing that started all the trouble in the first place has been safely removed to a realm beyond the domestic/national boundary. Yet the problem of domestic poisons, like the opening of the novel, *began* with the arrival of a story returning *from* the outside. Therefore, I feel that it is productive to read the closure of the novel as a commentary on the inefficacy of our own drug "solutions." Once the diamond/drug is placed outside the domestic space it is simply reinvested with the power to begin the cycle of the mystery all over again. Therefore this final announcement of the mystery's "cure," has buried within it the seeds of a repetition. By making exclusion the cure, it will continue to have buried within it, the trace of a poison, which by definition, must return.

Barry Milligan suggests that questions of opium consumption in the nineteenth century are centered around "anxieties about bilateral cultural exchange [as well as being] inextricable from matters relating to British territorial expansion and the very definition of 'Britishness'" . . . [56] We see these anxieties at work in the novel through the mechanism of moving the diamond out of England, along with the convenient death of the addict Jennings. In this way both of these "poisonous" and "foreign" bodies are momentarily excluded from the domestic space, and the Verinder family can claim that the family has now "recovered" not only its health but also its (national) unity.

However, as a result of its exclusion, no one knows where the diamond (or drugs) may turn up again. In our current "drug free" moment, this generates an all-encompassing paranoia and a round-the-clock alertness, which even today's worldwide narcotic squads confess they find hard to keep up with. The solution we thus suggest to ourselves is more vigilance, more alertness, and more surveillance. These policing activities "work" and are deemed "successful" insofar as they ensure that drugs are perceived, like Jennings, as marginal, and as long as they can show real proof that drugs are being actively excluded from the domestic/national space. This helps to explain the ways in which having "cured" itself of one drug, our culture is continually vigilant, always on the look out, ensuring that no new drug will return to replace the old. However, Collins's novel makes it clear that so long as we keep hiding the non-Self, burying it as far away as possible, in short, curing ourselves of it, and "re-covering" from it, it always *will* return. The non-Self will continue to return to us until we realize that we need not try to cure ourselves of drugs, but instead we must see that this non-Self is a legitimate part of the Self. We can then give up wasting all of our energy struggling against drugs and failure to recover, and instead we can move on to discover the knowledge that drugs are always going to be part of the inside. All we need to do is give them a place within our culture. I would suggest that Collins is suggesting that any culture that wishes to have a safe and healthy relationship with drugs needs to see that rather than recovering and curing ourselves of drugs by a process of exclusion/expulsion, (which is guaranteed to fail anyway), the drugged, unwilled, non-Self needs to be included in the culture and dis-covered.

What *The Moonstone* reveals is that questions of drug addiction and "the Will" can never be closed off finally, but will always reappear, and that if one drug is excluded, another has to come forward to replace it. The various attempts on the part of Betteredge to exclude Jennings, far from bringing an end to his poisonous presence, merely serves to underline his position as a foreign outsider which the family is dependent upon to solve the plague that is among them. Betteredge may want Jennings's story to go with him to the grave as a way of purifying the community, but paradoxically it was *from* the grave that Colonel Herncastle's "will" returned to bring scandal upon the family name in the very beginning of the novel. Betteredge may also wish to pin down the source of the various poisons that infected his domestic household, but as the conclusion of the text makes clear, no one can tell where the poison (the diamond) will turn up next. Its emergence and identification as a "poison" are not related to the diamond (or the drug) itself, but are connected to the ways in which we continue to label drugs as something "poisonous."

Fatal mistakes in the dark

The following historical analysis can serve as an example of the ways in which the drive to separate will/addiction, inside/outside, poison/cure actually exacerbates the drug problem rather than lessening it. Wilkie Collins began *The Moonstone* in January 1868; by June the House of Lords was embroiled in trying to pass the Sale of Poisons and Pharmacy Act.[57] On June fourteenth the Lords suggested that there were "good grounds" for adding opium to the provisions of the Act.[58] Lord Redesdale outlined how the Act would ensure:

> that poisons were to be sold only in a particular form of bottle, which would
> be known as the "poison bottle," and when it was made unlawful, not only to

sell poisons in other bottles, but to sell things not poisonous in "poison bottles," there would be far less risk than there was at present of persons been poisoned by mistake, as too many unfortunately were. Fatal mistakes were sometimes made in the dark, and these would be avoided by having a bottle of such a character that anyone who took hold of it would know it was the "poison bottle."[59]

Our cartoon characters Jeanine and Barry, as well as *The Moonstone's* Franklin Blake, know all there is to know about "fatal mistakes in the dark," but by legally defining the zone between the "normal" and the "pathological," government legislation, ostensibly *against* drug addiction, effectively brought it into being.[60] Antonin Artaud would have to repeat this point in 1925 by suggesting that drug laws do not abolish the desire for drugs—they simply "[a]ggravate the social need for the drug."[61]

Having passed the Pharmacy Act in an effort to prevent the poisoning of the community, the legislation had the opposite effect; within a few years "drug addiction" had been produced and was an acknowledged medical fact and social problem.[62] By 1880 the attitudes toward drug users had ossified into what they are today, so much so that an editorial in *The Times* (London) essentially rehearses the ideologically constructed anger that is today reserved for the (black) mothers of crack babies:

> Many more people take powerful medicines; and variations in the action of these medicines are more carefully observed than at any former period. Whatever may be the truth about the increased susceptibility to stimulants, it is certain that they were never so largely consumed; and it is believed by those well able to judge that the abuse of stimulants by women is such as to amount to a very serious social evil.[63]

The 1868 act thus desired to circumscribe a drug-free zone with the consequence that a population who before had merely had "drug behaviors" that often went unnoticed were now criminalized as addicts. By 1886 *Lancet* also indicated that drug addiction was now commonplace: "It is now the exception, instead of the rule to find a man or a woman of middle age who is not more or less addicted to the abuse of morphia. . . ."[64]

Collins's text reveals the ways in which drugs can never be removed from the culture and that what is placed outside will be immediately recreated inside. *The Moonstone* thus offers us a critique of our own drug rhetoric, which, because it demarcates where the forbidden zone begins, literally produces a population that can legally and morally be described as a menace to society.

What other possibilities are available? What would it take to start talking about drugs differently? Drugs, as Franklin Blake shows us, provide us with a "stupidity" that appears to leave us without will or language, but that also offers us a chance to laugh and to forget, at the same time reminding us that the Self will always be the non-Self, the criminal, the addict. By providing us with this knowledge, drugs prevent both us and our cultures from ever being finally closed and stabilized; so, rather than hating drugs, we should be grateful to drugs for allowing us to remain open to revision. Every time we try to ossify our position on drugs, drugs simply abandon these constructions and slip away to a more open and comfortable space.

In *Opium: The Diary of his Cure,* Jean Cocteau reverses our culture's reading of drug addiction. For Cocteau, as for Collins, what is damaging is not the desire to hold on to drugs, but the desire to hold on to the Will. If in *The Moonstone* the crime can only be solved once the critical faculty of sense, law, and the will have been put aside, for Cocteau it is the space of opium that is "intelligent" while the waking conscious mind is "stupid." The reversal occurs in that opium, which Picasso told Cocteau was "the least stupid smell in the world," is "intelligent" insofar as it provides us with "stupidity."[65] In the same way, Blake can only (re)discover the diamond and learn that he is the thief, when he is "stupid" and on opium.

Cocteau says that when returning from the effects of the drug, the awakening person returns to consciousness, which is a return to stupidity and the tyranny of sensible reason and the Will: "Once a poet wakes up he is stupid, I mean intelligent. "Where am I?" he asks . . . Notes written by a poet who is awake are not worth much."[66] For Cocteau, intelligence (the belief in free will) should be seen as stupidity, and only once we are free from reason and law can stupidity reveal its insights. For Cocteau, the solution, as in *The Moonstone,* is not to struggle against drugs, (like Betteredge, the Verinder family, and their lawyer Mr. Bruff do). Nor should we try to struggle against the Will, but simply, as Franklin Blake discovered, thanks to Jennings, we can pass into the stupor of stupidity, for only then, like Franklin Blake, can we begin to see clearly. As Cocteau says, "The living language of dreams, the dead language of waking. . . . We must interpret and translate."[67]

Our current, intelligent, sensible response to drugs, ("the language of waking"), as we know too well, is, in practice, a deadly logic. Let us then follow Cocteau's suggestion, and realize that it is the language of stupidity/nonsense that could provide us with an alternative response to drugs, one which could be truly liberatory insofar as it would sidestep the propaganda of the free will. We should now be able to understand Cocteau when he suggests how he "remain[s] convinced, despite [his] failures, that opium can be good and that it is entirely up to us to make it well-disposed."[68] Separated by almost a century, but subject to the same antidrug rhetoric as Collins, Cocteau would like us to understand that to put an end to the "problem" of drugs we "must be cured not of opium but of intelligence."[69]

Chapter 2

"A Creature Without Species": Constructing Drug Users

Are you not, then, much like some fantastic novel that insists on coming to life, instead of staying *written?*

—Charles Baudelaire "The Poem of Hashish"[1]

The media depicts users as losers, but losers who are somehow always winning.

—David Lenson[2]

This chapter focuses on our construction of the drug user and the drugged self. Ranging from discussions of Baudelaire's hashish eater to Stevenson's *Jekyll and Hyde,* this chapter examines how we actively construct the drug user as something that no longer possesses a Self as we do. Focusing on Stevenson's text, I shall examine how Jekyll's other Self, his Hyde, is actually perceived by Hyde as perfectly normal and natural, while it is only Jekyll who wishes to see him destroyed. Like us, Jekyll will go to any lengths to rid himself of his "drug problem," even if it is clear that he must destroy himself in order to do so. This chapter will try to steer us away from following Jekyll's solution to our own drug problem.

With the passing of the Pharmacy Act and the emergence of the pathology of addiction it was not long before doctors began to see visible signs of this "disease." In 1893 Dr. William Huntly noted that the opium addict can be identified by "the glazed look, the dry discolored skin, the head sunken forward, the emaciation, and . . . premature aging."[3] How do we recognize our drug users? How do we construct the categories of "drug user" and how do these categories get used by us? While trying to take a slightly off-center look at these constructions, I will also try to locate other categories, and other ways of seeing the drug user that might enable us to bring drug users not further away from us, but closer to us. If the solution offered by Wilkie Collins was to position ourselves closer to drugs rather than further away from them, then perhaps we should do the same with the drug user as well. We will have to lose our desire to want to make drug users into, as Burroughs says, "a creature without species," and instead bring them indoors, invite them in, and recognize them simultaneously as one of the family *and* as a drug user.[4]

Unlike Franklin Blake's archaic and somewhat Romantic ingestion of laudanum, Conan Doyle's *The Sign of the Four* opens with the now archetypal vignette of the drug user rolling up their sleeve and mechanically injecting themselves with a hypodermic syringe:

> Sherlock Holmes took his bottle from the corner of the mantelpiece, and his hypodermic syringe from it neat morocco case. With his long, white, nervous fingers he adjusted the delicate needle and rolled back his left shirtcuff. For some little time his eyes rested thoughtfully upon the sinewy forearm and wrist, all dotted and scarred with innumerable puncture-marks. Finally, he thrust the sharp point home, pressed down the tiny piston, and sank back into the velvet-lined armchair with a long sigh of satisfaction.[5]

This paragraph alone is enough to substantiate William Burroughs's comment, speaking of Holmes, that "[t]he world's greatest detective could not have survived a urine test."[6]

Doyle's opening paragraph, like Holmes, stands very much alone, and refrains from any moral judgements on the scene that it presents to us. The reader's need for some explanation or framing of this scene is immediately satisfied by Watson, who begins the second paragraph: "Three times a day for many months I had witnessed this performance, but custom had not reconciled my mind to it."[7] What we tend to notice, I think, is that Watson has been exposing himself regularly not to cocaine, as Holmes has, but to Holmes's actions. Watson has been getting angry at what Holmes has been doing three times a day for many months and even though he has regularly witnessed Holmes injecting, he is still not used to the sight. Unable to build up tolerance to this sight, it would seem that his moral outrage and anger toward Holmes operates as a kind of antidote and prevents Watson from becoming addicted, or habituated to Holmes's drug use. In fact, the more Holmes injects, the more irritable Watson becomes: " . . . from day to day I had become more irritable at the sight, and my conscience swelled nightly within me at the thought that I lacked courage to protest."[8] Contrary to *our* expectations, Holmes is not presented as a drug-crazed wreck who can no longer function; on the contrary, it is Holmes's "masterly manner" that prevents Watson from registering his moral objections to Holmes's behavior.[9] Finally, Watson does interfere, having been strengthened by the wine he has with lunch: "it was the Beaune which I had taken with my lunch."[10] The wine thus gives him courage to speak to Holmes about his drug use. Having thought about his objections for many months, all Watson can say is "Which is it today . . . cocaine or morphine?"[11]

Holmes's response to this very factual question is simply to offer the answer: "It is cocaine . . . a seven-per-cent solution. Would you care to try it?"[12] Watson responds by excusing himself not because of any moral objection but simply because of the weakness of his own body due to an injury in the Afghan campaign: "No, indeed . . . I cannot afford to throw any extra strain upon it."[13] Watson's answer then prompts the first objection to cocaine in the text, which, quite naturally, comes not from Watson but from Holmes himself: "I suppose that its influence is physically a bad one."[14] However, that is as far as the objections go, and the rest of his comment elaborates on why he *continues* to use cocaine: "I find it, however, so transcendentally stimulating and clarifying to the mind that its secondary action is a matter of small moment."[15] The difficulty for us at this point is that we have a reliable anti-crime detective offering us a prodrug position. Notice that what bothers Watson as well is not that Holmes's drug use makes him unfit for the job on moral grounds, but simply on physiological grounds:

> But consider! [said Watson] Count the cost! Your brain may, as you say, be roused and excited, but it is a pathological and morbid process which involves increased tissue-change and may at least leave a permanent weakness. You know too what a black reaction comes upon you. Surely the game is hardly worth the candle. Why should you, for a mere passing pleasure, risk the loss of those great powers with which you have been endowed?[16]

Interestingly enough, Watson does not object to Holmes being a cocaine user *and* a representative of the law. This is a startling absence for us, because by our standards Holmes would have already have fallen at the first hurdle because his *impossible* position of being a drug user *and* an enforcer of the law would instantly disqualify him as a reliable narrator, let alone as a detective.

A brief contemporary example is all we need to substantiate this point. In March 1999 the BBC reported that an internal investigation revealed that known criminals who were under arrest were offered large quantities of drugs by the police department if they confessed to crimes they had not committed. By collaborating with the police in this way, the Department could produce impressive figures to show that West Yorkshire police were doing a good job of tackling crime. Now, the only reason that this story is newsworthy at all is precisely because the West Yorkshire police have placed themselves into that impossible space that Holmes occupies: they cannot be detectives and offer people drugs. Such a deconstructive act on the part of the police has to then be met with moral and legal outrage so as to unblur the boundaries between drugs and the law.[17]

This objection is strangely absent from Doyle's text. Even though Watson is upset by Holmes's drug use, he does not call the law and get him thrown out of a job. While the cocaine may produce "tissue-change" as Watson calls it, Watson has no problem at all with Holmes being a drug user and a detective per se. In fact Watson reveals that his concern for Holmes is not ethical and moral but simply friendly and medical: "Remember that I speak not only as one comrade to another but as a medical man to one for whose constitution he is to some extent answerable."[18] Holmes does not dispute any of Watson's arguments and also "did not seem offended" by his remarks.[19]

The other thing that makes this text reverberate with oddities is that even though Holmes is obviously injecting regularly—according to Watson's observations—the question of being addicted to cocaine is not even raised while the reason for Holmes's cocaine use is simply a way of avoiding boredom. As soon as Holmes's mind can be occupied, then he simply will not need the drug: "My mind rebels at stagnation. Give me problems, give me work, give me the most abstruse cryptogram, or the most intricate analysis, and I am in my own proper atmosphere. I can dispense then with artificial stimulants."[20] A little later Watson inquires if he has any case currently under investigation and Holmes simply replies "None. Hence the cocaine."[21]

Comically enough, Holmes does express concern over one "shocking habit" and that is "guessing": "No, no: I never guess. It is a shocking habit. . . ."[22] At this point the case of *The Sign of the Four* truly begins and the cocaine is not referred to again until the end of the story. Once the case is finally closed the novella ends with Watson getting a wife and Jones getting all the credit for solving the mystery, and Watson asks Holmes what is left for him: "'For me . . . there still remains the cocaine-bottle.' And he stretched his long white hand up for it."[23] In short, once the mystery is solved and stagnation threatens to descend once more upon Holmes so the cocaine must be called upon. Doyle's text thus reveals that cocaine was not always seen as a drug that would destroy your life, but was something that could be taken at will and abandoned if a more stimulating activity comes along to replace it. The horrors of addiction are also startlingly absent from the text.

Baudelaire on Hashish

In his 1850 essay "Wine and Hashish Compared as a Means to achieve a Multiplication of the Individual's Potential," Baudelaire points out that hashish initially *seems* to be a way of accessing more life: " . . . temporal and existential proportions are disturbed by the multiplicity and intensity of your feelings and ideas. It would *seem* as if you were living several lifetimes in the space of an hour."[24] Hashish, which will cause "no serious harm," induces not a loss, but "an intensification of one's individuality."[25] If we feel that drugs cause problems, for Baudelaire, hashish actually appears to resolve them: "Every philosophical problem is resolved. Every difficult question that presents a point of contention for theologians, and brings despair to thoughtful men, becomes clear and transparent. Every contradiction is reconciled."[26]

Were this as far as it went, Baudelaire would seem very strange to us in his unqualified support of hashish. However, having gone to such lengths to praise it, he has to travel an equal distance in condemning hashish. He does this not by directly judging it as a bad drug but by comparing it to wine. In his poem "Get Drunk" Baudelaire makes it quite clear that we are to get drunk on whatever is available: "On wine, or poetry, or virtue, as you will. Only, just get drunk."[27] Interestingly enough for all of its power to allow access to an "intellectual paradise" of "boundless bliss," hashish is conspicuously absent from this list.[28] According to Baudelaire, the effects of hashish must be condemned because "(despite the wealth of benevolence that it seems to cultivate in the heart—or rather, the brain—of man) . . . it is 'antisocial'. . . ."[29] Unlike Collins, who was willing to reveal that foreigners need not be strangers, Baudelaire is eager to prove that hashish is a foreign habit: "Hashish does indeed come to us from the Orient; the stimulating properties of hemp were well known in ancient Egypt . . . India . . . Algeria and Arabia."[30] In contrast, wine, unlike the alien hashish, is French and therefore "profoundly human."[31] The easy framework of colonialism is ready at hand for Baudelaire to "explain" the two substances, and we are not shocked to learn that while wine, "the soul of the Nation," is "industrious," it is hashish, "the other," that is "essentially lazy."[32]

Baudelaire slips neatly into our own categories regarding drug users when he informs us that hashish must be condemned because it "belongs to the class of solitary pleasures; it is made for the pitiful creatures with time on their hands."[33] In contrast wine "yields fruitful results" while hashish is paradoxically both "useless and dangerous."[34] In marked contrast to our own position on the subject of alcoholism, Baudelaire feels that if "hashish destroys" the Will, then wine "exalts the Will."[35] Wine for Baudelaire "is a physical support, hashish is a suicidal weapon."[36] To Baudelaire, taking hashish means that you have "strewn your personality in all directions and now you are having a bit of difficulty in putting it back together again."[37] In contrast to his earlier pronouncements that hashish intensified life, now it does so at a very high price and this is a "just punishment" for the "ungodly waste of so much nervous energy."[38] While the drug may not effect a person's health, Baudelaire makes it clear that a man who can do "nothing but dream" cannot really be said to be "in good health."[39] Part of the reason for this is that in taking hashish "it is the Will that is attacked, and the Will is the body's most precious organ."[40] Putting aside Baudelaire's lack of medical knowledge, it seems strange that he would position the Will as an "organ" that, like a nation, can be "attacked" or defended. For Baudelaire, the error in taking hashish is that "man is forbidden to disturb the primordial conditions of his existence, or break the equilibrium between his mind and his environment."[41] Thus this drug user is someone who destroys a natural condition, substituting an artificial paradise in its place. The drug, even though it is "useless," is strong enough to crumble a nation: "If there were a government in whose interest it was to corrupt its subjects, the only thing necessary would be to encourage the use of hashish."[42] The drug user's garden of false delights is thus placed in stark contrast to the "real" worlds made by poets who, "through constant work and meditation, through the conscientious use of our Will . . . have made ourselves a garden of true beauty."[43]

The paradox that is exposed here is rather unsettling. When we listen to Baudelaire tell us that wine exalts the Will, for example, or that wine is industrious and is a physical support, we know, thanks to Alcoholics Anonymous (AA) and the Twelve Step Program, that such views on alcohol are completely wrong and dangerous. If we can now see that Baudelaire has constructed wine in a way that we find unacceptable today, we must make the next logical step and ask ourselves how his constructions of the hashish user (and our parallel construction of drugs) might also be misplaced. While we have actively rewritten Baudelaire's script for wine, we have left his script for the drug user completely unrevised. Having rejected all he says about wine, we have chosen to cherish his view of drug use as the truth about drugs. Imagine the following scenario: you enter an AA meeting and proceed to get them to accept Baudelaire's view of wine. A difficult task. Then walk into a Narcotics Anonymous meeting and Baudelaire's view of drugs will no longer be laughable, but will be the main currency of the debate. Where do we have to stand in order to see that maybe Baudelaire was "wrong" about drug use?

Baudelaire's analysis of hashish offers us a nice place to start reconstructing what it is that we think of our own drug users. It is clear from Baudelaire's work that his framework enables him to present himself as being industrious and creative and patriotic, while also showing how one can bolster their Will by drinking wine. For Baudelaire, there is no contradiction between celebrating wine and the notion of hard work, while segregating hashish as an antisocial drug. The same positions are in use today whereby alcohol advertisements extol community, warmth, sociability, and connectedness, while drugs and drug users are condemned as destructive, dangerous, antisocial, and antihealth. The Metropolitan Police recently ran an advertising campaign in England that showed a photo of a young man injecting himself, and below this simple image were the words "Your car stereo just shot up his arm" (see figure 2.1). Such messages perpetuate an image of the drug user as a social threat who, like some urban wizard, can transform your personal possessions (gotten through honest hard work) into a short-lived experience of pleasure. Another advertisement showed another young man with his eyes in shadow, accompanied by the text: "I only mug people when I get desperate. I get desperate every 36 hours" (see figure 2.2).

The objective is to realize that any drug, as well as its users, are not inherently social or antisocial in themselves in some chemical way, but are written as such by us. It is easy to imagine that if to Baudelaire, wine is "the soul of the Nation," would not hashish be the substance of choice for the patriot in the "Oriental" nations that Baudelaire lists? One can, with a little effort, imagine the mirror image of Baudelaire's text in which *hashish* would be seen to strengthen the (National) will, while foreign wine threatens to undermine the Nation's abilities.

Moreau and Hashish

In his closing remarks on hashish and wine, Baudelaire singles out Jean Jacques Moreau who, he says, has been foolish enough to suggest that madness could be cured by the use of hashish. He concludes that "[t]he doctor who dreamed up this fine system is hardly what could be called a philosopher."[44] What is surprising about this is that while Moreau's ideas come remarkably close to Baudelaire's, the distinction is that Moreau is wholly convinced that hashish, far from being "useless and dangerous," as Baudelaire believed, was in fact a very useful medicine. This throws the construction of hashish even further off its axis, as Moreau's research undermines Baudelaire's notion that the drug is only of use to the solitary delinquent. Moreau's work *Hashish and Mental Illness* (1845) was seen to be at odds with a popular opinion like that of Baudelaire. As Lasegue points out Moreau's work "goes beyond the customary scope of current publications. Moreau has embarked upon an unknown path, and even though his contentions sometimes verge upon incongruities one should not forget that they have this in common with all works of essential originality."[45] While this is indeed a generous review, Moreau's work certainly stands opposed to the model set up by Baudelaire. For example, whereas Baudelaire unquestioningly articulated an East/West divide in his drug classification, Moreau is careful to redress the

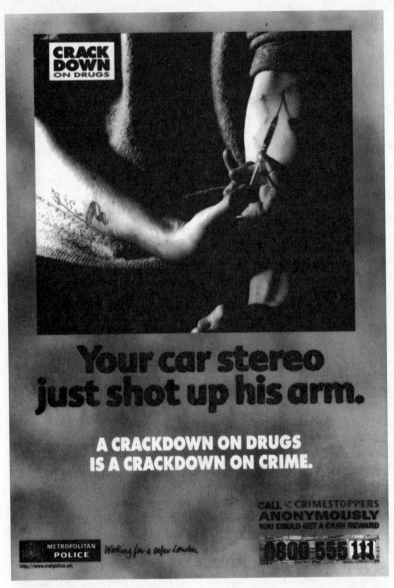

Figure 2.1. Transforming technology (permission of Metropolitan Police [UK]).

balance somewhat. In 1843 Moreau published his treatise on transcultural psychiatry, "Recherches sur les Alienes en Orient" and concluded that, unlike Baudelaire " . . . one ought not to form an unfavorable idea about

Figure 2.2. The hollow spectre of drugs (permission of Metropolitan Police [UK]).

hashish. It is the same with hashish in Egypt as it is with wine and alcoholic beverages in Europe. The use of it is equally common. Almost all Moslems eat hashish . . . and, yet, *it is extremely seldom* that one encounters persons upon whom the hashish has the disastrous effects we have spoken about here . . . wine and liquors are a thousand times more dangerous."[46] It seems almost gratuitous that Moreau would have to tell us that when it comes to his opinion on hashish, his "words have frequently been met with disbelief."[47] How can we then relocate our own position so that the drug user becomes "common" and beneath notice, rather than a heavily stereotyped public enemy?

Framed as a medicine, Moreau's taking of hashish can be labeled by him as an "experiment," rather than one of Baudelaire's solitary pleasures of a delinquent, and the drug, rather than breaking or destroying anything, is seen as helping to solve the mystery and painful sufferings of the mentally ill.[48] The drug enables Moreau to enter into the foreign territory of madness by providing him with a convincing disguise. Indeed, Moreau develops this notion of the drug as a kind of spy by referring to it as an "agent provocateur."[49] In contrast to Baudelaire's assertion that hashish destroys the Will, in Moreau we see how even though the patient may be "misled . . . by delusions or hallucinations . . . (the normal person) still remains one's own master."[50] Rather than losing control, for Moreau, hashish offers the user a copy of madness through which he can "comprehend the ravings of a madman . . . but without having lost the power to evaluate the psychic changes occurring in the mind."[51] Unlike Baudelaire's sense that hashish undermines control, to Moreau, hashish generously offers control.

Concealing Drug Pushers

Moreau and Baudelaire's different readings of drugs really center around the question of control and the loss of control. While their concerns were physiological, our social concerns about drugs are also focused around the issue of control. The task that we generate for ourselves on our relationship to drugs is always a narrative in which we are constantly struggling for control. We must constantly be alert and observant, always on the lookout for anything that might endanger the Self or its representatives. We never place drugs directly in view; we ensure that they are always kept out of sight and then employ our energies in trying to uncover them. Drugs, and those who would use them, are always already a potential threat, never present, never absent, but always lurking in the liminal space of the possible. This translates into a sense that drug users are ingenious at concealing themselves, their desires, and their drugs. The hidden specter of drugs is thus always conveniently on hand as evidence that it is an enemy that needs to be controlled. For example, in an advertisement put out by the Partnership for a Drug-Free America, the question of surveillance and control is paramount.

The image shows a group of eight happy white children closely grouped together, with the question, "Can you spot the drug pusher?" appearing over their heads. I was hoping to be able to reproduce this image, which was made by the Partnership for a Drug-Free America, but I was told by their permissions department that what I was saying about the advert in my text was, "inaccurate" and that my book was not "a mechanism for reaching [the] goal" of reducing the demand for illegal drugs, and therefore they felt they could not allow me to reprint the image. As we can see, the ideology of the anti-drug position seems to allow no room for analysis or critique. It would appear that the truth of the anti-drug position must be swallowed whole and cannot be interrogated.

The implication of the advertisement is that the drug pusher/user is so devious that no amount of looking will be enough to seek them out. Having invited us to look hard at the picture for signs of a drug pusher, we then search the children's faces for signs of drugs. Somewhere beneath that innocent exterior of health lies an evil drug pusher just waiting to spring to life and infect/addict all of the other innocent children. The advertisement is actually asking us to do something very strange: it is asking us to hallucinate in order for us to see not children, but drug pushers. Fearing that normal children are really drug pushers also implies that we are in the grip of some kind of paranoia. This wide-ranging network also ensures that the field of drugs spans the range of our moral field of vision insofar as children (innocence) and drug pushers (evil) occupy not just the same terrain, but in this case, even the same physical body. The hope that the advertisement holds out to us—albeit a false promise—is that if we could examine the picture well enough, the drug pusher would be found and the problem will go away. Yet by pushing the pusher out of the picture we perpetuate the mystery, allowing our "disgustful curiosity" for drugs to remain. Having (obviously) failed to "find" something that was never there in the picture, the text tells us that "[w]e all know what drug pushers look like." Yet this is not because we have any "real" experience of them, whatever that would mean, but because of a *fiction:* "We've seen them often enough on the television." The media has therefore told us what to look for.

If the young children are transformed into potential time-bombs of drug use because of "some innocent looking classmate," then schoolchildren may look innocent but that may just be a front to push drugs. In the same way that Utterson and Lanyon find it difficult to keep track of Hyde, so the parent is up against an almost impossible challenge, since children whose friends use drugs are "eight times more likely" (to match the number of children in the picture?) to use drugs. Anticipating our exhausted response the advertisement asks: "How do you beat odds like that?" The solution is that parents are advised to put *themselves* in the picture: "Get to know your kid's friends—and their parents." Like the empty unspeakable space occupied by

Hyde, drug pushers occupy an arena that cannot be detected visibly—a fact "proved" by the indisputable realism of this photograph—but that have the power to destroy the innocence and purity that surrounds them. It is surely crucial that the children are also all white; if there was one black child in the picture it would upset the narrative of the advertisement, for then the text and image would seem to identify the pusher clearly enough. The "solution" to the problem then is for "strong willed" parents to put themselves into the breach, thus short-circuiting the pusher's ability to dismantle the healthy group of children.

However, we could also read it like this. Imagine a community of children who have no interest in drugs and some parent starts pushing themselves into their lives, quizzing their friends and even their parents about drugs. The advertisement suggests that if the parent does this, then the likelihood of a pusher getting to the children is reduced. Yet what we realize is that the parent, by entering "into the picture" actually becomes the drug-information pusher. The advertisement also asks parents to ask your kids "how they feel" about drugs. Now, assuming that they have not been "told" what to feel by DARE, or the Partnership for a Drug-Free America, how can they respond? Let us assume that they respond "innocently" by saying that they feel that drugs are nobody's business but the person using them, or that drugs are not evil, or that drugs are not a problem to them. At this point the dialogue with the children would break down, because these opinions about drugs are "wrong" and the children are not entitled to these kind of opinions and will have to be "educated" into having the right feelings and ideas about drugs.

The advertisement rehearses the same issue that was explored in *The Moonstone,* whereby the cultural response to the problem of the drug is to try to keep a distance between the drug and the innocent domestic space of the family/child. However, we need to apply Collins's logic to this situation also. In *The Moonstone* the problem is resolved by collapsing the distance between drugs and the family. Hence if we are also to free ourselves of the problem of drugs we need to *collapse the distance* between ourselves and drugs, not preserve it. The solution that we need to try in this case is to allow children/ourselves and drugs to become *closer,* rather than getting exhausted while repeatedly failing to keep them isolated.

Princess Diana on Drugs

During the summer of 1992 *The Times* ran a story entitled "Princess speaks up for addicts." Coming in the wake of the Conservative government's White Paper "Health of the Nation," the article outlined the Princess of Wales's call for increased research into "the causes of drug addiction," in which she "pleaded for greater understanding of addicts."[52] Speaking at a conference on addiction in Glasgow, which has a very high number of AIDS cases, the Princess of Wales spoke of the "horror, evil and violence" of drug dependence. To begin with, it is surely a problem when someone has to "speak up" for addicts. Who or what has deprived them of a voice? Only the powerless need defending, and by speaking up for addicts (and possibly putting words in their mouths), such an action only ensures that they stay powerless. What is it that we fear addicts will say if allowed to speak? The Princess's characterization of the addict that we see here is thus dependent upon evoking a composite image of Stevenson's notorious evil addict Mr. Hyde, who is permitted *carte blanche* access to the back alleys of the British imagination.

This image is reinforced when she discusses the truth of addiction by offering what could be taken as a summary of Stevenson's story: "Addiction removes any semblance of social behavior. An extreme evil surfaces in people who may previously have seemed pleasant."[53] The Princess goes on to argue that we need to understand "the origins of addiction," striking out against "self-appointed moralists" who "from behind a cloud of cigarette smoke" claim "that addiction was a weakness."[54] This, at first, really sounds promising—maybe the Princess will suggest that drug addiction is *not* a weakness. In an attempt to reverse the stereotype of addiction as a moral weakness, the Princess goes on to state that "[s]ome studies had indicated that half the prison population was locked up as a result of addiction and dependency. Yet those ensnared were often sensitive, creative people."[55] Having stated that addiction should no longer be seen as a moral weakness, and that many addicts are "sensitive and creative people," she undermines her early promise for a different way of reading addiction when she asserts that like the Victorian hysteric, the "sensitivity" of the individual is the very flaw, like childhood weakness, that makes people susceptible to drugs and addiction in the first place. Strangely enough, the gateway drug in this whole process of decline and the catalyst of addiction is not marijuana, or even alcohol or cigarettes, but stories:

> . . . lively imaginations had long chosen to hide in fantasy worlds for protection rather than face a raw and real world. Imaginative children lose themselves in fantasy worlds through stories. Later they might choose to escape through Ecstasy, uppers, alcohol and addiction.[56]

This is really quite a wonderful analysis: that sensitive imaginations are actually the catalysts of drug use. Having said that the addiction is horrible, she then speaks (as if describing the unknown yet terrifying Hyde) of the "almost incomprehensible horror which drug addicts wield."[57] What is horrible, the addict or the addiction? If *addicts* are horrible, she cannot know precisely because the horror of *addiction* is almost incomprehensible. The truth of drug addiction is unspeakable at the same time that it must always be spoken of, while it can be neither comprehended nor apprehended.

What *is* horrifying is that the Princess of Wales could address a conference of delegates from 54 countries on the evils of addiction by drawing an analogy between the power of stories that lure sensitive minds (i.e., children), and the decision to take a range of pharmacological substances. The message is that literature, in setting up unreal worlds to which children can escape, habituates them to the need for drugs. Is this any more or less strange an assumption than Moreau suggesting that hashish could cure mental illness? The Princess states that not all children are susceptible, but only those who are sensitive; a weakness that paradoxically empowers them to take control because they can then "choose to escape" through drugs. The use of "choose" is itself misleading because she feels that the use of drugs is not a choice but a weakness, which, as in the nineteenth-century disease model of addiction, is rooted in the sensibility of the addict. Like Ezra Jennings's "femininity," or Hyde's "weeping like a woman," the Princess's formulation returns the causes of addiction back onto the hysterical tendencies of the addict who cannot choose anything but to be addicted.[58] Far from speaking up for addicts, she is simply reconsigning them to the pseudoscientific cul-de-sac where we wish them to remain. Her formulation, rather than speaking up for addicts, merely silences them. Such a model also neutralizes any attempts to rethink addiction.

As in the nineteenth-century disease model, the addict is still seen to be suffering from two things. First, we believe that addicts are victims of their own diseased will (sensitivity), making addiction a personal failing, and second, they are suffering from a medical condition that places them firmly under the scrutiny of the medical and legal establishment, making their addiction a disease that can (possibly) be cured. As in the Victorian scenario, our own addicts can only lose. If they do not respond to medical treatment and suffer a relapse, the medical establishment can argue that the patient's will is diseased, in which case the addict will be referred to a psychiatrist. If medical treatment is successful, then the cured addict becomes the embodied truth of the ability of medicine (or will power) to overcome addiction. Berridge and Edwards point out that the nineteenth-century model was identical to our current model:

> [a] strong moral component ensured a disease theory which was individually oriented, where the addict was responsible for a condition which was somehow also the proper province for medical intervention. Opium eating was medicalized; but failure to achieve cure was a failure of personal responsibility, not medical science. . . . Health was equated with self-discipline.[59]

Having asserted in her opening statement that we can no longer continue to perceive addiction as a weakness, Princess Diana goes on to say that it may be "worthwhile exploring some characteristics of addicts so that vulnerable people can be helped away from allowing themselves to be sucked into the habit."[60] Addiction is here seen as some kind of mental quicksand into which people allow themselves (or is it choose?) to be sucked/throw themselves. The habit itself is anthropomorphized into a living object and the question of will displaced. The vulnerable person is perceived as lacking the necessary will to fight addiction, because their will has abandoned them, having surrendered its strength to the other side, to the habit. We believe that this willpower is now in the hands of the habit that has the strength to pull one into itself. The rationale is that addicts are divided against themselves and will be cured if they can wrestle their will away from the drug and place it back where it belongs: in the Self. The sense that without the Will the Self is empty contributes to the popular conception of the junkie with his or her burnt-out eyes revealing only a hollow Self (see figure 2.2). Unlike the burnt-out addict, whose brain has been cooked by drugs, the Princess tells us that in opposition to the fictional world of escape and literature/drugs, the "real world" is preferable because it is "raw."[61]

What if we suggested that the drug user is not trapped in drug addiction but is silenced and trapped by being deeply embedded in a fiction of drug use that is itself circular and slippery. Instead of questioning the Princess's formula, Professor Fred Edwards, director of social work for Strathclyde, in Scotland, praises the Princess's speech on drugs for its *accuracy,* stating that in his professional opinion "she had a strong grasp of the issues involved."[62] Here, as in all of the popular discussions of drugs, it is the notion of control ("a strong grasp" of the issues) that becomes synonymous with truth. The Princess's speech outlines how a call to modernize and change our attitude to addiction simply rehearses a Victorian fiction, revealing the ways in which contemporary culture still perceives the addict as suffering from a weak will.[63]

A rhetoric that positions the Will as less than it could be is thus the fulcrum that in recent years has provided a framework through which to channel discourses regarding both AIDS and drug use. The two main (perceived) risk groups in the AIDS scenario are IV drug users and homosexual men, and it would seem that addiction and sexuality are often felt to be consanguineous. As Sedgwick has pointed out, these two categories of subjectivity have traditionally, since the nineteenth century, been one of the main arenas for presenting examples of the Will gone awry.[64]

As regards homosexuality and drug addiction, the subject's lack of Will is understood as a turning inward, a narcissistic denial of life whereby the drug user desires a mirror image of the self. This emerges either through the hallucinatory phantasm of drugs—in which a nonproductive pleasure is carried out within the borders of one's own body—or else through the choice of same-sex partners. These actions are then read as visible signs of a diseased will. The two groups collapse into each other, with both junkies and homosexuals being perceived as engaging in endless rounds of pleasure for its own sake. As Leo Bersani points out, "the act being represented may itself be associated with insatiable desire, unstoppable sex."[65] The role of the addict, who only lives to score more drugs, merges into the image of the homosexual who spends night after night leaping between anonymous sexual encounters. In both groups sexuality becomes an addictive disease, and the desire for IV drug use blurs into HIV. Our culture thus persists in the belief that what makes such subjects at risk from AIDS is their unwilled behavior, in which the Self has been invaded by a loss of will. The loss of will means that the Self, like a castle with its drawbridge down, or, as Susan Sontag says, like a form of "high-tech warfare," can now be invaded by the foreign virus.[66] In this scenario, as a "cure" for AIDS, the control of the Will through abstinence is seen to be the only way that we can guarantee against HIV infection.

The Will is thus seen as the repository of the Self and sense, and by "removing" it with drugs, the body is left without its will, and is a dead, senseless body, as if drugs had put the body's defense system to sleep. The cure for both drugs and AIDS is the enunciation of denial and will ("Just Say No"), which at the level of awareness programs is read as the need to be awake, alert, and armed with information. As we saw with the Princess of Wales, addicts (either drug addicts or homosexuals addicted to unsafe sex), are placed at the center of a rhetoric that allows them no space in which to speak differently about their position. They are always given plenty of space to repeat and reinforce the current rhetoric, for example by confessing, but no space is made for them to offer a route that would lead away from the current discourses. We say that addicts lack the willpower to do anything but get high, and like homosexuals (and like the Victorian undeserving poor who do not deserve charity), they are perceived as having no agency, unable to exert their will because it is consumed by their addiction. Paradoxically we seem to have constructed drug users as having *no* agency, as well as being configured as wishing to willfully infect/destroy/addict the rest of the population. They have no will, which is why they are addicts; but their condition then provides them with a dangerous (superhuman) willpower that is intent only on harm.

Seeking Mr. Hyde

The seeming density of the rhetoric that aims to keep the drug user in place does not prevent us from locating moments where the rhetoric does unravel, or gets into difficulties. While Robert Louis Stevenson's *The Strange Case of Dr. Jekyll and Mr. Hyde* seems to offer a simple binary of good/healthy vs. evil/drugs, the novel actually articulates a position on drugs at odds with what we want drugs to mean in our own culture.[67]

As William Burroughs has said, the addict is always a "creature without species" and Hyde is described in the novel as a "creature" who is inhuman, and "inorganic."[68] Hyde's origins are similarly invisible: "his family could nowhere be traced; he had never been photographed. . . ."[69] Obviously, the addict, as in the case of the Princess's speech, must be asked to play a vital cultural role, while simultaneously remaining absent and invisible, thus leaving more space for us to give free reign to our own wild constructions. The origins of the enmity toward the drug user are also untraceable. As Jeykll's servant Poole tells us, "there was something queer about that gentleman— something that gave a man a turn—I don't know rightly how to say it. . . ."[70] There is a "curiosity as to his origin" as the addict makes "an impression without any nameable malformation."[71] While all of these factors "were points against him . . . not all of these together could explain the hitherto unknown disgust, loathing and fear with which Mr. Utterson regarded him."[72] While Hyde may be strange to these characters in the novel, none of these constructions are really very strange to us, and in fact we can feel quite comfortable with these positions, for we like our addicts to be shady, incomprehensible figures. We also like to feel disgust, loathing, and fear when it comes to our own drug users.

For Jekyll's companion, Mr. Lanyon, the drug user operates on him with a "disgustful curiosity."[73] His friend Utterson is also troubled both by his "ignorance" as well as his "knowledge" of Hyde.[74] As we saw in Collins, Stevenson's addict is demarcated by a zone of unintelligibility:

> "He is not easy to describe. There is something wrong with his appearance; something displeasing, something downright detestable. I never saw a man I so disliked, and yet I scarce know why. He must be deformed somewhere; he gives a strong feeling of deformity, although I couldn't specify the point. He's an extraordinary-looking man, and yet I can name nothing out of the way. No sir, I can make no hand of it; I can't describe him. And it's not want of memory; for I declare I can see him this moment."[75]

What puzzles and so keeps Utterson's attention, as well as preserving our interest in the narrative, is that the addict's image cannot be placed:

> . . . even in his dreams it had no face, or one that baffled him and melted before his eyes; and thus it was that there sprang up and grew apace in the lawyer's mind a singularly strong, almost an inordinate curiosity to behold the features of the real Mr. Hyde. If he could but once set eyes on him, he thought

the mystery would lighten and perhaps roll altogether away, as was the habit of mysterious things when well examined.[76]

Allowing Hyde/addict to be known, and to be normal, would obviously make the mystery "roll away," but it seems that this is precisely the thing that we do not want to happen. In short, it seems that we desire to preserve what Jekyll/Hyde perceptively locates as his "nameless situation."[77]

If Hyde can be described, it is via his lack of a stable physique: "The few who could describe him differed widely, as common observers will. Only on one point were they agreed; and that was the haunting sense of unexpressed deformity with which the fugitive impressed his beholders."[78] The only thing we know about Hyde is that he "had no shape . . ." and has only a deformity, and even his lack of shape is unexpressed.[79] Insofar as he is occupying a cultural position that is outside of our binary thinking of good/bad, innocent/pure, he is literally unthinkable. Because he is a term beyond our logic, as we have constructed it, everyone is confused by his existence. He blurs our logic, and as such his position threatens to dismantle the "roots" of our thinking, in the same way that the vision of Hyde shakes Lanyon's life "to its roots."[80] We therefore cannot allow the drug user to become "possible." The survival of our "logic" requires that the addict remain veiled.

Our culture quite readily sets up a binary of good/innocent vs. evil/drug addicts, but in the novel this easy division is thrown into question—the two positions that we make available to ourselves are both revealed as inadequate. As Jekyll points out, "I was no more myself when I laid aside restraint and plunged in shame, than when I laboured."[81] The Self on drugs thus slides *between* the work ethic of self-control *and* the antiproduction of dissipation and self-centered pleasures. Jekyll circumvents this problem by having not one nature as we do, but by having two natures, saying that if he could claim "to be either, it was only because [he] was radically both."[82] In the same way that Sergeant Cuff was unable to perceive the duplicity at the root of the mystery of the moonstone, Hyde's duplicity also makes him invisible to detection: "Mr. Hyde had disappeared out of the ken of the police as though he had never existed."[83] Jekyll himself states that as a result of being able to hide within the drug (as well as physically hiding away in his laboratory/pharmacy) he "did not even exist."[84] That his drug offers itself as a "cure" is signaled by the fact that Hyde speaks of the "strange immunities of [his] position."[85] The drug thus makes him into a criminal, at the same time that it provides him with immunity to detection, in the same way that in *The Moonstone* we saw how laudanum makes Blake both guilty *and* innocent of the crime/not crime that he committed.

So instead of us writing narratives in which the sick side is guilty and the healthy side is innocent, we should blur the healthy and the sick, mix them, confuse them, join them, so that we then have at least two more positions available: that of the healthily sick, and that of sickly health. Jekyll even suggests as much, saying that he understands fully how the addict is placed both inside and outside the cultural discourse when he tells Utterson that: "[He is] painfully situated . . . my position is a very strange—a very strange one. It is one of those affairs that cannot be mended by talking."[86]

Our rhetoric asks us to turn away in disgust from the drug-using self, yet when Jekyll sees himself on drugs in his mirror, he responds not with repulsion but with a calm attraction: " . . . when I looked upon that ugly idol in the glass, I was conscious of no repugnance, rather a leap of welcome. This, too, was myself. It seemed natural and human. . . ."[87] On another occasion he tells us that the other self seems "none the less natural to me."[88] While we wish to assume that Jekyll is the good side and Hyde is the evil that must be destroyed, Jekyll tells us that in fact they are balanced and that "both sides of me were in dead earnest."[89] The suggestion, contrary to the usual reading of the text, is that the Self on drugs can, must, and should be accepted as an equally natural and legitimate part of the human self.[90]

In contrast to the Self on drugs as being natural, Jekyll makes it quite clear that it is not Hyde who is sick so much as the normal Self/Jekyll that is sick. Having "drank off the potion" Jekyll experiences a "grinding in the bones, deadly nausea, and a horror of the spirit that cannot be exceeded at the hour of birth or death. . . ."[91] One would then expect to be told that the horror of Hyde overtook him, however, Stevenson's text then continues " . . . and I came to myself as if out of a great sickness."[92] What Stevenson is suggesting then is that it is the sober, virtuous Self, which, far from being the cure is, in itself, "a great sickness."[93] The drug thus enables Jekyll to cure himself of the "sickness" of his Self. Just as in our own rhetoric of addiction, this sickness (the Self) will return, as Jekyll finds out, so the only real cure would be to realize that these two poles (and maybe more) of the self will *always* be in constant circulation. As such they cannot be policed against, and any demarcations between parts of the Self/non-Self are doomed to fail. Stevenson's text reveals that even if we reverse the terms of the binary so that the Self is a horrifying sickness and the drugged self is healthy, they will still insist on spilling over into each other.

Toward the end of his life Jekyll is in a position where he has to take the drug in order to be "himself"; *without* the drug, Hyde always returns. Thus, this is the reverse of his initial experiment. Stevenson is suggesting that our attempts to exclude drugs from the Self only serves to reinforce half of the picture. As Jekyll found out to his detriment: "when the attempt is made to cast [the non-Self] off, it but returns upon us with more unfamiliar and more awful pressure."[94] Jekyll realizes that the two sides of the Self can never be kept separate, and that in fact there may be more than just two sides to our sense of Self:

> . . . man is not truly one, but truly two. I say so, because the state of my own knowledge does not pass beyond that point. Others will follow, others will outstrip me on the same lines; and I hazard the guess that man will be ultimately known for a mere polity of multifarious, incongruous and independent denizens.[95]

Stevenson's text thus points to our own failure—we persist in attempting, through a rhetoric of what Jekyll refers to as a life of "virtue, effort and control," to keep good and evil, healthy and sick, innocent children and evil drug pushers, in two separate areas. While Jekyll learns from his failure, realizing that there may be parts of the Self, or even versions of the Self that are "incongruous" with each other, we persist in trying to carry on Jekyll's already failed experiment, first by limiting ourselves to only two selves, and in addition by trying to keep the good and the bad separate from each other.[96]

Stevenson's text is thus a word of advice to us to end our folly of the healthy/sick binary and move to a place where some of those "incongruous" selves can come to light and be together. At one point in the novel Utterson attends a party at Jekyll's home and "the face of the host had looked from one to the other as in the old days when the trio were inseparable friends."[97] I feel that Stevenson is suggesting that the Self and the drugged Self need not be separated, but should also become "inseparable friends" once again. Sadly, we insist on using the text as proof that we are right to blindly insist on our desire to keep healthy and sick as eternal enemies. Some might argue that this would be a great thing to do if only cocaine "in itself" were not such a deadly and powerful drug. Once again, while we imagine that the drug that Jekyll makes is malicious and evil, Stevenson tells us quite clearly that Jekyll's drug "was neither diabolical nor divine."[98] Quite simply, the drug has no power of its own on either side: the only power it has is the power we ascribe to it.

Jekyll tells us that the object of his experiment was to cast out the Other so that the Self would no longer have to acknowledge the "extraneous evil" of the other Self, something that he finds out is impossible.[99] However, what Jekyll learns is not that the use of the drug is "wrong" (such a label would be meaningless), but that any attempt to close off the link between the Self and its Other is doomed to fail. By the end of the story Jekyll is unable to accept that the Self could be composed of more than one side, and kills himself in order to destroy Hyde. Stevenson has left us with something to ponder by telling us, with no trace of irony, that in comparison to Jekyll's suicidal behavior, Hyde's "love of life was wonderful."[100] Jekyll, like us, is quite prepared to kill himself to get rid of "drugs," while Hyde's "love of life" is wonderful in that he wants more possibilities and more positions of the Self to be in existence. Unlike Jekyll, who wants to close down the Self—and finally succeeds—Hyde always wants to keep the Self open so that we stand a better chance of finding some of those "multifarious" avenues that Jekyll was aware existed, but was unwilling to open.

When we come to the end of Jekyll's narrative, there is a sense that we are meant to feel relief that Hyde has been destroyed; however, we should be sad that an opportunity to rewrite our relationship to drugs has been lost. The addict is supposed to be feared but not understood or seen: like one of Jekyll's poisonous letters, the addict must always be "destroyed unread."[101] When Jekyll reveals his Hyde to Lanyon, he prefaces the revelation by telling him that if he "so prefer to choose" then "a new province of knowledge" could be opened up to him.[102] Unfortunately, neither Lanyon nor our culture's reading of the novel has attempted to open up this new province of knowledge.

In its current state, the circumference of our knowledge of drugs and the Self has led, like Jekyll's experiments, "to no end of practical usefulness." However, if we look at this sentence (and the novel) in the mirror in which Jekyll saw his Hyde, we realize that Stevenson has offered us an opening in the rhetoric of drugs. An opening that, on reflection, could be infinitely beneficial: drugs can offer us *"no end"* of practical usefulness."[103]

The Dangerous Supplement

In Virginia Woolf's *To The Lighthouse,* Mrs. Ramsay is off to the local shops and asks the laudanum addict Mr. Carmichael if he wants anything:

> But no, he wanted nothing . . . he would have liked to reply kindly to these blandishments . . . but could not, sunk as he was in a grey-green somnolence which embraced them all, without need of words, in a vast and benevolent lethargy of well-wishing; all the house; all the world; all the people in it, for he had slipped into his glass at lunch a few drops of something. . . . He wanted nothing, he murmured.[104]

In contrast to our hollowed-out image of the addict, this is another costume that we sometimes utilize: someone who is full, completely satisfied, and without lack or need. A contemporary example can be found in the film version of Kim Wozencraft's novel *Rush,* in which a large, overweight black heroin dealer sits languidly on a leather sofa and intones softly and slowly how, once she shoots up, Kristen (Jennifer Jason Leigh) will feel "all un . . . necessary." While an image such as this appears at first to be much more benign, it is simply the other side of the image of the solitary wicked drug taker who is empty, burnt out, and continually craving. This image of Mr. Carmichael, for example, represents that part of our drug logic in which we imagine that such pleasures as this all-encompassing benevolence can and must be fake, and that very shortly he will have to pay the price for his pleasures. We cannot allow this image to remain as some kind of truth about drugs—whatever it might be—but it must always be constructed in our minds as a moment of hubris, or arrogant self-confidence and ignorance of what we "know" to be the real evil and power of drugs. In *Trainspotting* Renton makes a similar point: "People think it's all about misery and desperation and death . . . but what they forget is the pleasure of it. Otherwise we wouldn't do it. After all, we're not fucking stupid. . . ." Once again a comment like this is not allowed to escape from the narrative unquestioned. The end of the film, when he chooses life (as opposed to drugs), makes it clear that the narrative has successfully undermined this position and exposed it as an empty promise. The narrative seems eager to confirm that drug users *are* stupid. The opposite of the "full" contented drugged self is the empty and discontented self. In Wozencraft's novel *Rush,* the heroine, Kristen Cates, informs us that while on cocaine she became "perfectly, completely empty."[105] On the one hand, we construct this emptiness that is also a kind of fulfillment. On the other hand, we construct the image of the sick, dying junkie who is totally empty, hollow, and unfulfilled. This stereotype emerges in *Trainspotting* through the figure of Andy, dying sick and alone in his filthy (and empty) apartment. It would seem that for us the drug user is both a presence (the satiated, "full" drug taker) and an absence (the hollow, sick junkie).

Clearly, the addict, in Jacques Derrida's terms, is a "dangerous supplement."[106] The supplement is dangerous because while it completes the unity of the system, it also draws attention to the fact that the system was always inadequate and incomplete and will remain so. This concept is at work in our own cultural construction of drugs whereby the family is perceived as natural and self-sufficient yet constantly in need of the addict to unite itself against. At the same time that the family wants to exclude drugs by fighting against them, the culture brings them into the family with constant reminders to "Tell Your Children" about the evils of drugs.[107] As we also saw with the case of Hyde, the supplement, because it exists neither completely inside the system nor completely outside of it, is left to be represented in two opposing ways. First, as Derrida points out, "[t]he supplement adds itself, it is a surplus, a plenitude . . . the *fullest measure* of presence."[108] In Stevenson, this operates in the way that Hyde is the center of our attention, the focus of the narrative, the object of our curiosity par excellence. On the other hand, the supplement "adds only to replace. It intervenes or insinuates itself *in-the-place-of;* if it fills, it is as if one fills a void . . . its place is assigned in the structure by the mark of an emptiness."[109] This is obviously also seen in the ways in which Hyde, while being the center of attention, is never described, cannot be placed, and must forever elude our gaze. As Stevenson says, Jekyll/Hyde's position (by being neither of nor outside the system) results in "the strange immunities of [his] position."[110]

Trying to speak of the drug addict will always be hard because of its position/non-position in our frame of reason. For example, as nearly everyone in Stevenson's novel who sees Hyde tells us, they cannot "describe him" or what he looked like, let alone say what he means.[111] As Utterson utters, "What can the man mean?"[112] The supplement/drugged self confounds our sense of reason so that like the houses to which Hyde retreats, "it is hard to say where one ends and another begins."[113] For Derrida, the supplement, like the drugged self, is always "alien" and "exterior," coming to Nature from the outside.[114] The drug addict is therefore an excess that our logic can neither do without and expel, nor completely absorb. To put words in Derrida's mouth: "Reason is incapable of thinking this double infringement. . . . The [drugged Self] is neither in nor out of Nature. . . . The [drugged self as] supplement is equally dangerous for Reason, the natural health of Reason."[115] This accounts for Lanyon dying after seeing Jekyll/Hyde: his logic, and everything he relied upon to reasonably structure the meaning of his world has been "shaken to its roots" by coming face to face with the supplement.[116] The supplement is indeed dangerous. As Derrida points out (although he is talking about Rousseau), what kills Lanyon is that he "neither wishes to think nor can he think that this alteration does not simply happen to the self, that it is the self's very origin. He must consider it a contingent evil coming from without to affect the integrity of the subject."[117] Lanyon says that he will die "incredulous" and it is true that he is unable or unwilling to believe (as we find it hard to believe) that the drugged self could be a valid and "natural" part of the Self.[118] The supplement "breaks with Nature," and like Jekyll's strange (legal) will that keeps Utterson awake at night, making him break his regular routine, the supplement "is properly seductive; it leads desire away from the good path, makes it err far from natural ways, guides it toward its loss or fall and therefore is a sort of lapse or scandal."[119] Drugs, like the drugged Self, are also infected with the "logic" of the supplement, which account for the ways in which drugs are always seen to be leading us away from Reason (and reasonable behavior).[120] This bifurcation that marks the supplement also sheds some light on the ways in which drugs are endlessly hailed by their supporters as "plants of Nature," and endlessly condemned by their adversaries as chemicals, poisons, and artifice. One side wishes to place drugs on the inside, the other wishes to place them on the outside. The trouble is that drugs and the drugged Self will continually resist both of these positions: as a dangerous supplement they undermine any clear distinction between natural *and* alien, foreign *and* domestic, inside *and* outside. The drugged body and drugs are thus often marked by their inability to be pinned down.

If the drug addict cannot always be located by sight, the chances of us being deluded by the addict are dramatically increased. An example of drugs' amorphous status can be seen in a recent article in the *Los Angeles Times,* in which Charlie J. Parsons of the Los Angeles FBI demonstrated how South American cocaine smugglers mix drugs with fiberglass to produce innocuous looking household objects.[121] As with the freckled faces of the children that may have, buried within them, a hidden desire to push drugs, so Parsons shows us how a dog kennel is not used to conceal cocaine, but *is* cocaine. The fear of being deluded by drugs is still very strong as the kennels are "near-perfect replicas" of kennels sold in the United States. This metamorphosis, and this (chemical) mixing of the domestic/pure, and the foreign/toxic, "made the drug all but undetectable by traditional methods." Parsons noted that "This investigation demonstrates how cocaine can be molded into any imaginable shape or form and shipped into any port in the United States." In his conclusion, Parsons said that the investigation had made him "look at some products in a new light. Anything that's made out of plastic or fiberglass, I'm a little suspicious." Even the normal world of inanimate objects now needs surveillance and detection just in case domestic objects turn out to be drugs. These objects offer the same problem to a discourse based on binaries: these objects are beyond binaries, and as such are strange because they are neither dog kennels nor drugs, but are simultaneously both: hence they are (almost) immune to police detection, as Hyde was also immune to police detection. In Stevenson's text, Hyde also escapes the finality of our condemning gaze and judgment while the drugged Self often "promises itself as it escapes, gives itself as it moves away."[122] If the drugged Self were merely the opposite of logic and reason then it would be easy to locate, but the supplement "is maddening because it is neither presence nor absence. . . ."[123] Like Hyde, who is neither the breath nor the mirror but "the stain of breath upon a mirror," the drugged Self is simultaneously "desired and feared."[124] In the moment at which we try to grasp the drug user with one hand, so with the other hand, we place it beyond our own reach.

In the same year that Stevenson wrote of Jekyll's experiments with his powders, Dr. J. K. Baudry described the effects of cocaine poisoning in terms that, in the light of this chapter, should now sound to us not as a medical fact, but simply a fiction that the suicidal Jekyll, and ourselves, persist in believing:

> The most alarming poisonous effects of the drug are: debasing and enslavement of the Will, a general demoralization which is as diabolical as it is indescribable, and which tends rapidly toward depravity and to the development of everything that is degrading and ignoble in human nature.[125]

It is the firm belief in *this* kind of fiction that becomes a dangerous "drug" and it is the users of *this* kind of drug that, as Burroughs points out, constitutes the real "public health problem number one."[126]

Chapter 3 🔖

"Pleasures Impossible to Interpret": Freud and Cocaine

the genuine philosopher . . . lives "unphilosophically" and unwisely, above all, imprudently.

—Nietzsche[1]

To average bourgeois common sense I have been lost long ago.

—Freud[2]

This chapter moves us into the discourses that claim to offer us the truth about drugs: medicine and psychology. By focusing on Sigmund Freud's early writings on cocaine I aim to explore how Freud held positions on cocaine that do not fit with our current positions. What we see in Freud is an attempt, like Collins and Stevenson, to keep the meaning of drugs open, even when all of the signs asked him to narrow his range of meanings. In the face of professional opposition, Freud adamantly maintained his position that cocaine need not be dangerous. Given that the rest of Freud's work has been used to cure drug users, I will suggest that his troublesome writings on cocaine have gone unheeded because Freud continues to seriously undermine and question our discourses about the meaning of drugs.

One month before Stevenson wrote *Jekyll and Hyde* in September 1885, an article appeared in *Lancet* that described a technique whereby a solution of cocaine could be applied to the larynx. In support of the suggestion that *Jekyll and Hyde* was written under the influence of cocaine, Lloyd Osbourne, Fanny Stevenson's son, said that his mother constantly read *Lancet*: "my mother glued herself to it . . . with a view of keeping up with the advance of medicine and gaining some hints that might help [Stevenson]."[3] The article that appeared in *Lancet* a month before Stevenson wrote the novel was an abstract of the lectures on cocaine that Freud had delivered to the Psychiatrische Verien on March 5, 1885.[4] Freud was not alone in his suggestion that cocaine could be a panacea for the medical community. As Schultz points out, by 1884 "[a]n avalanche of papers appeared in the world's medical literature describing the use of cocaine, not only for local and regional anesthesia, but also as a cure for acute coryza, gonorrhea, vomiting of pregnancy, seasickness, hayfever, opium addiction, sore nipples, vaginismus, whooping cough, neuralgia, dysentery, asthma, syphilis, and angina pectoris."[5]

It is my intention at this juncture to suggest that when we read Freud's comments on cocaine, what we see is someone who is anxious to ensure that the meaning of cocaine remains open. The conventional way of reading Freud's work on cocaine usually falls into two camps, which usually meet at various points. The first way is to treat the work as juvenilia, engaged in by an eager young student whose genius was not yet mature, and can thus be discounted. This disables the text while enabling the commentator to humor Freud's fanciful statements, skipping over them so as to spend more time on Freud's "real" mature work. The second way is to treat the work not as innocent juvenilia from someone who as yet knew no better, but to read it as a highly conscious, dangerous, and irresponsible endorsement of a drug that in their opinion is "obviously" dangerous. E. M. Thornton is a good example of the second approach and his statements nicely summarize the first position as well. Although, for reasons which will become clear, he opposes the first approach: "The behavioral eccentricities displayed by Freud in the nineties and dismissed by Jones [Freud's biographer] as the harmless peccadilloes of a man of genius, *must now be given a more sinister interpretation.*"[6] Why? What do we gain by giving the events of the cocaine episode a sinister interpretation? More important, what do we lose access to by doing this?

What I wish to suggest in this section, however, is that these positions are not very useful if we want to unravel our own drug rhetoric. The first position prevents us from taking Freud seriously, while the second asks us to take it so seriously that we have to listen to the statements on cocaine as the rantings of an addict, so that once again they can be dismissed. As Thornton says, it is obvious from what Freud says about cocaine that these writings are "not the preoccupations of a normal mind."[7] In a sense we have to try, even though it is hard, to steer a middle path that allows us to cut ourselves off from our safe moorings on either of these shores and be brave enough to venture off with Freud as he pursues his work. If we do this without being tempted to run back to our safe haven, I think that what we can see in Freud's work on cocaine is someone who, seeing that the drug was rapidly being hemmed in and fixed into a very formulaic rubric, was actively attempting to defend the drug against this conceptual imprisonment. By approaching the work in this way, Freud's comments on cocaine become much more useful to us.

Freud's contemporaries essentially succeeded in pushing aside Freud's desire to keep the meaning of the drug open, with the result that we have now lost a remarkable opportunity to see cocaine differently. By fixing the meaning of cocaine and fastening it onto addiction we have lost the chance to allow cocaine to mean anything but addiction and death. This chapter hopes to suggest that we need to reopen Freud's initial line of inquiry, and essentially "reopen" the range of meanings that Freud was trying to ensure remained in circulation.

In retrospect, Freud said that the cocaine episode was an "allotrion" (from the Greek, *allos,* meaning other, or a turning away from the norm) and that like a perversion, it was a side path, and not the main route.[8] But more important, it was and still is, quite literally, an allotrion: a turning away from the norm regarding how the "meaning" of cocaine can and should be constructed in our culture. Moreover, Freud realized that the only way to get around the deadening weight of commonsense was to take a side route that would enable him to sidestep conventional "wisdom." He also tells us that it was "a side interest, though it was [also] a deep one."[9] I feel that while it has been assumed by Jones and others that this remark permits us to dismiss the work, and that Freud is encouraging us to do so, the reference to an allotrion actually is a clue to what Freud thought he was doing. In short, only by going against the norm, and by going around the conventional wisdom and avoiding saying what he was supposed to say could he hope to keep the meaning of cocaine open and "free" from being locked into a pernicious chain of significations. Freud, in this sense, is following Nietzsche in that the allotrion, which also can mean a "hobby," allows him to come closer to locating a new terrain in which cocaine (and us) could run and be free. I think that Freud was aware that very often a perverse thought is the best way to get around rigid constructions or "problems." By doing so, although he almost wrecked his career in the attempt, he has left behind a trace that should, hopefully, allow us to resist any easy positions regarding cocaine.

In his "Three Essays on the Theory of Sexuality," Freud writes that "Perversions are sexual activities which either (a) extend, in an anatomical sense, beyond the regions of the body which are designated for sexual union, or (b) linger over the intermediate relations to the sexual object which should normally be traversed rapidly on the path toward the final sexual aim."[10] However, as Kaja Silverman points out, "All other sexual activities belong either to the category of 'fore-play,' in which case they are strictly subordinated to 'end-pleasure,' or perversion."[11] Silverman refers to perversion as "the temptation to engage in a different kind of erotic narrative, one whose organization is aleatory and paratactic rather than direct and hypotactic, preferring fore-pleasures to end-pleasures, and browsing to discharge."[12] In this sense then, Freud is desirous to engage in a different kind of narrative for cocaine, one whose organization is not fixed by common sense and the rush for end-pleasure. Going beyond the norm is exactly what Freud wished to do with the meaning of cocaine. Obviously, I think this is why the cocaine papers have been so very hard to hear with any degree of accuracy, in part because we no longer subscribe to Freud's frequency regarding cocaine. He is offering us a cultural reading of cocaine that is quite simply no longer available to us and cannot be heard for what it is: a seriously perverted attempt to protect the drug from any of the charges leveled against it.

Two people who stirred Freud's interest in cocaine are Theodor Aschenbrandt and W. E. Bentley. In the September 1880 issue of *The Therapeutic Gazette*, Bentley outlined how in 1878 he had written an article that suggested that "if the victim of either opium or alcohol could find a preparation that would produce his accustomed stimulus without leaving a feeling of depression, he could, with the aid of very little exercise of his will, abandon his vice and regain his normal condition. In the erythoxylon coca we find that very article. . . ."[13] From the very beginning cocaine is being framed as a cure, and not as the poison that we "know" it is today.

Bentley's work discusses the story of a man in 1879 who had had an opium habit for five years: "I put him on coca . . . In the October following, I met him and he assured me that he was entirely relieved of the habit. . . ."[14] *The Therapeutic Gazette* also outlines in June 1880 the work of Dr. Palmer, who had also conducted research on curing opium addiction with cocaine, and the *Gazette* cannot understand why "it was not sooner recommended." It goes on to suggest that although many drugs have not been widely experimented with, it is the duty of "educated practitioner[s]" to "interest themselves in investigation into the possibilities of the newer remedies."[15] *The Therapeutic Gazette* then concludes that "*The Louisville Medical News* says in referring to Dr. Palmer's paper 'One feels like trying coca, with or without the opium habit. A harmless remedy for the blues is imperial.' And so say we."[16]

Aschenbrandt had conducted many experiments using cocaine, which again resulted in very favorable results. He cites the work of Schildbach and Mantegazza, who suggested that "even if coca were nothing more than a stimulant . . . it still seems to surpass all usual stimulants in harmlessness and agreeability. . . ."[17] Aschenbrandt then details how he administered the drug to a battalion that he was working with; the result was that several soldiers who had been sick or tired would become "cheerful and strong," and rather than relapsing to their former condition, "maintained the best state of health in the division."[18] If these comments are not quite strange enough for our ears, he adds that "the influence of cocaine on the body is *more benign* than that of the alcohols or cold coffee."[19]

When we come to Freud's *Uber Coca* (1884) the first difficulty that the reader will encounter is that the text is not easy to locate. Peter Gay suggests that "The best German edition of Freud's psychoanalytical writings is *Gesammelte Werke, Chronologisch Geordnet.*"[20] Unfortunately *Uber Coca* is not to be found in the *Gesammelte Werke*. For those texts that are not included in the *Gesammelte Werke*, Gay suggests that we may turn to the "handy Studienausgabe"; unfortunately, this also "omits some *minor* papers."[21] Turning to the *Standard Edition of the Complete Psychological Works*, a work of "international authority," according to Gay, we find a collection that "introduces each work, even the slightest paper, with indispensable bibliographical and historical information."[22] Yet again the cocaine papers are not included. It is also frustrating to discover that *Uber Coca* is also excluded from Gay's *The Freud Reader*. Moreover, the Robert Byck edition that I use for my research has been out of print since 1974. The cocaine episode does not appear in *The Standard Collected Works* and was only published in English in 1963 in Vienna by the obscure Dunquin Press. Robert Byck points out that the historical library of the Yale University School of Medicine did not list the Dunquin Press edition in its catalogue.[23]

Moreover, by comparing the standard edition of Freud's letters to Wilhelm Fleiss, edited by Anna Freud, with the more recent edition, edited by J. M. Masson (1985) we can see how many of the references to cocaine were removed. For example, if we look at the letters of June 12, 1895, we notice that Freud's remark, "I need a lot of cocaine," has been deleted. The standard edition of the letters, entitled "The Origins of Psychoanalysis," begins in 1887, whereas Freud's major letters detailing his work with cocaine were written in 1884–86. The letters to his fiancée Martha Bernays would also be a crucial source of information surrounding this episode. Unfortunately Ernst Freud has published "only an alluring selection of some ninety-three."[24] What is it about Freud's work with cocaine that makes it so uniformly absent? Is there some fear that this text, if allowed to escape from obscurity, will somehow poison the Freudian canon?

Freud openly said that the work with cocaine was an allotrion, yet Ernest Jones suggests that the cocaine episode was nothing more than a "surreptitious short-cut," which, by framing the allotrion as secretive and artificial, as well as lazy, suggests that it is not the "real" way of achieving something.[25] In the same way that Jekyll refers to Hyde as "a thick cloak" that can be discarded at will, Jones desires that the cocaine episode be perceived as merely an ornament and not the essence of Freud's career.[26] Ernest Jones also wishes to reinforce the sense that the cocaine project was perverse:

To achieve virility and enjoy the bliss of union with the beloved he had forsaken the straight and narrow path of sober "scientific" work on brain anatomy and seized a surreptitious short cut: one that was to bring him suffering in the place of success.[27]

So, sobriety is on the side of virility and success, while cocaine occupies the space of impotence, suffering, and failure. Jones' interpretation of this part of Freud's *oeuvre* has been accepted insofar as the cocaine project has not been allowed to come into contact with, or enter into, the Freudian canon.

Before writing *Uber Coca*, Freud felt that Martha was weak and pale, so he sent her cocaine "to make her strong and give her cheeks a red colour."[28] Looking forward to visiting her he states: "Woe to you, my Princess, when I am come. I will kiss you quite red and feed you till you are plump. And if you are froward [*sic*] you shall see who is the stronger, a gentle little girl who doesn't eat enough or a big wild man who has cocaine in his body."[29] The economic significance of cocaine for Freud emerges in a letter to Martha in 1884, in which he says that they only need one "lucky hit" to be able to "think of setting up home." Freud hopes that his interest in cocaine will turn out like the gold chloride method he invented: "less than [he] imagined, but still something quite respectable."[30] This focus on Freud's economic position is also another way of dismissing the work as being of real value insofar as he was simply in a rush to find anything that would make him rich. In short, many critics take Freud's material concerns at this stage of his life as a way of undermining the validity of his statements about cocaine. As Gay points out, Freud is simply hoping that cocaine will assist him in what he referred to as "the chase after money, position, and reputation."[31]

In the work on cocaine up to and including *Uber Coca*, Freud, like Aschenbrandt, presents the drug as a potent source of strength, and as a natural and unharmful substance. Freud suggests that cocaine is a "potent" stimulant that can enable one "to hold strength in reserve to meet further demands."[32] Linking cocaine with hard work, he sees it as generating a healthy body, one conducive to the growth of the Victorian family. Blurring the line between Sherlock Holmes and Dr. Livingstone, Freud describes himself in *Uber Coca* as both an "investigator" of cocaine and an "explorer."[33] Cocaine is a "magical substance"; it can make him "strong as a lion, gay and cheerful."[34] Whereas we know that cocaine leads us down paths that flow away from nature, for Freud cocaine is also capable of restoring him to a state of Nature. Not only can Freud feel "quite calm with a small dose of cocaine," the drug is not debilitating, and in fact enhances bodily strength: "I won't be tired . . . I shall be traveling under the influence of coca. . . ."[35] To "understand" cocaine, Freud decided to measure its effects on the strength of muscles and reaction times to stimuli. For the purpose of the former he used a dynamometer and found that with cocaine he noticed "a marked increase in the motor power of the arm"; moreover, "results achieved under the influence of cocaine even exceed the maximum under normal conditions."[36] Freud also concluded that "under cocaine my reaction times were shorter and more uniform than before taking the drug."[37] This parallel between cocaine and health and work/creativity is developed when Freud offers us examples of men who find themselves able to write after taking cocaine. One male patient was able, after treatment, "to write a long letter" and awoke the next morning "ready for work" while a "young writer . . . was enabled by treatment with coca to resume his work after a longish illness."[38] Another example tells of a writer "who for weeks before had been incapable of any literary production and who was able to work for 14 hours without interruption after taking 0.1g of cocaine. . . ."[39]

Uber Coca opens by establishing the geographical and historical origins of cocaine. The background that Freud offers serves to place the drug firmly within the realm of Nature in that cocaine begins life as a "plant" in South America. Not only is it seen as "an indispensable stimulant" to some ten million people, but it also contributes to the economy of the region: "The large-scale production (allegedly 30 million pounds annually) makes coca leaves an important item of trade and taxation. . . ."[40] Freud outlines how, among the Peruvians, the "divine plant . . . satiates the hungry, strengthens the weak, and causes them to forget their misfortune."[41] While Freud is writing this article in the hope that the drug that he is (re)discovering will win him his reputation and will thus erase his current economic "misfortune," it is not surprising that he tells us how coca leaves were "offered in sacrifice to the gods . . . and were placed in the mouths of the dead to ensure them a favourable reception in the beyond." The only difference with Freud is that he hopes his pronouncements on cocaine will earn him a favorable reception from his colleagues in this world.[42]

The main problem for Freud later on was that in *Uber Coca* he positions himself implicitly as a *defender* of the drug. Freud tells us how Garcilasso de la Vega, the historian of the Spanish invasion, "endeavored to defend coca against the ban the conquerors laid upon it."[43] One can here detect Freud considering his own skeptical audience, who like the Spaniards (and ourselves), would "not believe in the marvelous effects of the plant, which they suspected as the work of the devil. . . ."[44] Freud attempts to win a favorable reception for cocaine by separating it from the devil and magic and placing it firmly into the category of a natural drug conducive to the work ethic. He even relates how the council of Lima changed its policy when it became clear that "the Indians could not perform the heavy labour imposed upon them in the mines if they were forbidden to partake of coca."[45] Possibly looking forward to his own fame and the generalized acceptance of the drug among the medical profession, Freud concludes proudly that "the coca plant has maintained its position among the natives to the present day; there even remain traces of the religious veneration which was once accorded to it."[46] By inserting his (re)discovery of the drug into the initial discovery of Peru and the coca plant, Freud the "explorer" hopes that he has found his "treasure." One thing that is interesting about these parts of the narrative is that Freud opens up many contradictory positions for himself: he can be a detective, a defender of the indigenous Peruvian population, a historian of the Spanish invasion of the country, a defender of the drug, *and* an explorer. Only by proliferating our positions can the meaning of cocaine be opened up and here we see Freud attempting to do just that. In contrast, all that remains for us today is one position: that of the soldier constantly fighting an invasion by an evil drug that threatens to overwhelm us at every turn. How much better if we could occupy Freud's position with cocaine giving us the strength to explore further and locate even more positions.

All of Freud's later pronouncements on cocaine are basically variations on these original themes. The drug is pastoral in origin; "it thrives best in the warm valleys on the slopes of the Andes," it has religious associations, it is conducive to the economy both as a product and in its contribution to labor power, and can restore strength, while eliminating the need for food.[47] Freud does note that Weddell and Mantegazza suggest that an "immoderate use of coca leads to a cachexia characterized physically by digestive complaints, emaciation, etc., and mentally by moral depravity and a complete apathy toward everything not connected with the enjoyment of the stimulant." Freud dismisses these problems as being caused by weaknesses in the individual user.[48]

In order to represent the drug, and himself, as "respectable," Freud minimizes the extent to which the drug could be interpreted as possessing weakening or "feminine" qualities. Probably anticipating a negative reception, Freud attempts to suggest that cocaine is not a "narcotic," pointing out that most of the contemporary evidence is in agreement with his categorization: "only the elder Schroff refers to cocaine as a narcotic and classes it with opium and cannabis, while almost everyone else ranks it with caffeine, etc."[49]

Another striking difference between Freud's understanding of cocaine and our own knowledge can be found when we examine Freud's experiments with cocaine. In every case Freud asserts that the drug produces no artificial effects: on the contrary, the drug brings forth a self more natural than Nature. The drug produces natural results that, Freud tells us, will not interfere with the workings of the body or the body politic. The natural plant provides "a lasting gain in strength" and "[o]ne . . . feels more vigorous and more capable of work. . . . One is simply normal, and soon finds it difficult to believe that one is under the influence of a drug at all."[50] The drug and the body have now collapsed into each other to the point that one cannot distinguish where the natural body ends and the artificial drug begins. Cocaine becomes the body's supplement, without which it is unfinished and incomplete: for Freud, the body can only be Natural *with* drugs.

Freud hopes that the cocaine project will be acceptable to his colleagues insofar as it is encased in an economy that leads back to the good path, rechanneling desire away from the pathology of narcissism and addiction into respectability and work. Possibly aware that his flirtation with cocaine would be seen as a perverse activity, Freud is careful to ensure that his interest in cocaine is in no way linked to iatrogenic auto-affection. He goes to great lengths to assure us not only of the naturalness of the drug but also of the naturalness of his desire for cocaine. For Freud, the "euphoria" that cocaine produces is not unnatural: " . . . the mood induced by coca in such doses is due not so much to direct stimulation as to the disappearance of elements in one's general state of well-being which cause depression."[51] In Freud's framework cocaine does not artificially stimulate the body by introducing something alien into it (our own position); on the contrary, the drug actually removes bad things from the body, leaving behind a normal self. Far from bringing forth some horrendous monster (as our culture and Jekyll fears), Freud suggests that the effects of cocaine are so minor that we may overlook the benefits of this alkaloid: "[the] absence of signs that could distinguish the state from the normal euphoria of good health makes it even more likely that we will underestimate it."[52] Moreover, far from cocaine producing an altered state, the alteration is barely perceptible—what Freud defines as "the absence of any feeling of alteration"—and that when on cocaine, "it is difficult to believe that one is under the influence of a foreign agent."[53]

In a letter to Martha, written under the influence of cocaine, Freud tells her of how Joseph Bruer told him that "hidden under the surface of timidity there lay in [himself] an extremely daring and fearless human being." Freud responds that he "had always felt so, but never dared tell anyone. . . . I always felt so helpless and incapable of expressing these ardent passions even by a word or a poem. So I have always restrained myself, and it is this, I think, which people must see in me."[54] In the same cocaine-inspired letter, Freud feels that he may also have unleashed "something alien in [himself]" and dismisses ideas about things in his personality that are "hidden under the surface." Claiming instead that he is merely "making silly confessions to [Martha], my sweet darling, and really without any reason whatever *unless it is the cocaine that makes me talk so much.*"[55] Freud is unwilling to carry on writing if the work has no reason to be written, but this letter also implies that what Freud is writing, because it is a drugged confession, given without his conscious consent, is somehow lacking in rationality and logical reason, and can be discounted. He almost fears his own position in that he is making a case for cocaine that the "alien" part of himself knows must be permissible, yet the powerful drug of common sense asks him to question himself. It as if he almost cannot quite believe what he is saying about cocaine and even though he is dismissive here, he stands by his "alien" idea throughout his life and never retracts any of his major pronouncements on cocaine. In a sense he is right: the stance that he is making on cocaine is "extremely daring."

For Freud, cocaine does not displace Nature but allows Nature to be more Natural. Having positioned the drug as natural, he goes on to reveal how it is not destructive of (natural) willpower, but actually increases willpower:

> One senses an increase of self-control. . . . During this stage of the cocaine condition, which is not otherwise distinguished, appear those symptoms which have been described as the wonderful stimulating effect of coca. Long-lasting, intensive mental or physical work can be performed without fatigue. . . . [56]

Although Freud discovers that cocaine displaces the natural desire to eat and sleep, he dismisses this point insofar as the needs of the body can be overridden, allowing the mind to operate with greater (and not fewer) degrees of productivity:

> While the effects of cocaine last one can, if urged to do so, eat copiously and without revulsion; but one has the clear feeling that the meal was superfluous. Similarly, as the effect of coca declines it is possible to sleep on going to bed, but sleep can just as easily be omitted with no unpleasant consequences. During the first hours of the coca effect one cannot sleep, but this sleeplessness is in no way distressing.
>
> I have tested this effect of coca, which wards off hunger, sleep and fatigue and steels one to intellectual effort, some dozen times on myself. . . . [57]

Strangely enough for our ears, Freud also asserts that the drug does not undermine self-control. In fact, Freud suggests that we even feel an aversion to using it, and that we would have to force ourselves to keep taking it: "It seems to me noteworthy—and I discovered this in myself and in other observers who were capable of judging such things—that a first dose or even repeated doses of coca produce no compulsive desire to use the stimulant further; on the contrary, one feels a certain unmotivated aversion to the substance."[58] Freud even cites the drugs' nonaddictive properties as the reason why cocaine has not "established itself in Europe" in spite of "some warm recommendations."[59] Moreover, cocaine is recommended by Freud because it actually cleans up after itself, leaving the body exactly as it was found, leaving no trace of itself behind: "[the drug] left no sign whatsoever that the experimenter had passed through a period of intoxication" nor does it leave any trace of "depression."[60]

At this point Freud discusses how "[i]t was inevitable that a plant which had achieved such a reputation for marvelous effects in its country of origin should have been used to treat the most varied disorders and illnesses of the body."[61] Unlike in *Jekyll and Hyde* where we like to think that the powder caused Jekyll to become hysterical, Freud claims that "according to Caldwell . . . [cocaine] is *the best tonic* for hysteria."[62] We tend to imagine that cocaine upsets the natural balance of the body, yet Freud suggests that it can actually return the body to a natural harmony, returning one "to a normal desire to eat" in the case of "gastronomic excesses."[63] Bulimia would thus be a case of a natural desire that becomes unnatural, but could be returned to a natural state through the intervention of cocaine. The drug offers a "permanent cure" for "dyspeptic complaints," and where there is a "chronic lack of appetite . . . the use of coca restored the patient to health."[64]

For Freud, the naturalness of cocaine could only be of benefit to a capitalist economy:

> a good many of the authors who have a written on coca regard it as a "source of savings"; i.e., they are of the opinion that a system which has absorbed even an extremely small amount of cocaine is capable . . . of amassing a greater store of vital energy which can be converted into work than would have been possible without coca. If we take the amount of work as being constant, the body which has absorbed cocaine should be able to manage with a lower metabolism, which in turn means a smaller intake of food.[65]

Whereas we "know" that the use of cocaine leads to emaciation and the degeneration of the body, for Freud cocaine actually assists in "limiting degeneration of the body."[66] For example, Freud cites the case of one doctor who had a patient suffering from "chronic lack of appetite [and] and advanced condition of emaciation and exhaustion."[67] Contrary to our current expectations, this person was soon "restored . . . to health" by administering cocaine. Freud also presents cocaine in a favorable light by revealing that not only is cocaine a friend to the body, it is also a friend to other medicines. As an example Freud shows how cocaine is extremely useful in treating syphilis because the drug can protect the patient from the side effects of mercury. Although Freud does admit in *Uber Coca* that the model of cocaine as a source of savings has been "disproven," he goes on to argue that the case of the starvation of La Paz. For Freud, this event has the authority of an experiment "carried out by history itself" that seems "to contradict this conclusion" because only the inhabitants who had "partaken of coca are said to have escaped death by starvation."[68] Once again the implication is that cocaine is so natural that it can imperceptibly supplement food, working for, not against, human survival.

Concerned that cocaine will be connected to addiction, sensitivity, and "weakness," Freud outlines how the drug can in fact be used as a cure for morphine addiction. Interestingly enough, this is knowledge that he has gained from America:

> In America the important discovery has recently been made that coca preparations possess the power to suppress the craving for morphine in habitual addicts, and also to reduce to negligible proportions the serious symptoms of collapse which appear while the patient is being weaned away from the morphine habit.[69]

Freud also asserts that "The treatment of morphine addiction with coca does not, therefore, result merely in the exchange of one kind of addiction for another . . . the use of coca is only temporary."[70] Contrary to our understanding of cocaine, the drug actually leads one away from addiction, not toward it. Not only does the drug strengthen the body, it also actively fights the morphine on behalf of the body: "coca has a directly antagonistic effect on morphine."[71] So while it can work alongside the curative effects of mercury, it also knows how to work *against* morphine.

Freud suggests that cocaine could also be used to cure people of addiction to alcohol. In *Uber Coca* he states that in America cocaine has been used to treat "chronic alcoholism" with a degree of "undoubted success."[72] Freud goes on to discuss several other case studies conducted by W. E. Bentley, in which "coca was responsible for the cure."[73] Having suggested earlier that coca can be a cure for syphilis, Freud also suggests that cocaine functions as an aphrodisiac, reinscribing cocaine into the realm of familial desire by asserting that it can be of use in cases of "functional weaknesses" (i.e., impotence).[74] Despite our current vantage point that tells us that drugs dismantle the family, here cocaine is seen as a cure for the failing heterosexual family, facilitating procreation and the repetition of "natural" desire.[75]

Uber Coca opens up a chain of supplements, for once it was written, Freud continually added to it, either to offer improved suggestions or to revise certain aspects. In effect, he persisted—much to the annoyance of his contemporaries—in keeping the meaning of the drug open. In February 1885 Freud republished *Uber Coca* with an addenda in which he confirmed some of the points made in the 1884 text. While we are certain that cocaine use can only be destructive, for Freud the range of possibilities is more diverse. For Freud there is a "diversity of individual reactions to cocaine," and while some people "showed signs of coca euphoria," there are "others who experienced absolutely no effect."[76] Obviously these statements point accusingly to the holes in our own rhetoric whereby drugs operate within a uniform and constant pattern. He also continues to remind his contemporaries of cocaine's efficacy in cases of "morphine collapse" and states that "subcutaneous injections" of cocaine are "quite harmless."[77]

By 1886 reports of cocaine "addiction" were appearing and Erlenmeyer openly accused Freud of unleashing "the third scourge of mankind."[78] As we have seen, Freud viewed cocaine in terms of self-control and health, but the accusation that it leads to addiction now brings these metaphors into contact with late-nineteenth-century metaphors that were actively constructing addiction as a loss of self-control, passivity, and weak morals. Freud has to then deal with the fact that many reports "of the toxic effects of cocaine were received . . . from eye and throat specialists [in which] cocaine began to get the reputation of a highly dangerous drug whose use over a long period of time produces a 'habit' or 'condition similar to morphinism.'"[79] In response to these criticisms Freud defended himself in *Craving for and Fear of Cocaine* (July 1887). In this paper Freud never confesses that he ever made any errors in judgment, and conversely continues to defend the drug. In the paper he cites the case of Dr. Hammond who, like Freud, was also eager to "test the truth of reports appearing recently in the journals that have aroused a great deal of fear."[80] Hammond's work makes it clear that "the first authors who reported on the use of coca among South American natives had greatly exaggerated its noxiousness. . . ."[81] What bothers Freud is that these reports "were repeatedly warmed over and served anew, without reference as to source, and thus inspired the currently prevailing bias."[82] Dr. Hammond was injecting cocaine "repeatedly" and Freud draws our attention to the fact that he could "give up the drug whenever he wished."[83] Dr. Hammond was also using cocaine to treat a woman who was suffering from Graves' disease; similarly Freud notes that "she was able to discontinue its use without any difficulty."[84] Freud states that in spite of all the criticisms, his "original statements had in no way been invalidated."[85] Freud then suggests that this "agitation against the new alkaloid . . . has gone much too far:"

> *All reports of addiction to cocaine and deterioration resulting from it refer to morphine addicts,* persons who, already in the grip of one demon are so weak in will power, so susceptible, that they would misuse, and indeed have misused, any stimulant held out to them. *Cocaine has claimed no other, no victim on its own.*[86]

Adding that far from being addicted when he was using cocaine, he experienced "more frequently than [he] should have liked, an aversion to the drug . . ." arguing instead that of all of the criticisms, few "can hardly be attributed to the alkaloid" itself.[87]

Unfortunately, many physical disorders begin to emerge that Freud cannot dismiss. He concedes that "Another set of observations must, however, be characterized unequivocally as cocaine poisoning because of their similarity to symptoms which can be produced experimentally by an overdose of cocaine: stupor, dizziness, increase of pulse rate, irregular respiration, anorexia, insomnia and eventually delirium and muscular weakness," but feels that these are "rare occurrences."[88] While acknowledging that cocaine poisoning is possible, Freud is still concerned with keeping cocaine separate from the question of addiction. The same kind of logic is applied that was used with morphine addicts, because while there is this "one unreliability of cocaine," it is a flaw that "must be attributed to the drug itself."[89] Freud implies that this is not so much a problem caused by the drug, as by the patient. The varying effects that can occur with cocaine whereby "one does not know when a toxic effect will appear" is dependent finally not upon the chemistry of the drug, but of the person, and of "the sensitivity of certain individuals to cocaine."[90] Freud concludes that "the reason for the irregularity of the cocaine effect lies in the individual variations in excitability and in the variation of the condition of the vasomotor nerves on which cocaine acts.[91] In *Craving for and Fear of Cocaine,* Freud states that although individual reactions to the drug may occur, it is clear that "the possibility of toxic effects need not preclude the application of cocaine to attain a desirable end."[92] In the same way that Burroughs will develop the notion of drugs and immunization, Freud knows that if we are to reach a "cure" for the drug problem we will have to endure a period of toxicity if we are to reach a desired goal.[93] By reading Ernest Jones's comments on *Craving for and Fear of Cocaine,* it is apparent that Jones is intent on minimizing Freud's statements. For example, Jones tells us that "[m]any must have at least have regarded him as a man of reckless judgment," and Jones feels that Freud's "sensitive conscience passed the same sentence."[94] Peter Gay tells us that "When Fritz Wittels declared in his biography that Freud, concerning the "mistakes" of the cocaine episode, had "thought long and painfully just how this could have happened to him," Freud denied it: "False!" he wrote in the margin."[95] It is tempting to think that Freud would respond in the same way to Jones's remark.

Craving for and Fear of Cocaine (July 1887) was the last piece that Freud wrote on the topic until the cocaine dreams of 1895 and 1898. Freud felt that his first year in practice was his "least successful and darkest year" as a result of simultaneously trying to ensure his own "material existence as well as that of a rapidly increasing family."[96] As Bernfield points out "[i]n this situation he found himself simultaneously rejected by the leaders of the Vienna Medical School as the propagandist of the foreigner Charcot, and on the national scene accused of the greatest irresponsibility and recklessness [due to the cocaine episode]."[97] In 1898 Freud discusses "The Dream of the Botanical Monograph." The text of the dream is very brief:

> I had written a monograph on a certain plant. The book lay before me and I was at the moment turning over a folded coloured plate. Bound up in each copy there was a dried specimen of the plant, as though it had been taken from a herbarium.[98]

Contrary to the universal blame to which he had been subjected, Freud interprets the dream as essentially exonerating him from the blame that was directed at him in the 1880s:

> What it meant was: "After all, I'm the man who wrote the valuable and memorable paper (on cocaine)," just as in the earlier dream I had said on my behalf: "I'm a conscientious and hard-working student." In both cases what I was insisting was: "I may allow myself to do this."[99]

As with Stevenson's Dr. Jekyll, who asked Lanyon to ensure that Hyde gets his "rights" after his death, Freud sees the dream as "a plea on behalf of [his] own rights."[100] The dream of "Irma's" injection also operates in the same way for Freud. This dream, which was to become the first specimen dream in *The Interpretation of Dreams* (1900) concerns a patient who is suffering after receiving an unclean injection from Freud. Freud asserts that the meaning of the dream is that "Irma's pains had been caused by [my colleague] Otto giving her an incautious injection of an unsuitable drug—a thing I should never have done . . . I never did any harm with my injections.[101]

While he is desirous to free himself of the blame for the suffering of his patients, Irma and Fleischl, Freud's reading of the dream can also be read as his attempt to separate his "cure" (cocaine) from the "poison" that it had become. It would appear that in spite of the general sense that Freud had behaved irresponsibly, Freud never believes that his opinions or his statements on cocaine are irresponsible. Like Hyde, who has no interest in confessing, Freud cannot satisfy his detractors and confess that he has made a professional mistake because as far as he is concerned no mistake has been made. This very refusal to confess appeared to infuriate Freud's contemporaries, seeming to prove to their minds that he was after all guilty, irresponsible, and perhaps mad. This, to me, is the reason for excluding *Uber Coca* from the Freudian canon because it resists being made into part of the story that we now want to tell about cocaine. As David Musto reminds us, "Freud never publicly retracted his broad endorsement of cocaine. . . ."[102]

Avital Ronell feels that Freud became involved with cocaine "for the sake of some unplumbable purpose," and in *Crack Wars* says that "[t]his is not the place to analyze that fatal encounter."[103] In his recent biography, Peter Gay suggests that "cocaine held some uncomfortable, not wholly acknowledged meaning for [Freud]," who was at the same time "intent on minimizing the effects of the affair upon him."[104] Although it only occupies one page in Gay's 800-page text, we are told that this "misadventure remained one of the most troubling episodes in Freud's life."[105] Notice too that like Jones, Gay almost imperceptibly assumes that Freud's work with cocaine must be framed as a "misadventure" (or as in Ronell's remark, a *fatal* encounter) or that it is merely an "episode." Writing from within a historical moment in which the meaning of cocaine has been both fixed as well as substantially altered from what Freud was hoping for, Ernest Jones is retrospectively empowered to present us with a picture of Freud as a dangerous drug-pusher. In his words, "he pressed it on his friends and colleagues, both for themselves and their patients, he gave it to his sisters. In short, looked at from the vantage point of our present knowledge, he was rapidly becoming a public menace."[106] Jones also dismisses *Uber Coca*, suggesting that "it might well be ranked higher as a literary production than as an original scientific contribution."[107] Moreover, what bothers Jones, and what prevents the work from being taken seriously, is the degree of closeness that exists between Freud and his subject. What makes Jones anxious is that Freud is speaking with a "personal warmth as if he were in love with the content itself."[108] Ernest Jones also insists on framing the work as something less than normal/correct. For Jones, the cocaine episode was a "foolhardy episode" that Freud (apparently) exacerbated by his constant "evasion and confusion of the issue."[109] Notice again that what Jones sees as evasion and a deliberate attempt to confuse the issue is considered as perhaps a strategy on Freud's part by which he can refuse to allow the work to be fixed into the frame that Jones and many others were trying to impose upon cocaine.

Recently E. M. Thornton has taken this dismissal of the work even further, suggesting that *all* of Freud's theories should be discarded for they are "not the preoccupations of a normal mind," but instead are the product of a paranoid coke fiend with "poisoned brain cells."[110] Thornton even suggests that on the subject of the cocaine episode, Freud engaged in "deliberate mendacity," which is conveniently located as "simply another symptom of his addiction" to cocaine."[111] His conclusion is that Freud's entire *oeuvre* is the product "of his cocaine usage and had no basis in fact," being merely the sad product of his "drugged brain."[112] In his bibliographical essay, Gay notes the existence of some critical works on Freud and cocaine, but divides them up into those that are "dependable" (including the Byck edition that I use) and those like E. M. Thornton's *Freud and Cocaine: The Freudian Fallacy,* which in accusing Freud of being a drugged charlatan, is no more than a model of "the literature of denigration."[113] While Gay may be disturbed by

Thornton's conclusions, they essentially share Jones's opinion on the cocaine episode. For Thornton it was a mistake, a foolhardy episode, an error, irresponsible behavior, deception, a perversion of science, and something not worthy of our attention, but worthy of condemnation.

Freud wanted to keep the book on cocaine open and prevent it from being closed. He insisted on a perverse course, preferring foreplay to endpleasure, preferring browsing to discharge. Jones says that he can easily see that from his "current vantage point," Freud was becoming a public menace, but Jones can say this not because he has a vantage point, but because that is all that he is being allowed to see. In a sense his vantage point, like our own "vantage point," is nothing more than a "disadvantage point" from which we can actually see very little. What would it mean to read against our own "vantage point" and *with* Freud? Hopefully in this chapter I have tried to show that Freud was trying to keep the meaning of cocaine open for us. While the book was eventually closed and the narrative closed off, we should try to drift away from our (dis)advantage point and locate other places from which to get a different view of the history of cocaine. This would enable us to construct a future in which we can look forward to a better relationship with drugs. Instead of a war on drugs, maybe, like Freud, we can even become a little bit "in love with the content itself."

Of course such a suggestion places me right back where Freud was: now I am being irresponsible and a public menace, and even if I think that I am merely being anti-antidrug, you can claim the vantage point and thereby know that I'm *really* being prodrug/anti-health. My concern is that we are reading Freud's texts on cocaine not with an eye on what is flawed in our own perceptions of drug addiction, but we read them in order to bolster up own current framework, so that the position that we have settled on will look as if it has always been the only viable position. To enter into what Jekyll/Hyde suggested was a "new province of knowledge," we have to set ourselves adrift from our current vantage point, allowing ourselves to wander off into new uncharted waters, as Freud was trying to do. Yet we resist and assume that such an action, far from being to our benefit, would mean giving up the reassuring security provided by the framework of our current (dis)advantage point. In short, we keep ourselves thinking along the same lines by ensuring that we only conceive of new positions of knowledge as something to be feared, rather than as something to be desired. We tell ourselves that abandoning our current vantage point—in essence, our foothold—would entail becoming addicted, losing our grip, moving out of our depth, getting in over our heads. But that is precisely what we should be doing.

Chapter 4

"The Doctor Does a Good Job": William Burroughs's Critique of Control

Control can never be a means to any practical end, it can never be a means to anything but more control

—William Burroughs

In 1969 William Burroughs made the following prediction in his novel *The Wild Boys:* "The uneasy spring of 1988. Under the pretext of drug control suppressive police states have been set up throughout the Western world. . . . [T]he police states . . . maintain a democratic façade from behind which they denounce as criminals, perverts and drug addicts anyone who opposes the control machine."[1] This prediction, which sadly came true, raises the central issue of this chapter: the question of control. Whether it is control of bodies, races, or drugs themselves, our drug discourses since the mid-nineteenth century, both in England and America, have all aimed themselves at this target. Often the question of control is not limited to controlling our habits; it becomes the control, surveillance, and imprisonment of whole sections of society. Whether it was the fear of the Chinese and opium in the 1920s or the superhuman PCP user in our own moment, control is usually carried out and justified in the name of restraining a violent minority group. While the question of race will be dealt with more extensively in the next chapter, for the moment I would like to examine the possibility that in the case of drugs the application of control on any front will always be counterproductive. Through an examination of Burroughs's ideas about control, I aim to explore in this chapter how we have to let go of our belief in the efficacy of control.

A recent health pamphlet on heroin put out by the Do it Now Foundation uses a quote from William Burroughs's novel *Junky* for its epigraph.[2] The title of the pamphlet, "The Junk Equation," is also from Burroughs. The leaflet obviously wishes to use Burroughs to authorize its position on heroin, but there are various ellipses in the passage that belie the supposed truth of a simple equation about heroin. One of the ellipses concerns marijuana and alcohol. Here is the quote as it appears in the leaflet: "Junk is not . . . a means to increased enjoyment of life." Yet if we look at the novel, the quote actually reads "Junk is not, *like alcohol or weed,* a means to increased enjoyment of life."[3] Considering that the Do It Now Foundation also publishes leaflets on marijuana and alcohol use, it would be very difficult to allow this part of the quote to remain. It also reveals how the foundation must edit the truth if it is to produce a junk equation that makes sense. The comment that weed can lead to an "increased enjoyment" of life flies in the face of how Do It Now also desires to see marijuana as a problem drug. While they want to utilize those moments in Burroughs where he offers some kind of validation of what we want to hear about heroin, he must be partially silenced if he tells us things that do not quite fit.[4] My point here is to suggest that while the Do It Now Foundation wants to teach us about the junk equation (i.e., junk = death), their equation is not the only equation possible. Moreover, by making this the only available equation, it means that junk *does* lead to death because there is nowhere else for the narrative to go. However, the leaflet does expose a possible exit from the limited self-fulfilling prophecy of our junk equation. While informing us that heroin is "an identity, a vocation, and a pastime, a master, lover, and a friend," they also suggest that "heroin is just about everything to every addict, all the time. Everything, that is, except legal, safe and free." The pamphlet then moves on to discuss the horrors of addiction, as it must. But surely if heroin were legal and free, it would also be a much safer drug than at the moment. As Dr. John Marks has pointed out, "Drugs are not forbidden because they are dangerous. They are dangerous because they are forbidden."[5]

As far as drug control is concerned, Burroughs feels that the junk equation also affects the doctors, administrators, and law enforcement officials who similarly become "addicted" to junk. For William Burroughs, it is our unquestioned faith in the efficacy of control and surveillance that keeps us tied to our drug problem. The only solution to the drug problem is to cure ourselves of the pleasure and satisfaction that we get from exerting control. The junk that the health/police establishment gets addicted to is more dangerous than heroin: they get addicted to the truth. This process of seeing drugs in either/or terms, and as something that must at all costs be controlled constitutes our addiction to control, which for Burroughs is worse than any drug addiction. If we use words to control drugs ("Just Say No"), then we are in the grip of a "word authority, more habit forming than heroin."[6] One way out of this impasse is to read "junk" and "addiction" not only as something that can occur to the drug user. Burroughs feels that "there are many forms of addiction" and addicts and nonaddicts alike are prone to "addiction."[7] This would explain why he often says that drugs are a not a kick, but "a way of life."[8] It is always assumed that he is referring to the street addicts' "lifestyle," but he also means that junk is a way of life for all of us, addicts and nonaddicts alike: "hooked or kicked . . . [all] come in on the junk beam."[9] What we see in Burroughs is an expansion of the use of "junk" so that it comes to include the behavior of hooked and clean alike: "I am using junk as a basic illustration. Extend it."[10] Addiction thus occurs to those who use drugs, and those who push drugs, as well as those who would wish to control addiction or cure addicts. Burroughs informs us that "Non using pushers have a contact habit, and that's one you can't kick. Agents get it too."[11]

If we then begin to realize that social workers, academics, and law enforcement officials have "a contact habit" and are addicted as much as the addicts they hope to cure, we come closer to finding a way out of the labyrinth of addiction. All of the bureaucratic and institutional positions that hope to do some good for addicts but do not include themselves in the equation represent for Burroughs a form of addiction to what he calls "white junk—rightness." As he points out, "Assuming a self righteous position is nothing to the purpose unless your purpose be to keep the junk virus in operation."[12] Burroughs has made it clear that rightness is articulated by control through language. In Burroughs's texts, control, speaking in the voice of Mr. Martin, outlines the situation: "I am not an addict. I am the addict. The addict I invented to keep this show on the junk road. I am all the addicts and all the junk in the world. I am junk and I am hooked forever."[13] The virus that control produces is "an obligate cellular parasite," which forces the host to a point where they always have to be right. According to Burroughs, "This right virus has been around for a long time, and perhaps its most devoted ally has been the Christian Church: from the Inquisition to the Conquistadores, from the American Indian Wars to Hiroshima, they are RIGHT RIGHT RIGHT . . . the Christian Church has given the virus a nice long home. . . ."[14] Any attempt to cure the host of its parasite results in hysterical outbursts of control and repression: "Hell hath no more vociferous fury than an endangered parasite."[15]

What we often say about addicts—"they just do not want to be cured"— applies equally well in this case. Even though it would be in the host's interest to be rid of the Right virus, it refuses to expel the parasite that by now has reached a stage of benevolent symbiosis with the Host. Burroughs feels that the language virus keeps us alive only so as to be able to reproduce itself. It has also reached the point at which we are no longer able to recognize that the parasite is our enemy. Yet how do we attempt to cure the Host of its Parasite, how do we cure ourselves of this disease that continually makes us mechanically repeat the rhetoric of Just Say No? A word of advice from Burroughs:

> Probably the most effective tactic is to alter the conditions on which the virus subsists. That is the way various manifestations of the RIGHT virus have disappeared in the past, as in the Inquisition. Conditions change, and that virus guise is ignored and forgotten. We have seen this happen many times in the past forty years. With the RIGHT virus offset, perhaps we can get this show out of the barnyard and into Space.[16]

By making us aware that power survives in language, he points us to the need to free ourselves not from drugs, but from the restrictions of language.

Burroughs suggests that language is quite literally a virus, and seeing as how the Latin root of "virus" is "poison," it is this virus that has caused us to become sick. If we are excessively fond of control and in fact we "dote" on control, then Burroughs's work is precisely an antidote, curing us of the poison of language, and so curing us of our addiction to control. Unfortunately, we behave exactly like the addicts that we so easily condemn when we stubbornly resist being cured, vehemently holding onto our cherished beliefs ("drugs *are* a problem, drugs *are* a threat") like an old junkie hoarding his morphine. As Burroughs asks, imagine a junky who has been addicted "for several thousand years. Control that habit . . . ?"[17] Our civilization is that junkie, a culture addicted to control. Burroughs, however, is on a mission, "Operation Rewrite" as he calls it, and it is a medical as much as a political operation. One aim of Operation Rewrite is to cure us of a sickness that causes us to imagine (and eventually believe) that drugs are a problem and a menace. In an interview in Tangier, Burroughs outlined his view that getting away from words was the only way to evade control. Such a step forward, away from words, is a step that, according to Burroughs, must be made "in silence."[18]

> Gregory Corso: "How does one take that 'forward step,' can you say?"
> W. S. B: "Well, this is my subject, and what I am concerned with. Forward steps are made by giving up old armor because words are built into you—in the soft typewriter of the womb you do not realize the word-armor you carry. . . ."[19]

The story about the dangers of drugs is repeated by doctors and law enforcement officials who rarely cease to remind us, lest we forget perhaps, that we all have to keep up the constant fight against drugs. No one is allowed to suggest that we stop the story. When Alice attended the Mad Hatter's tea party, the only way to get a clean cup was to move to the next seat, yet in our drug scenario we tell the story in such a way that everybody has got a dirty cup. Each moment is tainted with a trace of drugs and so the movement round the table goes on and on, with doctors, politicians, confessing addicts, the media and academics, assuring us that eventually we will all have clean cups, and then we can sit down to tea. What would happen if we moved away from this endless fiction, which after all is how many people see the world of heroin use, and refuse to tell the story in this way? What if we kicked our control habit? However, as soon as one suggests that perhaps drugs could be perceived differently one is accused of being prodrug, anti-health. We can only say yes to telling ourselves about drugs in this way, and as Reeves and Campbell point out, the drug narrative is "is as much about saying 'yes' to the recovery operations and discriminatory systems of the modern control culture as it is about saying 'no' to drugs."[20]

For William Burroughs, the only thing that we should be saying "no" to is drug hysteria, not drugs. Ronald and Nancy Reagan told us that "nobody has the right to mind his own business" and promptly informed us that "Indifference is not an option. Only outspoken insistence that drug use will not be tolerated."[21] As if to prove that they are not addicted, the propagandists of free will openly declare that they have no tolerance for drugs. After all, is not a lack of tolerance the first sign of addiction? According to the Reagans, "This is a war, and anyone who even suggests a tolerant attitude toward drug use should be considered a traitor."[22] Yet for Burroughs it is quite plain that the war on drugs is a "colossal red herring" that is not even designed to succeed.[23] In "General Security: The Liquidation of Opium," Antonin Artaud offered an expanded view of this point by suggesting that "There is only one reason to attack opium. This is the danger that its use can inflict on society as a whole. BUT THIS DANGER IS NONEXISTENT."[24] For Artaud, any attempt to "solve the drug problem" "is not only impossible but also pointless . . ." and in fact can only "[a]ggravate the social need for the drug."[25]

What is strange about the war on drugs narrative is that it works on a logic that looks remarkably like the one that we say addicts are hooked into—the one that keeps them sick. We know that addicts are always in search of their next hit, preoccupied with getting money to score—and having gotten high, want to get even higher—the search for the ultimate high leading to a downward spiral of addiction, disease, and death. However, the war on drugs is a mirror discourse that also operates on the logic of "not yet," or "not quite enough." The story that we hear about the control of drugs is that something that we desired (or were supposed to have desired), which usually means capturing drugs or criminals, always gets away from us. In fact they must get away from us in order for us to continue our surveillance of them. We hear how the occupants of the destroyed and disbanded crack house will relocate somewhere else, or how the controls on drugs are not yet completely foolproof, and that if only they could be a little tighter, we might start to bring the problem under control.

Operation Re-Write

While the Do It Now Foundation takes its junk equation epigraph from *Junky*, it is in this same novel that Burroughs outlines the emergence of our contemporary hatred of drugs. In the novel, Will Lee decides to leave the United States just as the control virus begins to move in:

> When I jumped bail and left the States, the heat on junk already looked like something new and special. Initial symptoms of nationwide hysteria were clear. . . . This is police-state legislation penalizing a state of being . . . the anti-junk feeling mounted to a paranoid obsession, like anti-Semitism under the Nazis.[26]

Burroughs knows that it is always time to move on, out of the binary of addiction and cure: "I Don't Want to Hear Any More Tired Old Junk Talk and Junk Con . . . The same things said a million times and more and there is no point in saying anything because NOTHING Ever Happens in the Junk World." As a result, Burroughs decides that "We don't want to hear any more family talk, mother talk, father talk, cop talk, priest talk, country talk or party talk. In short, we have heard enough bullshit!"[27] Addicts, as well as the addict's enemies, keep the whole Junk Con on the road, because "no matter how you jerk the handle results always the same for given co-ordinates."[28] Hence Burroughs asks us to find new ways of thinking and knowing drugs, but this can only happen if we start talking about drugs differently. We have to "Shift Co-ordinate Points/ Shift Linguals/Cut Word Lines."[29]

    When *Naked Lunch* was first published in 1959, Burroughs wrote a preface entitled "Deposition: Testimony Concerning a Sickness," the effect of which, when the novel came to trial, was to place the text within a moral framework. In 1991 Burroughs supplemented this preface with his "Afterthoughts on the Deposition," which substantially alters the meaning of the word "junk," which is used throughout the novel. In the first preface Burroughs had said that "the junk virus is public health problem number one of the world today. Since *Naked Lunch* treats this health problem, it is necessarily brutal, obscene and disgusting. Sickness is often repulsive. . . ."[30] As could be expected, this statement was seen as proof that Burroughs's intentions in the book were conventionally moral insofar as he was attacking "junk." However, in the "Afterthoughts," he explains:

> When I say "the junk virus is public health problem number one of the world today," I refer not just to the actual ill effects of opiates upon the individual's health (which in cases of controlled dosage, may be minimal), but also to the hysteria that drug use often occasions in populaces who are prepared by the media and narcotics officials for a hysterical reaction.[31]

The result is that "junk" as a worldwide problem refers not so much to opiates as to those who would either cure everyone of their addiction or punish them (metaphorically or literally) for being addicted or for taking opiates: "Anti-drug hysteria is now worldwide, and it poses a deadly threat to personal freedom. . . ."[32] Hence it is the "junk virus" (i.e., the discourse of control) that really represents the "public health problem." The point is that any of the criticisms that Burroughs makes of "junk" go in two directions at once. He is attacking not just drugs (as he managed to convince the jury), but also the junk virus of control. For example, one short passage in *Naked Lunch* makes it clear that the control addicts are "the junkies": "Red Necks in black stetsons and faded Levis tie a Nigra boy to an old iron lamppost and cover him with burning gasoline. . . . The junkies rush over and draw the flesh smoke deep into their aching lungs. . . . They really got relief. . . ."[33] Racism, like hate, or even the ideology of prevention and cure, is dangerously addicting. We could read *Naked Lunch* as a critique of heroin as a "bad" way of life, but Burroughs is more interested in critiquing those of us who buy The Junk Con of The Cure, Educational Prevention, and "Just Say No."

In *Naked Lunch* Dr. Benway, an "expert [in] control," tells us how the junk con is perpetrated on the rest of us: "The subject must not realize that the mistreatment is a deliberate attack of an anti-human enemy on his personal identity. He must be made to feel that he deserves any treatment he receives because there is something (never specified) horribly wrong with him."[34] The addict is then faced not with a single enemy, which would be relatively easy to handle, but with a whole army of intellectuals and administrators who through their impartial research and scientific proof reassert the addict's status as "a creature without species."[35] The addict is simultaneously in need of cure and salvation, and only under this disguise can "[t]he naked need of the control addicts . . . be decently covered by an arbitrary and intricate bureaucracy so that the subject cannot contact his enemy direct."[36]

In her study of William Burroughs, Robin Lydenberg envisions Burroughs's writing as an example of Paul De Man's theory, which holds that "authority depends upon the fiction of reference or meaning, and authority can be undone therefore by exploding such fictions, not by producing a new myth or reality—by telling yet another story—but by exposing the fictitious character of reality as a narrative process and so rendering language useless for purposes of domination."[37] The whole point of *Naked Lunch* is to tear off the disguises that control hides behind, thus helping us to see that our antidrug rhetoric is not health, science, or morality, but raw coercive power. Burroughs is suggesting that control addicts, by keeping us limited to an either/or universe, are on the side of death and are an antilife force. As Burroughs said, the real theme of *Naked Lunch* is "the Desecration of the Human Image by the control addicts who are putting out the virus."[38] Control makes us line up in opposition to drugs, but I would suggest that control is less interested in drugs, and is more interested in ensuring that the rest of us stand properly in line and hold out our arms to show our allegiance to the drug-free body. To this end, it is not drug users—a very small number of people—but the population at large who are the main focus of control. While this conclusion may seem rather bizarre, we can remind ourselves that it is the addict Hyde who has "strange immunities" from police detection.[39]

If we are trapped by control, then in Burroughs's schema the junkies are immune to control, and lead the way in showing us how to move beyond our current limits. The drug addict goes outside of control and "exists in a painless, sexless, timeless state."[40] As well as cutting addicts off from the word, heroin also cuts them off from need: "Junk short-circuits sex. . . . when I have a H or M shooting habit I am non-sociable."[41] Junk therefore allows one to get away from the social and move into a physiological space, which is experienced as being outside of language. For Burroughs, this freedom from the word allows the body to be free. Burroughs suggests that "perhaps all pleasure is relief" and here it would seem that the relief is release from the body and pain, or what he calls "momentary freedom from the claims of the aging, cautious, nagging frightened flesh."[42]

In *Cities of the Red Night* Burroughs presents us with a group of outlaws and criminals whose "addiction conveys immunity to the fever."[43] It would appear that heroin is a cure for the virus of control, an antidote to those who suffer from the Right Fever. This virus/fever produces "fear" and in the same way that the ideology of health is transmitted from generation to generation, so "the virus information was genetically conveyed."[44] Burroughs tells us that since the "white race was fighting for its biological continuity . . . the virus served a most useful purpose."[45] The machinations of bureaucracy and medicine and law enforcement are therefore "all symptoms of The Human Virus."[46]

Burroughs is suggesting that we are addicted to what language offers us: a stable sense of Self, but for Burroughs this addiction to white junk is making us sick: "I felt the crushing weight of evil insect control forcing my thoughts and feelings into prearranged molds, squeezing my spirit in a soft invisible vise."[47] Therefore, the strategy to beat control is to undermine words. Only by letting go of control can we free ourselves from our "old as-sociation locks."[48] Only then will the drug problem disappear. The cure for Burroughs is always "Let Go! Jump!"[49]

The Ecstasy of Drugs

Drugs are conventionally seen as feminizing the user, turning a man from a stable Self into a hysterical weeping junkie, or at the least, a deviant from the male norm. This sense that taking drugs essentially castrates you in the sym-bolic order causes problems when the people taking the drugs are already scripted as castrated: i.e., when they are women. The result is a subject who is twice removed from the norm. She is once removed for being a woman, and then once more for being on drugs. The result of this framework is that the woman drug user is caught in a rhetoric that perpetuates her powerless-ness. For example, it was a commonplace strategy in the 1920s to perceive (white) women drugs users as passive, innocent victims being abused and mistreated by nasty foreign men. Marek Kohn's *Dope Girls* gives extensive evidence of how this horror story was deployed across England and America in the 1920s and 30s. The popular scenario was of the "susceptible" young woman, combined with the strong and seductive "Chinaman" who leads the woman astray. Many stories from the period serve as templates for this sce-nario: the case of Billy Carleton and Reggie De Veulle, or Freda Kempton and Brilliant Chang. The woman in these narratives is either a figure of pity, or the drugs increase her strength and power and she operates as an object of fear. As Kohn points out,

> a disordering of femininity underlies the young woman's downfall. She is the highly-strung, neurasthenic type believed to be vulnerable to artificial stimu-lants. Her neurosis has also destabilized her sexual identity: her bizarreness and brilliance make her neither a maiden nor a spinster, but a bachelor girl— a young woman with masculine attributes. She is thus vulnerable to the "ad-vances" of another woman. It does not require the modern meaning of "queer" to read this as a warning of homosexual seduction.[50]

While the narrative of the "yellow peril" and the "drug crazy Chinaman" has been dissolved so that we now see it for what it was—nothing more than the "racist garbage of Sax Rohmer," as William Burroughs says—narratives of fe-male drug use are still in operation, readily available, permitting us to "un-derstand" drugs *and* gender *and* race. For example, let us examine the recent case of the drug Ecstasy in England.

In *Ecstasy: Case Unsolved* Sheila Henderson asks us to join her in "saying no to certainty."[51] She agrees that sticking with uncertainty "isn't easy," but hopes that a look at the "genderscape" of the English Ecstasy culture in the 1980s and 90s will prove beneficial to our understanding of how to perceive drugs beyond the popular "opposition between fear and ease."[52] As many young girls started to spend large amounts of time dancing and taking Ecstasy, the media began to tell us what it all "meant." In spite of the changes made by feminism, and in spite of all the research into drug users, the media story seems to have remained unchanged since the 1920s. In the story of Ecstasy we once again see the lone, innocent white woman, "prone and helpless . . . preyed upon by men with an evil intent."[53] The narrative, as we have come to expect, has drugs featuring as "mere 'tricks', 'traps' and 'lures' to entice her into sexual danger."[54] In this narrative, the female drug user is here positioned as the victim. The cases of Leah Betts and Janet Mayes, who died after taking the drug, are then paraded as proof of how these young girls are the targets of those curious men with their evil intent. According to Henderson, the story is told like this:

> Acid House party punters were pagan "revellers" at "sex and drugs orgies"; drug dealers and party organizers were Acid House "Mr. Bigs" who preyed on their victims by seducing them with "killer music," Ecstasy and other "mind-bending" "sex drugs" with "devastating" effects. . . . [55]

Of course, those "devastating" effects were very quickly linked to the girls' sexual behavior. As *The Daily Express* reported:

> Teenage pill-poppers hooked on the Acid house music craze are trying out a new "love drug" nick-named Fantasy. The stimulant creates a feeling of energy and encourages promiscuity. . . . One drugs squad detective said last night: "We fear young girls who are tempted to use it will be taken advantage of by older youths and men."[56]

It was clear that Ecstasy was not physiologically addicting, but the story is not complete without the specter of unwilled behavior; the girls have to be "hooked" not on the drug, but on the music. Stories of "Spanish men" spiking the drinks of innocent young girls and rogues who would "lie in wait and rape" drugged girls were also drawn in to fill out the narrative.[57] The drug supposedly "increases promiscuity" and thus makes women vulnerable targets for rapists.

Yet a brief glimpse at the voices of the young girls themselves allows a very different picture to emerge: "We do fancy blokes at raves and enjoy flirting with them . . . but its like going back to when you were younger, you don't want to get them into bed, you're just friendly."[58] As for being raped or molested, this is not due to the drug, but would be due to the *absence* of it. Men on Ecstasy are not a sexual threat at all: "We were trying to find this rave in Ardwick in deserted flats somewhere. I remember me and [her female friend] being dumped by a cab in what felt like the middle of nowhere and seeing this gang of lads coming toward us. *Luckily* they were on 'E' so there was no problem (my italics)."[59] In short, "they felt safe at clubs, parties and raves," for the dance floor was no longer the disco meat market with women as objects of consumption, for now they were "actors in a huge social and sensual landscape."[60] Science, in the form of *The Journal of Psychoactive Drugs,* even came to the same conclusions: "It is curious that a drug which can increase emotional closeness, enhance receptivity to being sexual . . . does not increase the desire to initiate sex."[61] For girls, the rise of Ecstasy gave them, according to Henderson " . . . power. Power to revel in their own sensuality and sexuality, to conduct their relationships with the boys on their own terms. Power to be social in a way they'd never known before. . . ."[62]

However, as Henderson points out, these two positions for women both have problems: "Old fashioned girls duped into a dangerous sex-and-drug fest or post-feminist babes, active and powerful participants in a limitless sensual and safer sex zone."[63] In this sense the myth of the passive drug user, prone to sex slavery, rape, and abuse, circulates alongside a parallel discourse that says that the drug enables young women to be socially empowered and free from sexual harassment. Neither position, then, actually tells us anything: all either does is allow us to "understand" the other position.

In the film version of *Trainspotting* we see the two positions that are available for female drug users: Alison, the heroin junkie: a weak mother who only desires to shoot up after the death of her baby. Or, the intelligent self-empowerment of the underage raver/schoolgirl Diane, who engages in safe sex with boys in her parents' house. No pregnancy, no HIV, and no needles are involved. The challenge for us is to move beyond creating these binary discourses in which drugs mean either sensuality/empowerment and/or weakness/illness.

Coming Naked to Perception

Burroughs affirms Deleuze and Guattari's comment that "Language is made not to be believed but to be obeyed, and to compel obedience. . . . Language is not life; it gives life orders."[64] For Burroughs, " . . . words are still the principal instruments of control. Suggestions are words. Persuasions are words. Orders are words. No control machine so far devised can operate without words."[65] Burroughs feels that "Modern control systems are predicated on universal literacy."[66] Yet control can never be in control completely; it has to let something slip, and it is that slippage that then justifies intervention: "All control systems try to make control as tight as possible, but at the same time, if they succeeded completely, there would be nothing left to control."[67] Hence drug programs are designed only to constantly resist drugs and addiction, not to rethink the boundaries that produce the concept in the first place. To do so would involve questioning the very language structure that keeps control in control.

Burroughs shows us that language operates by producing a physical response in our bodies. For example, in *Naked Lunch* we constantly see humans turning into insects, centipedes, or worms. Normally addicts of some drug—be it Control or using them—these people are beyond metaphor: addicts are not *like* maggots or worms, or insects, they *become* these creatures before our very eyes. Burroughs is telling us that we believe so strongly in our metaphors that we literally put them into action, with the result that human-bugs then receive the treatment that bugs receive: they must be fought and exterminated. It is not drugs that transform the drug user's body, but language. Language is not *like* a virus in Burroughs's schema, it *is* a virus, and has to be treated as such: "the Word is literally a virus."[68] Burroughs has produced narratives that are essentially surgical: the skin has been cut, the organs are visible, the parasite is exposed and can now be removed.[69]

At one point Burroughs describes *Junky's* Lee as he becomes addicted: "While not exactly invisible he was at least difficult to see. . . . People covered him with a project."[70] The project in this sense is the metaphors that we use about the addict, metaphors that allow us to "know" the addict and the words that we use to block the exits to new vistas. Hence to see drugs "naked" would mean seeing them without the metaphors that the language virus puts out, and to which we have become so addicted. Burroughs refuses to feed our habit for metaphor: "I bring no junk words, no sick words from Jesus."[71] In order to heal us, he has to first take us "to the final place where the human road ends . . ." which involves also taking our metaphors to breaking point.[72] Burroughs dropped out of Harvard Medical School, but he preserved his doctoral function when he became a writer: the doctor always does a good job with his emetic fictions.

In his *The Hashish Eater* Fitz Hugh Ludlow felt that eating hashish meant that his body, along with History, were forgotten: "When the body is removed, the barrier to the Past goes also."[73] The break with the virus of control is also signified by a break in the power to narrate truth. In Ludlow's words: "What that truth was I strove to express to my companions, yet in vain, for human language was yet void of signs which might characterize it."[74] Like Ludlow, Burroughs has created a way of talking about addiction in a narrative space, in which the truth of drug addiction is constantly being thrown into question and is not interested in finding the right words, but in bringing an end to "the whole stupid game."[75] Of course we can always ignore *Naked Lunch* and hold onto our belief that language will allow us to arrive at the truth of addiction. We could also assume that we know what addiction really is and that there is no need to rethink the whole situation. All we need to do is keep going in the same direction: one more truth "fix" and we will have the whole thing wrapped up.

If the cure is active forgetfulness, what would it involve? Maybe it would begin with us asking different questions. What if addicts are not trapped, but in fact are free from something, as Burroughs suggests? What if, far from being out of control, being "outside" of control constitutes freedom *from* control. In that case, giving up drugs means leaving ourselves back inside control, and a return to sickness. What happens to our antidrug position if addicts are actually exercising their free will by getting away from the sickness that is control?

Perhaps we say that drug users are trapped because we cannot bear to think of them as free: that would make us the ones that are trapped. We say that addicts are trapped—yet they are also escapist or have somehow escaped from reality: how can it be both? They are both out of control (and we can then bring them back into control), as well as controlled by their habit (and we can then free them through our "cure"). However, for Burroughs it is the desire to control that is the real threat to our health: "You see control can never be a means to a practical end. . . . It can never be a means to anything but more control. . . . Like junk. . . ."[76] Burroughs tells us in *Junky* that "Morphine hits the back of the legs first, then the back of the neck, a spreading wave of relaxation slackening the muscles away from the bones so that you seem to float without outlines. . . ."[77] Instead of holding onto control as our only hope of solving the drug problem, we should learn to freefall, and, as with the effects of morphine, learn to float. However, we persist in trying to use control to cure ourselves. But control will only lead to more use of control, and the problem will only get worse the more we try to use control. As Burroughs warns us, "Try using junk as a means to something else. . . ."[78] implying that with the junk of control, nothing else can be done except exert more control.

Jean Cocteau states that "Everything one achieves in life, even love, occurs in an express train racing toward death. To smoke opium is to get out of the train while it is still moving. It is to concern oneself with something other than life or death."[79] With Burroughs, this concern expresses itself through his focus on the *between.* As with Burroughs's experiments with cut-up narratives in his novels *The Ticket that Exploded,* and *Nova Express,* the emphasis is on the new meaning that emerges out of concerning oneself with something other than binary thinking. The only way to escape the word virus is to enter the space between words and operate at a level of neither one or the other, but in the space where the one *becomes* the other. Drug addiction has to be deconstructed so that we cannot rest with the binary definitions of heroic existential exploration or neurotic nihilistic escape. For Burroughs, such a deconstruction would be the end of the drug problem in that control cannot function in such a spatial arrangement of narrative: "The Virus runs on hate It The Virus only lives in the Words-Love Hate. Only in Time. Out Space No Word is . . . I The Control Virus lives in The Word."[80]

As far as control is concerned, drug addicts are dangerous and therefore they must be "cured": hence we have outreach programs, education, pamphlets, support, and counseling advice to ensure that addicts are reprogrammed and brought back into the sphere of the normal and the healthy. If, as Burroughs is suggesting, we shift coordinate points to escape this virus, then maybe we should move ourselves to a new viewing position wherein the kind, caring doctor vaccinating masses of school children becomes instead a dangerous and crazy Dr. Benway getting children hooked on the propaganda of the "health/illness" binary. If this scenario leaves us and the medical establishment as the addicts who are in need of help, then Antonin Artaud suggests that we should turn to those outlawed patients, the addicts, for help. For Artaud, it is the drug addicts who hold the secret to our cure: they are, in his words, "wonderful doctors."[81]

Chapter 5

Planet Heroin: Women and Drugs

> and you put the heroin
> in my vein
> and take blood and heroin out
> and put it back in
> it is indeed fascinating
>
> —Pat Califia.[1]

Exploring the Heroin World

In this chapter I wish to examine the work of Marsha Rosenbaum, Elizabeth Ettore, and Carter Heyward to see how the subject of women and drugs is currently being constructed and understood.[2] I especially want to examine the limits that these three writers impose on our ability to reconstruct our relationship to drugs and the drug user. I will then look at Avril Taylor as well as Anna Kavan and Dr. John Marks to explore some possible avenues that could provide female drug users, and ourselves, with ways of talking about drugs and gender that would be truly liberating.

In *Women on Heroin* (1981), Marsha Rosenbaum says that if we are to "fully comprehend the draw of the heroin world" we must be prepared "to explore the heroin world itself."[3] Instead of placing us in a familiar space that would make it easier to think about drug addiction, Rosenbaum prefers to put us into an alien territory. She is setting up a situation in which addicts will obviously figure as the aliens, and we must be prepared to encounter many strange sights as we explore this dark continent, this alien world of planet heroin. The titles of the subsequent chapter headings, "The Heroin World and the Addict's Career," "Where are the Women?," and

"Getting In," sustain the feeling of this trip to another world. What is strange is not the Ridley Scott–like presentation of women's drug use, but the fact that having said she wants to understand women's heroin use, she then reverts to a metaphor that gives the game away. She does not really wish to "fully comprehend" it, she merely wants to "explore" an alien world. As long as she insists on it staying an alien world, then, it cannot be understood: it can only be observed, or misunderstood. If heroin use is indeed an alien world, why not get a local guide or ask the inhabitants themselves to show you around? Of course, drug addicts cannot be allowed to explain their world to us; *we* must explain it to *them*.

Rosenbaum's concern is with gender and drugs, but her framing of women's drug use seems to preclude any "full comprehension" of heroin. For example, it would seem that on her map of planet heroin there are only two places where the aliens can live: either the female addict is "a liberated woman who breaks through sexual barriers and functions alongside men in the heroin world. *Or* she is doubly oppressed and exploited as an addict and a woman."[4] Rosenbaum asserts then that we can "fully comprehend" female drug use, as long as it falls into this simple binary. If the residents of planet heroin do not live in one of these two areas, then such drug users either do not exist, or, are simply invisible to Rosenbaum.

Rather than attempting to understand heroin use, the text exposes how the role of heroin itself has also already been decided. In her narrative, heroin has been cast as some kind of heavy planet or a black hole that pulls women toward its deadly core, what Rosenbaum refers to as "the draw of the heroin world."[5] Such an approach, while providing excitement for Rosenbaum and the reader, has precluded any chance of locating another position from which to "understand" women's heroin use because it has already decided what heroin and heroin use "really" means.

In the conventional drug narrative, we are positioned as a subject who is to be disappointed and dismayed when drug users relapse and get drawn back into the heroin world. But why are we surprised when we have constructed planet heroin as a world in which the force of gravity is so incredibly superhuman and strong? Rosenbaum's thesis is that the use of heroin by women results in a "career of narrowing options."[6] The book then "reveals" how this is "true." Her text then follows the "career" of the typical woman drug user as she gradually gets "pulled" into the "gravitational force field" of planet heroin and is finally sucked to her doom.

According to Rosenbaum, it would seem that once the drug users are on planet heroin they are not alone, but join other prisoners: an indigenous population of male alien drug users. For Rosenbaum, female drug users "are either omitted or seen as peripheral members of predominantly male worlds, ornaments to lift the status and prestige of men, or money makers . . . [in short] women addicts must relate to the world of heroin where the pace, norms, values, and patterns are shaped by men."[7] Strangely enough, Rosenbaum positions the *male* addicts as conscious manipulators who are in control of the situation, and are even able to worry about shaping "norms [and] values." Having designated women drug users as belonging to an alien world, it is not surprising then that the research "reveals" the same conclusion. Rosenbaum discovers that the female drug user

> . . . scores higher on tests of pathology, is said to be insecure, frightened, anxious, confused about her role and status in society, hostile, rebellious, without motivation, manipulative, selfish, and aggressive! Women addicts are, it is claimed, more difficult, therefore to treat, and their drop-out rates reflect this, as they are much higher than men's.[8]

Rosenbaum goes on to point out that therapy for women often fails because it attempts to cure the women by resocializing them, which often means forcing them back into the social roles that they initially turned to heroin to escape. The result of these barriers to the woman addict, both in the shooting gallery and in the clinic, means that the female addict's career becomes "inverted":

> Heroin expands her life options in the initial stages, and that is the essence of its social attraction. Yet with progressively further immersion in the heroin world, the social, psychological, and physiological exigencies of heroin use create an option "funnel" for the woman addict. Through this funnel the addict's life options are gradually reduced until she is functionally incarcerated in an invisible prison. Ultimately, the woman addict is locked into the heroin life and locked out of the conventional world.[9]

This narrow "funnel," which represents their life on heroin, then forces them to be buried or drowned as their "immersion in deviance" increases.[10]

This alien world is not just a funnel, but is also constructed as an "invisible prison" from which one can assume only free will is the "key" to "escape." The end result of heroin use, as far as Rosenbaum can see, is that many women often believe "that they have replaced one kind of domination with another—male domination with domination by a drug whose insistence they cannot control."[11] As the narrative progresses, the drug user goes further downward, while the reader and the researcher remain immune to the gravity of planet heroin. It is as if they have will-powered energy boosters that allow them to pull themselves out of this fatal trajectory. We are allowed to watch in fascinated horror as the addict burns up on entry.

Elizabeth Ettore

In *Women and Substance Use* (1992), Elizabeth Ettore, like Rosenbaum, argues that women's circumstances "predispose them as a group to addiction and dependency."[12] In order to free them from this "bondage," Ettore—with the advantage of over ten years of drug research since Rosenbaum's—puts forward a model that would enable women to combat the gravitational pull of planet heroin. Instead of altering Rosenbaum's metaphors she accepts them as truth and then works to find a "solution" to the way that the metaphors pose the (metaphorical) problems.

Ettore is genuinely troubled by the growing tendency among several addiction theorists who she feels are "individualizing" and thus "depoliticizing" addiction through their solutions. In response to this, Ettore says that what is needed is a "collective social approach" to drug addiction.[13] The way to achieve this is by women "educating themselves to see that the control of our health and fertility is fundamental to the control of our lives."[14] Ettore then lists several self-help groups who could benefit from this approach, beginning with Narcotics Anonymous and Alcoholics Anonymous and then branching out to Emotions Anonymous and Sex and Love Addicts Anonymous. Ettore feels that while "the worth of these type of self-help groups must not be denied," she also feels that their format prevents "any development of a women's praxis."[15] In short, her model is fundamentally identical to Rosenbaum's and suffers from the same limitations. We are still on planet heroin, and the escape must come by women struggling against the pull of drugs by politicizing themselves.

Ettore's solution to the problem of drug use is for women to establish "more knowledge of and control over women's own bodies," control that will bring "a new sense of solidarity and strength as women evidence powers uniquely their own."[16] Ettore's model is one in which the body/spaceship wakes up just in time, grabs the controls and steers herself away from the pull of planet heroin by an exertion of will power. These women drug users, having rejected drugs, are then in a position to "develop separate, strong identities within a collective framework."[17] Once free of drugs, women are then wholly liberated and can formulate a women's praxis.

In the first model, Rosenbaum constructed the drug user as someone out of control, helpless, sucked into a funnel of narrowing options, while in Ettore's version the model/metaphor is one in which the drug user regains control through collective support, thus averting the tragedy. Yet, as Slavoj Zizek points out, what should concern us here is not which one of these positions is "true" (a "pseudo problem" for Zizek). We need to rephrase the question. For Zizek it is not a case of "What does the [drug user] signify?" but "How is the very space constituted where entities like the [drug user] can emerge?"[18] In a sense, then, it is more productive if we use these two very limited positions for women drug users (one super passive, the other super active) and treat them, in Zizek's words, "as two complementary versions of the same myth which interpret each other."[19]

While Ettore, like Rosenbaum, is assuming an antipatriarchal, anticapitalist position in her book, the rhetoric of free will that she employs would seem entirely consistent with hegemonic notions of a "stable" Self. Ettore is proceeding as if she knew what the Self is, and that all we need to do is take it back. Furthermore, by proposing that the solution is the exertion of will through empowerment and control, her response is in keeping with a "Just Say No" ideology, which understands drug addiction only in terms of will power, control, and weakness. In both cases, the "tragedy" of heroin is always being staged because the woman has "let go" of her will and allowed her self-control to be usurped by heroin and/or men. Such cures partake of the very logic that allows us to perceive of addiction as a problem. There is an assumption that Ettore's argument is radical and challenging, yet her desire to return the Self to normal parameters of behavior, desire, and stability is something that a "Just Say No" culture never ceases to remind us.

Homer's Lotus Eaters were quite happy to stay where they were and not return to Ithaca, and Ettore feels that female drug users occupy the same status of being dreamy, weak, and languid creatures. For Ettore, the "cure" for their condition is to "become disillusioned" so that women can wake up out of their drugged "sleep," and take control of their behavior with the result that "their substance use become[s] visible *as it is in reality,* not as it appears through male eyes."[20] It seems that "through male eyes" could also be read as "through the eyes of the drug," because, according to Ettore, it would amount to the same thing: a condition of sleep, ignorance, and weakness. The woman's "enemy" is men, drugs, or both. Ettore points out that it will be "in this light" that we can "awaken and [develop an] awareness" of women's addiction. The solution to drug addiction, then, is to create a space in which women "struggle to replace substance use, a form of pleasurable routine, with real feminist affirming practices," which would involve women "collect[ing] their strength," enabling them "to challenge hierarchical structures of power."[21] However, in her desire not to be misunderstood as pro-pleasure and by default, prodrug, she goes to great lengths to reassure us that she is "not advocating substance use."[22]

She expands upon her position by outlining how she intends for women to take pleasure not from drugs, but from empowerment, which again will be tied into the notion of a supposedly "free" Self: "pleasure [will be] linked [to] autonomy and empowerment."[23] For Ettore, if women are to rid themselves of patriarchy/drugs, they must "be vigilant" and "resist, [and] be aware" so that "[w]omen [can] replace what is perceived as pleasurable routines (substance use) with life-giving rather than life-threatening practices."[24] Once a woman learns to "master herself" she can be free, because for Ettore "[r]eal pleasure and freedom go hand in hand."[25] Again, this position asks women to renounce "bad" pleasures and replace them with healthy, controlled, productive, willed activities: activities that will set them "free." Heroin, or any unwilled activity, thus becomes a kind of pharmacological smoke screen, which "separates [women] from *their real female selves*."[26] In her model, drugs can only be represented as a form of ideological blindness that must be resisted and fought against.

Drawing unquestioningly on the popular view of drug addiction in which the Will collapses and the individual is powerless, Ettore speaks as if drug addiction were a form of retinal narcolepsy, whereas freedom from addiction involves being able to focus and awaken from the blindness that goes along with being duped by patriarchal ideology/drugs. The solution of empowerment, self-sufficiency, and will power thus becomes the cure, in which autonomous healthy whole Selves pursue pleasures (but not drugs) in an environment that is "free" from addiction, with the result that all women can then live "free" and "productive" lives. This is the ideal of Ettore's antipatriarchal response to addiction, and yet it fits perfectly into a patriarchal culture that thrives by generating exactly the same ideal subjectivity that Ettore wants women, and by extension all addicts, to "struggle" for. Ettore only sees drugs as a threat to the Will, one that must be combated with an exertion of "pure" will. Such an exertion also appeals to us because it appears to prove that the Will is free, or at least, is becoming so: we must "fight against" drugs, and we must "struggle against" addiction. The acronym for DARE, after all, stands for Drug Abuse Resistance Education. Ettore's position, by ostensibly mirroring the anti-addiction rhetoric, is thus unable to move beyond it.[27] The lessons that DARE aims to teach young children would feel quite at home in Ettore's model. According to a pamphlet put out by the Minnesota Bureau of Criminal Apprehension, the lessons of DARE are: "providing accurate information about drugs and alcohol; teaching students decision making skills; showing them how to resist peer pressure; suggesting health alternatives to drug use; and building self-esteem." Like DARE, Ettore is writing from within a structure which she is unwilling or unable to dismantle or critique.

In Ettore's work she uses subheadings such as "Seizing the Means of Production" and "Recognizing Empowerment as a Tool of Change;" these can easily be placed alongside Attorney General Hubert Humphrey's statement that DARE is a "tool" that can help children to "fight drugs." In both of these cases, the "cures," (one from the Sheriffs' Department and a $700 million dollar budget, the other antipatriarchal, anticapital) are squarely within a field that is actively hindering our ability to renegotiate our understanding of drugs.

Carter Heyward

In a recent collection of essays on the issues confronting lesbian and gay substance abuse, Carter Heyward opens by stating her position as "a feminist liberation theologian . . . [and] also a lesbian who is recovering from alcoholism and bulimia."[28] Given this kind of marginal subject position, we would expect that Heyward would be able to speak to us from beyond the usual frameworks that structure the talk about drugs. However, it soon becomes apparent that even marginal subject positions are infiltrated by the traditional rhetoric. Taking us back to planet heroin, Heyward begins by stating that "we [women addicts] are an alienated people" and that only by striving toward recovery and healing can this alienation be overcome.[29] We are, she says "captive to social forces that are in control of our lives, including our feelings and our values."[30]

I agree with Heyward here completely, but what if we take her statement further than she might like to go with it, and state that we are controlled by forces we have no control over, including forces that only allow us to articulate certain ideas about drugs? In that case, we should then perhaps begin to question what forces are at work that want us to articulate these positions. Otherwise, if we do not question our own solutions, we will end up back where we started. As with Rosenbaum and Ettore, I find Heyward's analysis unproductive for women drug users because it simply assumes that they are constantly being blinded by patriarchal drug plots that want to entrap and alienate them, and that somehow assuming a willed healthy position will be a "challenge" to patriarchy. This is not really the case, as power *needs* healthy willed subjects, and will not discourage any discourse that has this as its final goal.

For Heyward, the state of alienation that drugs bring is also, not surprisingly, a state of "powerlessness."[31] Therefore, she suggests that "both homophobia and addiction need to be understood . . . [as] a manifestation of alienation."[32] Thus homophobia is a social problem which must be "healed" (10) and addiction, which for Heyward springs from the very same roots, is not an individual disease, but a social "dis-ease" that can be "cured" if lesbians/addicts liberate themselves from oppression/drugs.[33] To this end, Heyward asserts that "the therapeutic tradition remains, uncritically, a product of patriarchal capitalism's preoccupation with the ego of the individual (white heterosexual male) as normative in determining mental health."[34] I would concur with this, but Heyward paradoxically challenges this "therapeutic tradition" with an antidrug rhetoric that patriarchal capitalism is quite happy to encourage.

For Heyward, the goal is to realize that we are always already connected to others, and that the recognition of this original connectedness is a way of overcoming the alienation that leads to addiction: the cure, once again, as in

Ettore or Rosenbaum (or even from the most generic patriarchal psycho-analysis), is a "creative struggle" that will be the "root of personal change and transformation."[35] This struggle, which for Heyward can be conducted through the 12-Step program, enabled her to go from an inauthentic, alien-ated self to her "most authentic, relational self."[36] Having spent time sug-gesting that there are particular issues for lesbians and addiction, it is interesting that when she attends her first AA meeting she listens to a *man* tell the group "my story," pointing out that in fact there was no difference at all between her addiction story and the addiction story of this man: "I knew that he and I were connected near the core of our humanness. . . ."[37] Heyward's healing process, parallel to Ettore's and Rosenbaum's will suppos-edly enable us to overcome drug addiction as we learn to struggle "against forces of alienation" with the result that "we are brought more and more to our senses."[38]

Julia's Story

In contrast to Heyward, Ettore, and Rosenbaum, we have a very strange case coming from Britain. The psychiatrist Dr. John Marks used to run a clinic in Widnes, Liverpool, in which drug users were granted a place on the pro-gram only if they promised to *stay* on the drug of their choice. While Marks had no feminist agenda for drug users his work turns out to be more far reaching than the above examples, and made proposals in how we could treat both men and women drug users that were far more "political" and "radical." Unlike Ettore, Heyward, and Rosenabaum, Marks' program had no intention of trying to make its patients quit, because it was clear to Marks that such strategies did not work. All the medical establishment need do is provide addicts with a healthy environment and with "healthy" drugs so as to ensure that they are getting pure, rather than adulterated, pharmaceutical heroin and cocaine. Marks' argument is that after a while users' lives will restabilize, and the addicts will slowly put their lives back together and give up their drugs in their own time: no amount of prison or psychoanalysis is going to change or speed up this process. All the medical establishment can do in the meantime is ensure that addicts stay healthy during their drug use, and as Marks says, it is a simple case of "drugs from the clinic or drugs from the Mafia":

> Cure people? No, nobody can. Regardless of whether you stick them in prison, give them shock treatment, put them in a nice rehab center away in the country and pat them on the head, give them drugs, give them no drugs— no matter what you do, five per cent per annum—one in twenty per year— get off spontaneously. They seem to mature out of addiction regardless of any

intervention in the interim. But you can keep them alive and healthy and legal during that ten years if you wish to."[39]

While it is well known to medicine that pure pharmaceutical heroin "is not by itself physiologically dangerous," this policy also ensures that the crime associated either with selling or buying street drugs is eliminated, along with the health risks associated with buying heroin on the street, which has been cut with cement, brick dust, talc, and so on.[40]

In 1992, an episode of *60 Minutes* covered the work of Marks' clinic. They showed the black American presenter (Ed Bradley) watch a white English pharmacist inject cigarettes with pure solutions of cocaine and heroin. Bradley is horrified and asks the pharmacist if he does not feel odd making what he feels are ostensibly "crack cigarettes." The presenter's shock is matched only by the pharmacist's calm response that there is nothing untoward or morally suspect about what he is doing. We are then introduced to Julia, a young woman about 26 years old. The American presenter points out that "although she doesn't look like it," she is a heroin addict and that Julia used to work as a prostitute to support her habit. However, she was then given a prescription by Dr. Marks for pure pharmaceutical heroin. She then tells us that she "stopped [being a prostitute] straight away." Unlike Ettore, Rosenbaum, and Hayward, who feel that Julia should have struggled against the drug, Julia actually *stayed with the drug* in order to survive. According to Julia, without her prescription she would "probably be dead by now." As a result of being *given* heroin, she can now hold a regular job as a waitress, care for her three-year-old daughter and have normal relationships. Quite simply, once the metaphor of planet heroin is abandoned, the destructive power of heroin seems to be lost. The result is that heroin is perceived in this narrative not as an alien planet, but simply as a regular part of our own world, while the residents, not surprisingly, are no different from us at all.

Julia's story is one that is not usually seen in the American debate about women and drug use. In most narratives the prostitute is kept in the distance and is always already out of reach, but in this narrative Julia was brought close, held tight, embraced, and was given what it was that she told us she wanted.[41] When she is asked why addicts should be *given* drugs, her reply is so simple as to be almost shocking: "So that they can be given a chance to live. Like everyone else." This kind of narrative is unpopular because it prevents us from telling so many of the other stories that we wish to tell about women and drugs. If we acknowledge this story as a truth in its own right, then we are unable to give space to our truth that drugs are equal to enslavement and/or a patriarchal plot. It also castrates our narratives regarding planet heroin, which assert that only by struggling against drugs can we hope to arrive at planet health. In Julia's narrative it is only by putting an end to struggling against drugs that restores her to health and freedom from prostitution. Ettore's argument that we should struggle against drugs (or what really amounts to making Julia struggle to get them) only serves to push her even further into prostitution and does nothing to move her toward "health." Michel Foucault says that we have to beware of thinking that saying yes to sex automatically means saying no to power, and a similar structure works with drugs: Ettore, Rosenbaum, and Hayward all feel that saying no to drugs also means saying no to patriarchal ideology. As the case of Julia makes clear, saying no to drugs would actually leave her firmly in the grasp of all that Ettore et al. want to free her from. Listening to and accepting Julia's demands for drugs actually helps to keep her away from prostitution and sickness, rather than making her sink deeper into them.

Obviously, Rosenbaum, Ettore, and Heyward are seriously trying to grapple with the problem of drug use. Yet if we are to move forward, we should consider how their positions are damaging women's lives and rather than serving to dismantle the drug problem, they are supporting the very structures of belief that perpetuate it. Let us briefly return to the case of Julia from the *60 Minutes* program. What would have happened to her if Heyward, Ettore, or Rosenbaum had been in charge of drug policy in Liverpool? It would not enter into their field of vision to think of *giving* Julia heroin, for this, in their minds, would have been adding to Julia's oppression under the forces of alienation. Ettore would have said it would leave her prey to patriarchy. Rosenbaum would have said it would simply push her further down the funnel and further into deviance, while Heyward would have suggested that Julia go to NA and try to struggle to become a healthy free and liberated person. We can assume that as Julia became "free" and unalienated so she would then, to use Heyward's phrase, be "brought to her senses," and choose not to take heroin or engage in prostitution. However, in complete opposition to these models, John Marks actually *gives* her heroin and Julia is able to function normally. According to Rosenbaum's framework, such a thing would be impossible: "Part of the addict-prostitute's difficulty in maintaining a regular routine . . . is due to her heroin habit, which prevents her from constantly keeping her wits about her."[42] However, Julia has a regular job, cares for her three-year-old daughter, *and* has an addiction to heroin. How can this be possible? Julia's case shows that drugs and stability are not mutually exclusive. In fact, easy, healthy, and *legal* access to heroin makes her life *stable*, not unstable, and allows her to make choices and explore options that had previously been denied to her and closed off by an inadequate, expensive, and unhealthy supply of heroin.

In recognition of the power of what *60 Minutes* had uncovered, the American government quickly exerted pressure on the British government to have Marks's clinic shut down. Mike Gray, the author of *Drug Crazy,* points out how "Friends in the Home Office warned Marks that the embassy was getting heat over the broadcast."[43] The result was that the clinic had its funding pulled in April 1995.[44] England was then asked to "harmonize" their policy on drugs with the American approach.[45] Marks continues to write and work as a psychiatrist but the clinic is no longer in operation.

Avril Taylor

Avril Taylor's *Women Drug Users* (1993) also offers conclusions very much at odds with the truths located by Rosenbaum, Ettore, and Heyward. Taylor's work is an ethnographic work that aims to study a group of woman drug users in Glasgow, pointing out that "no ethnographic study of female drug users alone has been undertaken anywhere."[46] Rather than "explore planet heroin," the study "avoids the pre-definition of what is to be considered relevant and aims at discovering the insider's view of [her] world."[47] Taylor suggests that such an approach is "particularly suitable for feminist research" because it has as its aim "the uncovering of women's own perspectives of their lives."[48]

One of the central positions held by Ettore is that women drug users are passive victims of patriarchal networks of power. Yet Taylor makes it clear that women drug users all engaged in an "active involvement" regarding their drug use: "the stereotypical image of women drug users as "passive victims" is thus refuted."[49] The tendency of most research is to suggest an *underlying* cause for drug use (in Ettore's case, patriarchy is at the root of women's drug use). What Taylor suggests, though, is that "[t]he evidence presented thus far cautions against the search for one overriding factor which can explain entry into illicit drug use."[50] For example, rather than evil male pushers being the cause of many women starting drugs, Taylor discovers that it was often a close female friend who introduced women to drugs. Moreover, entry into the drug world brought with it not a decline in status, but a rise in the women's self-confidence through acquiring a respected set of skills. In Rosenbaum's analysis the move to injecting was always treated as the barrier that, once crossed, meant only less control over their lives, but Taylor shows that for the women she studied, the move to injecting brought with it a sense of accomplishment. In the words of one woman: "I just done that, stuck it in and pulled it back and the blood all came into it and see because I had done it myself, I felt brilliant . . . I felt dead proud. . . ."[51] Other women also expressed this opinion, and according to Taylor, it was "a common reaction" when learning how to inject: "I became a pure expert . . . a lot of skill."[52] Taylor reveals that the move to injecting was not seen as another step in the horrid chain of addiction but a rational and logical decision based on economic considerations so that "the benefits of drug taking were to be continued and costs were to be kept to a minimum."[53]

Studies of male drug users tend to perceive that males engage in Odysseus-like feats to sustain their habits, while the older assumption that male drug addicts are weak and ineffectual is now generally applied to women users.[54] However much we may enjoy telling ourselves the story of the weak woman addict who cannot help herself, Taylor found that such a scenario is no more than a fantasy on the part of the researchers: "[W]omen are shown to be every bit as busy, every bit as involved in the business of maintaining their habit, as male users."[55] At this juncture it would be easy to argue that the risks and the excitement of the habit were what the women were "really" seeking, as does Rosenbaum. Yet here again our stereotypes are not upheld by Taylor's study: "[T]he women in this present study were aware of the risks they ran, there was no sign that the women welcomed them or found them intrinsically exciting."[56] Scoring drugs was far from being a dangerous and exciting challenge—it was often very mundane and ordinary: "For some women, shopping for drugs became part and parcel of shopping for other items, and was bound up in the everyday organization of the community. Scoring was often carried out at the same time as buying groceries, [or] nappies for the baby."[57] Many times drugs were bought from friends or from "respectable" members of society who were selling their prescription drugs, which as Taylor points out, lent "an air of normality to the proceedings."[58]

Many of the narratives that we like to tell about drugs would simply collapse if we switched drugs from special to normal and mundane, abandoning our horror stories about the dangers of drugs. However, we prefer to insist on them being the deviant substance and subject par excellence. If Mark's method had been allowed to extend to Glasgow, then these women could have simply gone shopping for diapers and groceries and on the way home stopped off at the chemist to pick up their prescription for heroin. No one is bothered by *these* kinds of drug deals; thus the drug "problem" would disappear into the crowd, as it did for a brief spell in Widnes, Liverpool under the guidance of Dr. Marks.

The other narrative we tell ourselves is that all "drugs" immediately disqualify the user from any sense of responsibility. But as one user points out, you cannot make these generalizations about "drugs" because while some drugs do eradicate clear-headed thinking, others actually allow you to keep a moral stance. One woman describes an episode of scoring, in which she makes the mistake of stealing from another woman who was selling: " . . . if I had had heroin or tems, I'd know what I'm doing. I won't do anything that I think I shouldn't do. But the downers I think they get you into more trouble. . . ."[59] Contrary to our position, the heroin or the tems (buprenorphine) would have allowed her a sense of perspective that the downers eradicated.

The other narrative that enjoys a wide circulation is the presumed link between drugs and crime. As Taylor says, we respond as if "there is some pharmacological link between the two."[60] Rather than the links being automatic and inevitable, Taylor again reveals how crime had to be *actively engaged in,* rather than passively fallen into. Even then, it was engaged in only after all other forms of economic survival had been exhausted: "rather than being driven into crime, the women made pragmatic choices about how they set about raising finance."[61] We tend to want to perceive drug users as disorganized and chaotic but Taylor suggests that if people are to survive as drug users, their lives "are far from chaotic, but require to be carefully planned and structured if their goals are to be achieved."[62] Moreover, like any good businesswoman, "[d]rug users are constantly on the lookout for ways to obtain money, and through this vigilance an acute awareness of opportunities for making money becomes developed."[63] We champion such behaviors on Wall Street, but when we see these behaviors in drug users, it is a sign of their sickness.

Prostitution is seen as the female addict's main economic activity and this belief upholds the "crack for sex" narrative that we have readily available to explain the power that drugs have over people's lives. However, Taylor points out that prostitution was only taken up as a last resort once all other economic avenues had been exhausted, and even then with reluctance. Contrary to our belief in the immorality of all addicts, the women that Taylor worked with did have rather conventional morals. Many of the women viewed prostitution as "shameful" and morally suspect and even looked down on other women who resorted to it. Many women treated prostitutes as sexual deviants whose behavior in fact had nothing to do with their drug use, and actually saw them as a strange exception rather than the norm. As one woman pointed out," I just don't know how they can do it. I think it must be something in some people. They just treat it like a nine-to-five job. Even when they stop drugs they go back to it . . . it's something in them." Another woman user said: "Not once have I ever, *ever* thought of going up the toon. Not once. I think you already have to have that in you."[64] In comparison to the prostitutes, these women see themselves as normal, psychologically healthy and moral. Why do we then insist on refusing to see them as they see themselves?

An important story that we also tell ourselves about women drug users is that they are disqualified from being functional mothers. Not surprisingly, Taylor's research reveals that this narrative is also unfounded. In fact, the women drug users had no less interest in being good mothers than any other mother. In Taylor's words, "[w]hat also becomes apparent is the falsity of the notion that women drug users are socially inadequate, isolated, or lacking in moral standards. An examination of their social relationships provides evidence to refute all these images."[65] Taylor's study reveals that women drug users make every effort to ensure that they have a maximum number of connections and drug-using friends in case of shortages in supply. One thing that drug users realize is that the more connections that they can establish around themselves, the more possibilities are available to them. Paradoxically in terms of our own approach to drugs and our attitude to drug users we take the opposite path. We close down possibilities, we cut ourselves off; we limit and restrain ourselves from opening up more possibilities or combinations of solutions.

We also like to imagine that drug users are selfish and will double-cross their mothers. After all, we believe that all they care about is the next fix, so that leaves us no room to think that they care about anything else. However, Taylor found that her subjects revealed a high degree of empathy for "each other's plight and [had a] willingness to be supportive." As she says, "bonds did develop . . . which also challenge views of drug users as self-interested and uncaring."[66] If the drug users were sometimes uncaring toward each other, Taylor found that what was happening was that the drug users were internalizing the straight perception of addicts as liars and untrustworthy people. In practice, however, the women "gave and derived support from other drug users."[67] Though our response to addicts is to resist helping them with *their* needs out of fear of somehow enabling them, such a response actually disables them. Taylor shows how the women would openly offer to help each other with everything from housing to offering drugs when needed. Rosenbaum felt that female addiction "often includes child neglect," yet Taylor found that these women addicts, like anyone else, have an active concern for the health and safety of themselves and their "weans" (babies):

> Judy: "Frances is going to try and come off tomorrow so I'm going to sit up with her and take care of the wean."
> Sally: "Karen's just had a big abscess which I telt her and telt her and telt her to go to the doctor aboot . . . 'You get up that hospital.' In the end I had to drag her to the nurse. These really young lassies that are up the town and they don't realize the dangers of AIDS. And I'm like that to them: 'Let me see in your pockets. Have you got Durex? Don't do it without Durex, you can get AIDS.'"
> Laura: "Lynne's been staying here. She has naewhere to go and she's my pal and I wasnae wanting to let her roam the streets, so I've let her in."[68]

These comments are of no use to us because they simply do not "work"— they are ineffective because they disarm the story we wish to tell about addicts, which is that they are somehow "Other" than ourselves. These comments do not work for us because they make addicts more like you and

I—more normal, even ordinary. If the narrative of drugs that we wish to tell is to continue, then the space between our subjectivity and the object of the drug user must remain as large as possible. While we call for drug users to become like us, to become subjects, we always insist on their otherness.

While we accuse drug users, and particularly addicts, of being solitary and deceptive, Taylor finds a large degree of "group solidarity" among women addicts, something that dismantles Ettore's notion of the women drug user as weak and disempowered.[69] It could be argued that treating "group solidarity" among addicts as a sign of empowerment is rather pathetic, because we "know" that it is only a false sense of empowerment rather than the real empowerment that Ettore, Heyward, and Rosenbaum would wish for. However, if the addicts see themselves as operating along lines of group solidarity, why should the researcher, or policymaker, armed with his or her own values, decide that the addicts' perceptions are wrong? Regarding the solidarity of addicts, Taylor found that the "most important rule in this respect was that one should never be a "grass." To expose or denounce another drug user to straight society, particularly but not exclusively to law enforcement agents, even to save oneself, was a serious misdemeanor."[70] Contrary to this belief, we encourage children to turn in their parents, or each other, to the police. From the drug user's point of view, straight society is hopelessly immoral, not only in getting children to do its dirty work, but also in showing no respect for a basic tenet of their own social and moral values. From the user's viewpoint, straight society discourages group solidarity and actively works to undermine it. From a drug user's stance, why should they trust us if they honestly believe that we are behaving in ways that they find morally reprehensible?

Taylor's study also dispels the notion of the drug user's lack of moral fiber. Taylor found ample "evidence of adherence to ethical and moral values."[71] While we like to suture addicts to narratives of promiscuity, Taylor found that promiscuity "was not a feature of the women's lifestyle. In this and other aspects of their sexual relationships, the women held conservative and traditional attitudes."[72]

Ettore argues that women need to see their addiction for what it is "in reality" and not see it through men's eyes. However, Taylor came into contact with women who wanted to use, and it was the men who morally opposed it. Some women therefore "had to hide their drug use for fear of the boyfriend's disapproval." As one woman points out, "Like if they don't take drugs they think you shouldnae. . . . He said, "If I found out for one minute that you're taking anything it is finished."[73] How do we place such a scenario into Ettore's framework? These men are disgusted by the women's drug use, and have zero tolerance for it. Are these men then somehow exempt from Ettore's suggestion that drug addiction is an arm of patriarchy? Are these men enlightened feminists who realize that addiction is a way of controlling women, or are they simply antidrug? Or is it that the women, by thinking that they want to use drugs, are somehow already caught by patriarchy and cannot see what they are "really" saying and doing? If it is the men who are exempt, then Ettore's thesis breaks down because it reveals that attitudes toward drug are not limited to gender (i.e., women *and* men can be against drugs). If it is the women who are exempt and are acting in bad faith by failing to recognize their true (drug-free) selves, then Ettore must dismiss the opinions of these real women in order to inject them with her own antidrug logic. In either case, Taylor has located something that cannot be absorbed easily into our usual framework.

We like to assert that addicts are "withdrawn" and "introverted" (both individually and as groups), yet we can see from Taylor that in fact it is *our* construction of drug users that forces them to stay away from us: we drive them away and then accuse them of being antisocial. One of Taylor's examples reveals this concept when a group of women were talking in a community center:

> One of the group, Fiona, had just had her children taken into care. Fiona was considered by other drug users as an exemplary mother, and there was considerable sympathy for her plight. This topic arose again, and the newcomer to the group, who had been chatting quite happily until that moment, turned to Fiona and said: "Are you a junkie? I may as well tell you that I've no time for people like you. I don't think you should be allowed to keep your children."[74]

The result of this attitude toward drug users, *and not the actions of the users,* is what drives them further and further into a corner from which they are unable and unwilling to leave. These opinions of drug users are obviously not only limited to other working-class women that the drug users would come into contact with, but extend right up to the educated research expert. As Taylor points out:

> I recently attended a seminar addressed by an "expert" in the drug field. During the discussion that followed, someone raised the point that from the presentation it would appear that drug users had fairly high intelligence levels. At this the "expert" replied: "I don't think I would say intelligent exactly, more that they have low animal cunning."[75]

This sounds like the kind of rhetoric that was used against African Americans over a century ago, yet it now seems permissible to use such language when referring to drug users. One of Ettore's arguments that is repeated across the antidrug response is that drug users are seen as "rejecting the traditional role of motherhood."[76] This argument is much more prevalent in the United States, with its dependency on the crack baby narrative, which, strangely enough, was not repeated in England with the same vehemence. While the drug-using mother "is generally regarded in negative terms," Taylor's study points out that once again the reality is a long way from the fantasy.[77] Taylor's drug users agreed that "the majority of *professionals* with whom they came into contact held [the] opinion, that drug use *per se* was evidence of a lack of complete fitness for the task of parenting. . . ."[78] Once again Taylor's findings are refreshingly banal and unexciting:

> Drug using mothers expect to adopt the traditional caring role toward their children. Where the demands of their drug using careers make this difficult or impossible, like ordinary mothers with jobs and careers, they try to ensure that their children will be well cared for elsewhere, and, like other mothers, they feel guilty about abdicating from full-time mothering because of commitment to a career.[79]

Once again the reality is that drug using-women are no different from ordinary mothers. Obviously, "as in any random sector of society," there are drug using mothers who do neglect their children, but again, the morality of the drug users surfaces and "[s]uch women are castigated by other drug users."[80]

In *Trainspotting* we are treated to the pleasing image of the junkie mother who is so high that her baby dies—although it is never clear why the baby actually dies: it is as if the simple fact of the mother using drugs is enough to kill the baby. Layered onto this image is her promiscuity as Renton tells us that the group of drug users is not really sure who the father is. This formulaic melodramatic construction of the addict serves everyone but the female addict. Imagine how strange it would seem to one of Taylor's women drug users to listen to critics and academics saying what a "gritty" and "realistic" portrait of Scottish drug addiction is deployed in the film.

Contrary to our construction of drugs as dismantling motherhood, Taylor shows that many of the women found that drugs actually assisted them in their role as mothers:

> Helen: Since I've had the wean . . . some of the reasons why I take it is . . . I've got all these bottles to make up and I've got to do all her washing and I'm feeling kind of tired and then I'll think, "I feel like a hit" and once I've had that I can go and do it all, dae the washing. It just gives me the energy.
> Laura: I felt that I could cope with her a lot better because I didnae know how to cope with a wean and I had [some drugs] to relax me a bit and I felt I could handle it a lot better. I used to take them for the sake of being full of it and having a good laugh but now when I've no got them I feel dead lazy as if I cannae dae my housework or cannae attend to the wean.[81]

Notice how both Helen and Laura see drugs not as working against their ability to be mothers, but really act as mother's little helpers. The drugs *give* them energy, and *give* them the ability to cope. In Helen's case, drugs are clearly polyvalent: on the one hand they can be taken for a "laugh" (play), but they can also help with the pressures of motherhood (work). Notice too how she says that *without* drugs she feels "lazy." We would say that she wants to be lazy and that is the reason she takes drugs. Far from being unproductive and undermining the logic of the domestic economy, drugs are here being utilized to the benefit of these women's domestic economy. Again, critics could respond that what these women are saying is naive and misguided because they are not intelligent or educated enough to know what drugs can really do. Unfortunately, such a criticism must simply discount these women's lived experiences of their drug use and replace it with a truth that we would prefer to see. As one woman points out, the fact that so many of the social workers have these educated opinions about drugs simply means that "they just grab all the junkie mothers, [and] all the junkie mother's weans."[82]

The women that Taylor worked with felt that the drug-using mothers were subject to being targeted by social workers and as a result they were under more pressure than regular mothers to prove that they were capable of looking after a child.[83] As Taylor points out, "the women believed that the images held of them by social workers were so strong that not only were they powerless to change such images, but no matter what they did, it would be interpreted as unacceptable behavior."[84] In order to deal with the effects of the social workers' attitudes toward them, the women often adopted "defensive attitudes and behaviors."[85] But as Taylor makes clear, these responses merely "confirm the negative images of them held by social workers and society in general."[86]

Paradoxically, the idea of taking away the child, far from helping the mother and child has the opposite effect. As one woman pointed out: "Look at Fiona. See since the weans got taken away, she's just gone doon and doon and doon. She's mad wi' it all the time and working up the toon noo to pay for her habit."[87] The healthy decision of the child care specialist "saves" the child, at the cost of destroying the mother's mental and physical health. In Dr. John Marks' program both Julia *and* her child were saved by administering heroin.

Marks also told us that no amount of drug enforcement or morality propaganda is going to make anyone, male or female, stop using drugs. He argued instead that most users will eventually decide to stop using on their own. Taylor's research repeats this argument, and extends it to include the consideration that trying to pinpoint the causes of drug addiction is as impossible as it is to locate the reasons for quitting: "[J]ust as there are various reasons for beginning to use drugs, there are a myriad of reasons for wanting to cease drug taking."[88] The other myth that Taylor's work exorcises, therefore, is the narrative surrounding quitting. None of the women that Taylor worked with said that "stopping drug use *per se* was a motivating factor."[89] Rather, it was the difficulties of the life that eventually drove the women to stop using. While we like to think that keeping up the pressure on drug users will eventually help them to quit, in fact this was seen by the drug users themselves as the least effective reason for stopping: "external pressures were regarded by the women as insufficient to guarantee success. . . . It was a commonly held belief among the drug using community that attempts based on these grounds were doomed to failure."[90] The only way that any woman was going to stop was if she was doing it for herself. We have come to accept the image of the drug user as "passive socially inadequate . . . chaotic, out of control . . . and inadequate, unfit mothers."[91] Taylor's research makes it clear that these images of the addict are nothing more than a misrecognition—a misrecognition, moreover, to which we then force the Other to conform. Taylor has made a crucial inroad into the field of drug studies by making several strange discoveries:

- the women played an active role in their own drug careers;
- their habit provided their lives with a degree of order and structure;
- decisions regarding their habit were made rationally and pragmatically;
- their drug use linked them to a supportive network of other drug users;
- attitudes of non-drug users prompted drug users to become detached from straight society;
- women drug users can be adequate mothers and have traditional expectations of motherhood;
- the drug lifestyle provided them with a set of skills and pride that had previously been denied them—skills that enhanced rather than undermined their self-esteem; and
- drug use opened up their options, rather than narrowing them down.

In some ways it is strange that these arguments have to be made. For example, it is completely unnecessary today to have to prove that black women are as good at being mothers as white women, or that black women can handle stressful jobs as well as white women, or that black and white women are equally intelligent. But when it comes to drug users, we are once again back on this kind of barren terrain.

Having opened up our field of vision a little more, thanks to Taylor, we can now hopefully begin to see that the "feminist" positions that Ettore and Rosenbaum are offering—far from being empowering for women—run the risk of *disempowering* women drug users. Of course this is not Ettore's and

Rosenbaum's desire, but it reveals the extent to which the discourses of antidrug rhetoric have the ability to seep into even the most level-headed attempts to find a solution to the drug "problem." What is useful from Taylor's analysis, however, is the ways in which it allows us—as well as addicts—to stand in another place from which to now view our current acceptable positions as strange, immoral, and even unhelpful.

Anna Kavan

Like Taylor, the British heroin addict and writer Anna Kavan similarly unravels our notions of what drugs may mean in her novel *Sleep Has His House* (1948). In the short story "Glorious Boys" Kavan asked "What exactly is it that's wrong with me? What is the thing about me that people can never take?" In her work Kavan addresses what it means to use drugs in a society that detests the drug user.[92] As with Julia, for Kavan, drugs provide a sense of purpose and health, and it is only when she is *without* heroin that she is "a lost child."[93]

Sleep Has His House begins with two separate prefaces. The first states that "If life be taken as the result of tension between the night and the day, night, the negative pole, must share equal importance with the positive day." The novella's preface sets out the ways in which the text will be constructed from the language of dreams and childhood:

> *Sleep Has His House* describes in the night-time language certain stages in the development of one individual human being. No interpretation is needed of this language we have all spoken in childhood and in our dreams; but for the sake of unity a few words before every section indicate the corresponding events of the day.[94]

The second is an extract from John Gower:

> ... in a strange land, on the borders of Chymerie ... the god of sleep has made his house ... which of the sun may naught have, so that no man may know aright the point between the day and night ... Round about there is growing on the ground, poppy which is the seed of sleep ... a still water ... runs upon the small stones ... which gives great appetite for sleep. And thus full of delight the god of sleep has his house.[95]

The first preface suggests how Kavan desires to resituate the focus between the day and the night. The second preface pushes further: the place that her fiction will occupy—the house of sleep—will not just be in the night as opposed to the day but will be in the space *between* the day and the night, a space on the marginalized "borders of Chymerie," a place so marginal that "no man may know aright the point between the day and the night."[96]

The house of sleep, like the space occupied by the drug user, is beyond binaries—it is neither day nor night. Resisting artificial closure, the fragments that Kavan lays before us in this novel never add up to anything: "Into the ephemeral images I dive, one after another: sometimes one crystallizes into a brief sharpness—never to permanence."[97] Feeling no desire to tell a story, Kavan is as uninterested in plot as if it somehow belonged to the daytime world of control. Control cannot enter the in-between space of "the house of sleep"; there can be no control over the narrative:

> "And so on: in considerable repetition, with varying details, of the basic situation; the central theme itself being subject to variation insofar as the attraction is not inevitable to darkness from light.
>
> For instance; the dream travels, quite briefly, through a picture sequence in which each view lasts only long enough for apperception before it is superseded." [98]

Kavan's text is loosely based upon her growth from the formless darkness of the embryo to life in the formless house of sleep, a trajectory which, as she says, is "subject to variation." The rest of the narrative never desires to gain any sense of direction, but wanders from one scene to the next, never fixing on any issue, never drawing any conclusions. Instead of a narration that produces truth, she prefers a narrative texture that erodes the moment it begins to stabilize into perception. At one point we are given a series of dream sequences, written, as she said, in the "night-time language of childhood," but none of these dreams are put to work; they are neither decoded, clarified, or explained. Cause and effect, which as Sedgwick points out, amounts to a belief in the causality of will itself, is here forgotten:

> B finally goes to her own room, stands for a minute fingers drumming the window-pane swimming in rain, then sits down on the bed, opens a book.
>
> The book opens with a thud of the front door . . . B turns the pages. Each one is exactly the same as the one before. She turns them faster and faster, running them over between her thumb and first finger, speeding them up into a bioscope blur . . . When she comes to the end she closes the book and puts it down on the seat of a railway carriage. The train is just roaring into a tunnel.[99]

As Kavan says in her short story "Among the Lost Things," "Basic essential things, always taken for granted, drift away and dissolve, get lost, change into totally different things."[100]

What if we adopted such a narrative strategy for our own perceptions of drugs and drug use? Such a willing suspension of belief would enable us to forget all that we know of drug use. Like Kavan, we should desire a space in which nothing is taken for granted, a space in which previously fixed positions can always be open to revision. Rather than categorizing and structuring our own positions we might follow Kavan, and in the words of Alexander Trocchi, unlearn our own positions and become strangers to our own truths: "I have unlearned. I have become a stranger."[101]

In the opening pages of the text we meet a child, only to lose sight of her: "A little girl with fair hair—she is unmistakably the child of her mother and so could be called B—peeps in through the open door, unnoticed by the grown-ups, then tiptoes away."[102] This child is drawn to alternative narratives at an early age, and here, as in adult life, the search continues:

> I learnt from the rain how to work the magic and then I stopped feeling lonely. I learnt to know the house in the night way of mice and spiders. I learnt to read the geography of the house bones. Invisible and unheard I scampered down secret tunnels beneath the floor-boards and walked a tightrope webbing among the beams. . . . Hidden by curtains, sheltered in cupboards, ambushed in foxholes between the tables and chairs, I transmuted flat daylight into my night-time magic and privately made for myself a world out of spells and whispers.[103]

Her magic, by allowing her to go beneath the floorboards, like her drug addiction, allows her to play among the foundations of the house. In the attic she refuses to walk on the beams, preferring to spin a tightrope that allows a performance of the between: what saves her is the world of imaginative play.

When she is sent off to school by her distant father, she realizes that if she is to stay in control of her world she will need a "stronger magic" and that she has to find "some private place where [she] could be at home."[104] She realizes that "because of [her] fear that the daytime world would become real, [she] had to establish reality in another place:"

> Out of my urgent need I found the way of working a new night magic. Out of the night-time magic I built in my head a small room as a sanctuary from the day. Phantoms might be my guests here, but no human could enter. . . . My home was in darkness and my companions were shadows beckoning from a glass."[105]

Voices and positions have been so unstable in this text that we cannot say with any certainty who is speaking, but the content represents an analysis of the positions of those addicts who, like Kavan, are seen to be "retreating" from the real world and the Law:

> Many people have said that retreats are undesirable and that they should be abolished because their existence constitutes a threat to the supremacy of the

authorities whose powers ought to be absolute. But when a man says that he is going into retreat it does not mean he is evading the law, which is an impossibility anyhow: it means that he is effecting a change of authority, a transfer from one set of laws to another set at least equally mysterious and severe—so that he is certainly not making an escape of any sort. All that these retreats do is afford an alternative code, no less exacting and quite as incomprehensible as the one held in more general observance.[106]

What is useful for us is the sense that Kavan recognizes that the drug user does not occupy some radically disruptive space; rather, the retreat of the addict is merely "an alternative code" that we can choose to occupy. Neither "inside" or completely "outside," the addict's position is that of the house of sleep, which, as Kavan told us in the preface, by being on the borders of Chymerie, means that no man can tell the difference between day or night. The binary opposition of poison/cure, the binaries that we would wish to keep firmly in place, are here displaced and neutralized.

The final description in the text is of the house of sleep where B now resides. Unlike our own insistence on black and white positions in the drug war, inside the house of sleep, it is always "twilight." The house, like the Self on heroin, "is really difficult to describe," and the location of the house is also between: One could say "that it's in the town," but some of the rooms "look clean into the country [and] it's no easier to give a description of the interior either:"

> Like most old places, this house has been altered and enlarged again and again so that the rooms are of all shapes and sizes and periods, opening one into another, or linked by galleries or flights of steps leading up and down in the most unexpected and unconventional way. [For example there is a] circular tower room . . . [which] appears to have been built on quite haphazard, as if the architect had overlooked the necessity for connecting it with the rest of the building, and had only added as an afterthought a crooked little staircase hidden away in a corner which you might pass a dozen times without noticing.[107]

The construction of this house of sleep is quite irregular and the normal rules of causality no longer apply: it is inconsistent as regards periods, fitted with "haphazard" and "crooked" ways that could easily be overlooked. This "irregularity of design makes it hard to find your way about the house. It's such a rambling old place, there are so many rooms, and all of them half-dark that you can never be absolutely certain that you've been into every one."[108] Unlike our current house, which only has two rooms— one for drug positions, one for antidrug positions—for Kavan, the architecture of her house opens up an endless series of discoveries and possibilities.

In the drugged zone of the house of sleep, "alterations were continually taking place in the outlying parts of the house, certain rooms changing their shape or position or even disappearing entirely, and other new rooms proliferating in different corridors. . . ."[109] B tries to figure her way around the house but realizes that the house operates on noncausal logic. Unlike our own (constantly failing) attempts to master addiction and drugs, Kavan learns from the house of sleep that control and mastery have always already failed:

> B herself is often surprized when she is wandering in the passages to find that she has come to a door which she has never seen before. And this is particularly apt to happen just when she feels that she has at last mastered the plan of the different floors.[110]

Kavan finds that in such a space, control is ineffectual: "The best way, as in all these obscure matters, is simply to accept the situation without enquiring into causality, which would most likely be incomprehensible even if brought to light."[111] Far from being alienated or lost, as we assume drug addicts always are, B feels that she is at home because "these constant unpredictable variations, which some people might find disconcerting, to her constitute one of the great charms of the house."[112]

While the adult, nondrugged logic of either/or would find the house disconcerting, for Kavan the house is charming and beautiful because of its constant unpredictability. As "charming" as the world of spells and whispers that she finds in heroin, and like a house that children would find delightful to play in, Kavan is now in a marginal zone that allows her to watch "the white sky children wreathing light-hearted dances in their playground."[113] Unlike the logic of the retreats or their opposite, the house of sleep embodies the antilogic of play and forgetting. She is not exiled from innocence by the "evil" of drugs, but is reunited with the openness and optimism of childhood: "Her companions are the many mirrors which hang all over the house . . . [and] in every one of these mirrors B recognizes the fair-haired girl who is her closest friend."[114]

As a house that is never ending, the house of sleep represents an architecture of deferral, a domicile of difference: It is, she says, "My home," and with that phrase, a heroin habit is rewritten as a habitat, a place in which she can live. A home that, for us in the straight world, is both strange and unsettling. The house is a source of pleasure because it is beyond description, and thus, like the tightrope in the attic, it becomes a text that hovers between the beams of power.[115] In our own world, in which our views on drugs are limited to one—or maybe two—positions, from the perspective of the house of sleep, this limiting focus is gladly eliminated: "What a variety of views there are too. That's what makes window-gazing from this house so delightful."[116]

Kavan tells us that "It's really impossible to mention even a fraction of the riches contained in a house so inexhaustibly rich with wonders from all over the world." Although she would like writing to go on forever, she closes the novel by telling us: "Well, the line has to be drawn somewhere: and that's why it seems useless to say any more except that no discriminating person would ever willingly leave such a house once they had taken up residence in it; or find any other house even tolerable afterwards."[117] For Kavan, only the possibilities of the house of sleep provide the scope for a healthy subject position, while it is our limited world of categories, binaries, logic, and limits that Kavan finds unhealthy and sick.

From Kavan's position then, the "cure" that Rosenbaum, Ettore, and Heyward are offering is thus transformed into a poisonous domination and a denial of the openness of the house of sleep. What happens to our knowledge of drug users when we see that Kavan's view of her own drug use cannot be accommodated into their framework? In short, Kavan makes apparent the inadequacies and limits of our own knowledge. Rosenbaum, Ettore, and Heyward must construct women addicts as "trapped" or held down by drugs so that they can then suggest a program of treatment that will free them and lift them up. Rather than being an alternative view of addiction that would cure our (mis)understanding of patriarchy and drug use, these strategies sustain a situation that is not working, and silence the possibilities contained in a narrative that could be based on the house of sleep. In their narratives, the woman addict has only an "escape" that is also an "inward focus," while she must be someone who is "inverted," spiraling down to planet heroin, deprived of free will and power. Having written the script for drug users, we then establish the "cure" by simply reversing our own narrative: we have decided that they are "falling," so we shall cure them by picking them up. We have decided that they are "slipping" so we shall provide them with a firm ground to walk on. Since we know that they are "trapped," we shall make sure that they "escape." We have constructed the scene so that drugs make them "alienated," so we can then drive them away from drugs toward an "authentic" self. Rather than recognizing these narratives as our fictions we put these cures into operation as if addicts really are "slipping," "falling," "trapped," or "inauthentic."

In both Kavan's and Taylor's works we discovered that the addict is not doing any of these things. What we see as "slipping," they perceive as stability/peace; our sense that she is "falling" is seen by them as a tightrope, something that supports the drug user and on which she can balance. Our view that she is "trapped" by heroin would make no sense to Kavan or Taylor's drug users for they see heroin as an entry into a world of play and a world of work : not a "prison" but a polyvalent "key." Rosenbaum, Ettore, and Heyward are thus asking drug users to give up a cure, not a poison. In short, we are asking Kavan and Taylor's subjects to hand over their key in return for our prison, to supplement stability and peace for our uncertainty and fear, and to replace balance and firmness with our slippage and sickness.

It would seem that we have arrived at a place where "knowing" that addiction is a "trap" results in a treatment program of enforced "freedom" that paradoxically harms the addict. The irony is that as the death toll increases every time we try to "free" someone, the statistics make it appear true that drug use really is what we say it is: Addiction is a trap that can only end in death. If Kavan, from within the house of sleep, sees addiction as her home, then, rather than tearing down the walls and demanding that she make herself homeless, we should perhaps offer to decorate her home and buy her furniture—maybe even go and visit. If she likes the house because of its haphazard aspects, we should perhaps encourage architects to come up with even more strange staircases and windows for her. If Kavan perceives addiction not as a falling but a "tightrope" that holds her up, then rather than distracting her with our shouts from below, maybe we should applaud the skill with which the balancing act is performed, and show our appreciation of her aptitude, bravery, and poise. Given the ways in which Kavan is rewriting drug use by placing it beyond judgment, and so refusing to condemn drugs, it is not surprising that reviewers perceived her work as offering not a "cure" to addiction, but its opposite, in the same way that Rosenbaum, Ettore, and Heyward would see Kavan's perspective as undermining their ability to empower and "cure" female addicts.[118]

Kavan tells us that she "knows all the sensational stories about drug addiction," and suggests that "[i]t is ridiculous to say that all drug addicts are alike, all liars, all vicious, all psychopaths or delinquents just out for kicks."[119] In fact, as Kavan has pointed out—far from her life being fragmented because of heroin—like Julia, it is the absence of heroin that would make her life a mess: "Without it she could not lead a normal existence, her life would be a shambles, but with its support she is conscientious and energetic, intelligent, friendly. She is most unlike the popular notion of a drug addict."[120] What aspects of power are at work that encourage us to feel that Kavan is promoting "unhealthy" or shocking and unacceptable responses to drugs? How do we know that what Kavan is saying is not a "sensible" approach to drug use?

In *The Diary of a Drug Fiend* Aleister Crowley suggests that "[we] have got to learn to make use of drugs as [our] ancestors learnt to make use of lightning."[121] His position on drugs, parallel to Kavan's and Trocchi's, is, he tells us, seen as sick by those around him: he illustrates this situation by telling the story of two children's fear of the sea:

They found themselves in danger of being drowned and thought the best way was to avoid going near the water. But that didn't help them to use their natural faculties to the best advantage, so I made them face the sea again and again, until they decided that the best way to avoid drowning was to learn how to deal with oceans in every detail. It sounds pretty obvious when you put it like that, yet while every one agrees with me about the swimming, I am howled down on all sides when I apply the same principles to the use of drugs.[122]

Maybe a useful strategy is not to resist drugs, but to learn to swim around in them. We may get wet, but at least we are unlikely to drown, and while our children are having fun safely splashing about near the shore, the rest of us can quite calmly get on with our swimming, or even teach others how to do the backstroke. Once in a while, we might go diving for pearls. As Kavan reminds us, "[e]ven the crooked lanes leading to the poorer quarters promise adventure and mysterious revelation."[123]

Chapter 6 🖾

Up from Drug Slavery?: Drugs and Race in Contemporary America

Casual drug users ought to be taken out and shot.

—Los Angeles Police Chief Daryl Gates,
U.S. Senate Judiciary Hearings,
September 5, 1990

Crack Fascists

In this chapter I would like to explore the various ways in which contemporary America responds to the intertwining issue of drugs and race. In particular I want to show how our "progressive" and "empowering" positions on drugs, by remaining firmly rooted in an antidrug position, are forced into standpoints that are not only racist, but are also disempowering. If we are to change what drugs and race mean in our culture, we shall have to abandon the truths that we hold onto about drugs and race. As long as we keep drugs and race together in one pathological mix, they will continue to explain each other and we will continue to generate an increase in the percentage of black and Latino males incarcerated for drug-related crimes. I would propose that our current psychological truths, like our enforcement laws and cures, are not explaining race and drug use, or helping to unravel it, but are producing and exacerbating these problems. I will argue that it is the preservation of our current ideas about drugs that is regressive—and racist—and that only by forgetting these current "truths" can we begin to see the emergence of less harmful ways of thinking about drugs and race: only an *anti*-antidrug position will allow us the space in which to achieve such goals.

We have come a long way from the simple measures of the Pharmacy Act of 1868: the drug war budget in 1981 was $1.5 billion; by 1993 it had risen to $12.7 billion; and in 1995 it dropped to $8.2 billion.[1] In addition to this the military had, in 1995, a drug enforcement budget of $700 million. Los Angeles can serve as an example of the scenarios that such spending inevitably produces. The chief of the District Attorney's Hardcore Drug Unit said of the city, "[t]his is Vietnam here," and those people who "one local mayor calls 'the Viet Cong abroad in our society'—are the members of local Black gangs. . . ."[2] Statements such as these signal that a military-style operation is currently being deployed to combat the enemy: drugs and black youth. In the minds of law enforcement, the two seem to be connected in a deadly ecology. In *Dope Girls* Marek Kohn suggests that the category of drugs allows racism to be deployed "in code" so that white hatred and fear of the African American community can simply transferred onto "crack."[3] The result of this transference, as Mike Davis points out, is that "[a]s a result of the war on drugs every non-Anglo teenager in Southern California is now a prisoner of gang paranoia and associated demonology." "Police," he adds, "now have virtually unlimited discretion, day or night, to target "undesirables," especially youth."[4] Nor is this racial coding of the drug war just a West Coast phenomenon. Ernest Drucker points out that in 1990 police SWAT team raids in New York, which were "all [in] Black and Hispanic neighborhoods," cost the taxpayers "$169 million." There were a total of 9,500 arrests, which amounts to $17,000 per arrest, more than "the annual cost of most residential treatment centers."[5] While these figures are staggeringly high, they are to be expected, given the degree to which we agree that drugs are a problem for particular racial groups. Since alcohol and tobacco kill over half a million Americans each year, one might expect a war on these drugs as well. But as Joseph McNamara, former Chief of Police in Kansas City, Missouri, and San Jose, California, points out, tobacco and alcohol manufacturers are not given life sentences; in fact, the government subsidizes them.[6] It is this embracing of legal drugs that causes the public to not perceive them as a problem in the same way that drugs are. Given this degree of repression and brute enforcement against drugs, though, our logic tells us to expect some drop in availability. However, as we can easily observe via the continued escalation of the war, "the reverse is true," since availability and price have burgeoned.[7] If the "reverse is true" and enforcement actually leads to a rise in availability in the long term, then surely we must change the direction of the current situation by reversing our current policy. Thus we should be aiming for less, rather than more, enforcement; lighter, rather than heavier sentences; talk of drugs as a friend, not an enemy; a closeness to drugs rather than a distance from them; and an active bringing of drugs into society, rather than trying to keep them out.

As we have witnessed throughout this book, the main problem we experience with drugs is precisely the difficulty of locating any kind of alternative discourses that would lead us out of our various narrative cul-de-sacs. When it comes to focusing on the question of drugs and race, these difficulties can be highlighted by the ways in which alternative discourses on crime have also been erased since the1980s. For example, in a 1988 interview, Joan Howarth of the American Civil Liberties Union noted that

> progressives have virtually deserted us on this issue . . . the Left has been largely shut out of the policy debate which is now framed by the Reaganite Right and its Democratic shadow. There is no progressive agenda on crime, and consequently, no challenging of the socio-economic forces that have produced the burgeoning counterculture of gang membership.[8]

The result of this absence of alternative discourses on drugs and race is that even thinkers who would at one time have been considered progressive have begun dancing to conservative tunes. Ishmael Reed, for example, in the late 1980s was urging the black working class to "take offensive against Black terrorists . . . the brutal crack fascists" and attacked white liberals for allowing "drug fascists" to prey upon "decent citizens."[9] Reed's solution to save black America from the black "crack fascists" involved the idea of "a curfew for 18–24 year olds and a much sterner community invigilation of youth."[10] Crack is fought with a crack down.[11] Congresswoman Maxine Waters, Democrat for the Watts-Willowbrook community in Los Angeles, also "reluctantly endorsed police sweeps and "street terrorism" laws."[12] The sad irony of this situation is that in the name of taking a firm stand against drugs, the black community must side with an antidrug rhetoric that has a brutal racism at its core. Today, the war on drugs remains a war on people of color, but it is a war that is also being waged by black people against other black people, who simultaneously believe that the real enemy is drugs.

During the height of the crack crisis, Harry Edwards, organizer of the Black Panther power protests at the 1968 Olympics and former Minister of Propaganda for the Black Panther Party, was asked how he would "turn around" a 13-year-old kid selling crack. His reply is telling:

> Edwards: The reality is, you can't.
> S.F. Focus: So then what?
> Edwards: You gotta realize that they're not gonna make it. The cities, the culture and Black people in particular have to begin to move to get that garbage off the streets.
> S.F. Focus: How?

Edwards: It means we have to realize that there are criminals among us and we have to take a very hard line against them, if we're to preserve our next generation and future generations. Even if they are our children.

S.F. Focus: So what do you do if you're a parent and you discover your 13 year old kid is dealing crack?

Edwards: Turn him in, lock him up. Get rid of him. Lock him up for a *long* time. As long as the law will allow, and try to make it as long as possible. I'm for locking 'em up, gettin 'em off the streets, put 'em behind bars."[13]

With this kind of a response from a radical African American spokesperson, it becomes easy to see that it is going to be hard to find a way out of the current impasse. As Mike Davis points out: "Black middle-class revulsion against youth criminality—indeed the perception that dealers and gangs threaten the very integrity of Black culture—is translated, through such patriarchal bluster, into support for the extremist rhetoric of the gangbusters. . . . It is a dismal sign of the times that once fiery nationalist intellectuals, like Reed and Edwards, can openly float the idea that a 'sacrifice' or 'triage' of criminalized ghetto youth (i.e., "the garbage") is the only alternative. . . ."[14]

As we saw in the last chapter on drugs and women, we often think of drugs as a chemical form of patriarchal ideology from which women must struggle to free themselves. For African Americans, the narrative metamorphoses so that drugs represent a form of white slavery that the real authentic black person must fight and struggle to be released and liberated from. The result is that the metaphors of enslavement are deployed in order to articulate the truth of what drugs really mean. African American women must struggle to liberate themselves from both the racial *and* the gendered narratives, in that they are supposed to free themselves from drugs and male ideology as well as the slavery of drugs. These narratives do nothing to help African American drug users; in fact they just give them more layers of truth, under which they become buried and trapped. Insofar as these positions are also currently held in place by African American psychologists and rehabilitation programs—which are genuinely trying to help the African American population—it may seem like a racist suggestion to want to dismiss these frameworks as unhelpful. However, the only other available alternative is to side with Edwards and Reed and their crackdown on the crack fascists, a rhetoric often even harsher than, but otherwise indistinguishable from, that adopted by the police.

The Emancipation Proclamation

What do these current truths about drugs look like? A good example of the state of the discourse on African American drug use is *Doin' Drugs: Patterns of African American Addiction* (1996) by William H. James and Stephen L. Johnson. Their analysis begins by suggesting quite accurately that "[t]raditional alcohol and other drug treatment programs have been unable to stop the wave of addiction that has engulfed the African American community."[15] However, having recognized that a change of direction and policy is desperately needed, they resort, in the very next sentence, not to a healthy abandonment of all that we hold nearest and dearest, but to a return to pushing these already failed programs harder and more vigorously. In their opinion "[a] coalition of the strongest resources in these communities, including families, churches, schools, and community agencies, is urgently needed to address such widespread drug use."[16]

These two sentences tell us much about the limits of our current position—within two sentences, James and Johnson try to move us toward the need for something new, only to find themselves dragged back to where they began. Obviously, in spite of the urgency and the honesty of their desire to change the situation, their conclusions leave everything unchanged. They assert that, given the scale of the drug problem, their book has been written "in the belief that an accurate portrayal of the present and historic realities of African American addiction will help African American leaders, communities, churches, and colleges and universities meet the challenges of urban addiction."[17] This is certainly an admirable goal, but the question is what would such an "accurate" portrayal look like? What tools will they employ in order to find an accurate portrayal of African American drug use? In many ways their position is already starting to get caught in the groove that Ettore followed when she said that women must see addiction not through men's eyes, but "as it is in reality."[18] As with Ettore's text, that strategy, instead of taking us away from the tired constructions of our current drug narratives, actually brings us back to their very heart. Here we can imagine that the parallel will be to see drugs not through *white* eyes, but as it is in reality. James and Johnson believe that tracing the roots of addiction to American slavery will help us to "better prepare a new generation of counselors, ministers, social workers, nurses, and physicians to face the epidemic of drug addiction in African American communities."[19] While desiring an accurate perception of drugs, they do not stop to question their use of the word "epidemic" for a condition that Stanton Peele has endlessly shown is *not* a disease; they continue to work squarely within the safe borders of generic drug-addiction theories.[20] For example, they repeat how the cure for this disease comes from a belief "in empowerment" and "mutual decision making" and "self-concern, pride and development."[21] Having prejudged drug use as alienating and fragmenting, James and Johnson respond by asserting that "African American heritage encourages traits like loyalty, honesty, and trust. . . ."[22] Now obviously we all believe in these qualities, but making them the cure for a disease that is not a disease does seem rather odd. What is more troubling is that this portrayal and response to the problem of drug use does not move us beyond our current position, but is actually speaking from within it, and thus actively reinforcing it. Paradoxically, the current thinking on drugs, which their approach supports, is openly acknowledged by James and Johnson as a way of thinking that has resulted in "thousands of African American men [ending up] in prison for drug charges. . . ."[23] To change our current thinking would mean to stop constructing drugs and race in these ways and find other less harmful narratives, but this is something that, try as they might, James and Johnson find themselves powerless to do.

Concurring with the above positions of Reed, Edwards, and Waters, James and Johnson assert that the African American community, once naturally homogenous, unified, trusting and loyal, has now been turned against itself by drugs, which have destroyed the original African unity and purity. They argue further that this situation is something that white people are quite happy to perpetuate because it weakens and divides the black race, and that politically conscious black people should fight against it. The contradiction, as I see it, is that this restoration of purity and organic wholeness can only come about by an antidrug position, something that white power *also* endorses. That is, the result is not the restoration of black organic wholeness, but in the perpetuation of an antidrug rhetoric and black incarceration. Insofar as James and Johnson see the war on drugs as a good healthy thing, they paradoxically find themselves enforcing a policy that in the streets, as Mike Davis and others have pointed out, is highly racist. If the antidrug position is a racist position, then an antiracist position that African American leaders and researchers could adopt would surely be an *anti*-antidrugs policy. Of course, the narrowness of the current discourse leaves no room for such a position because it would immediately be converted into a prodrug stance and would mean political suicide for people like Maxine Waters and Jesse Jackson. Black leaders and researchers thus find themselves left with only one option, which means that the ideological terrain of health/empowerment is now inseparable from a repressive and violent war on African Americans. The problem for James and Johnson, as directors of drug programs, is that they are left with an impossible rhetorical position: They desire to be supportive of the health of the African American community while simultaneously firmly supporting an antidrug position. Their construction of the drugs-as-slavery narrative presumably gets them out of a narrative impasse by making drugs into a chemical manifestation of the bad white slave system: the evil that must be fought against if blacks are to be free.

They suggest that "African American addiction is often evaluated without a close examination of the traditional uses of alcohol and drugs in Africa and without an understanding of the trauma African people suffered when separated from their ancestors, religion and homeland."[24] James and Johnson suggest that Africans had "highly evolved patterns of drug and alcohol use for religious, social and medical purposes." This provides the narrative root of their notion of an original, homogenous African culture in which drugs were only medicinal or spiritual or used to nurture, rather than to destroy a community.[25] Once these same Africans were brought to America as slaves, they lost touch with these organic behaviors and practices and replaced them with the unhealthy and impure American practices in order to try and cope with the experiences of slavery. As James and Johnson have it: "African American slaves . . . came to adopt the drinking patterns of the European American colonists."[26] The result, then, is that today's drug use among African Americans can be traced to "celebrations begun in the 1700s [that] contributed to the later development of certain destructive patterns of African American alcohol and drug use."[27]

This framework then becomes the narrative that we can then tell about African American drug use: We once had an original wholeness in which we made a healthy medicinal/spiritual use of drugs and alcohol. After being corrupted by the poison of slavery, we lost touch with ourselves and our behavior; forgetting ourselves, our history, and heritage, we began to model ourselves on white patterns of drug and alcohol use. As a response to being made slaves by whites, our drug use shifted from "social, religious and medical" purposes to the self-destructive patterns that we see today. If we are to be freed from this evil situation we must then cast off this fake white drug behavior and reclaim our heritage and our real Selves by a process of struggle against the mental slavery of drugs.

In order to sustain such a story of dysfunctional behavior for over 200 years it is incumbent upon James and Johnson to assert that a predisposition for drug addiction has now become *genetic.* They openly state that "there is evidence to suggest that genetic factors are very influential in the predisposition for marijuana addiction," but there is no evidence for this remarkable assertion at any point of their text.[28] In one way their story sounds very good and can feel even empowering. From that point of view, to criticize it can only mean that one is *against* black empowerment and *for* a continuation of black mental slavery. However, what if the problem lies within the narrative itself?

The difficulty here is that James and Johnson are reverting to the usual positivist psychological explanation of drug addiction as a pathology. Having been alienated by slavery, and now by its chemical equivalent, James and Johnson suggest that African American males come into their program having had "little experience with friendship and mutual support." The women come in, counter to Taylor's assessment, "as victims of sexual exploitation and other forms of victimization."[29] The philosophy of their program is then to strive toward organic wholeness and "help men and women move into a belonging relationship with other members and with the program."[30] James and Johnson tell us that their book is written with the aim of helping "African American people who are struggling to find hope, healing and recovery from the disease of chemical dependency."[31] Yet if we remember Taylor's analysis of Scottish heroin addicts, we realize how far their analysis is from being any kind of realistic portrayal. The difficulty that James and Johnson are setting up for themselves is that they are only allowing themselves to think of drugs through a preexisting framework that has been handed to them by the culture. To say that African American males and females have a genetic propensity for drug use because they have a history of slavery seems a dangerous mistake.

The result of their narrative is that stopping drug use somehow involves the removal of a historical blindness that allows the user to now come face to face with their real history and their real self. The sense that drugs equal some kind of false knowledge, history, and self, seeps out when they suggest how the withdrawal from drugs involves a process of "adjusting to dealing with real feelings and the reality of life without self-medication or numbing."[32] Having said that they want to move away from "deviance and pathology models," they conclude their chapter on the opiates by outlining how

> it is becoming increasingly clear that the home environment—where no mother or father figure is present, a parent is emotionally distant, a parent or guardian is an addict or engaged in criminal activity or infidelity, or a parent or guardian does not provide support for the family—is strongly associated with deviant drug-using behavior."[33]

Having decided that drugs constitute a space of ignorance, then the therapeutic group must be " a place of disease education." Perceiving drugs as a way to avoid contact with others, the therapeutic group will be " a place of understanding." Having exposed the truth that drugs are a form of slavery, the therapeutic group will replace this bondage with "a place of bonding." Finally, having determined that drugs are a way of blocking out the pain of living under the burden of a false sense of self/history, the group will provide "a place of self-discovery."[34] However, as we have seen, drugs are not really doing any of these things; in fact, drugs are doing nothing and can do nothing by themselves, it is we who give them their meaning. Our cures are based on illnesses that *we* have not only constructed, but that we have also misconstrued.

Climbing Mount Zion

While recognizing that current institutions are not doing enough to solve the scourge of drug use among African Americans, James and Johnson suggest that a vital weapon in the war against drugs is the African American church. Since slavery, they say, the church has always been there to help African Americans "toward freedom of mind, body and spirit."[35] James and Johnson's model becomes San Francisco's Glide Memorial United Methodist Church, under the guidance of the Reverend Cecil Williams. To confront the growing crack epidemic in San Francisco, Glide developed an 11-point plan for Afrocentric drug prevention. Not surprisingly the 11-points fit nicely with the narrative that James and Johnson have been constructing about the need to overcome mental slavery and get free from drugs:

- Gain control over my life
- Tell my story to the world
- Stop lying
- Be honest with myself
- Accept who I am
- Feel my real feelings
- Feel my pain
- Forgive myself and others
- Practice rebirth: A new life
- Live my spirituality
- Support and love my brothers and sisters.[36]

The central message of Glide is that "recovery is a miracle of healing and a social change movement": a miracle which involves working closely with "the police."[37] For the drug users, this healing process involves learning about the gravity of planet crack by recognizing and making yourself pow*erless* in the face of "the power of addiction."[38]

The other example of the churchs' role in the struggle comes from the Mount Zion Baptist Church in Seattle. Much of the research for *Doin' Drugs* was provided by Mount Zion and the organization that they have set up called the Cocaine Outreach and Recovery Programs (CORP), formed in 1989: "CORP is sponsored by the church and has developed an Afrocentric approach to recovery from drug abuse."[39] If the Glide model attempts to "reconnect the individual to his or her culture and self-pride," CORP "endorses the disease model of addiction (a physiological disease that is primary, progressive and fatal) and attempts to find the root cause of the addiction and to get the disease into remission." They conclude that the African American church should be the "wall of defense against drug use."[40]

The problem with adopting the disease model, is that the disease model of struggle, liberation, and freedom quite simply makes getting off drugs a lot of hard work. The struggle to climb to the top, where freedom is supposedly waiting, is essentially constructed as an endless struggle, which, in its magnitude, makes recovery only obtainable by a superhuman effort of will. Why is it that we cannot see the connection between setting up drug use as a huge mountain to be scaled, and the fact that "[m]any of the most respected inpatient treatment centers report that over 70 per cent of their crack cocaine patients relapse one year after program completion"?[41] Surely the high rate of relapse is due not to the power of the drug—a power that we ascribe to it in the first place—but to the insistence with which we assert that drug addiction is a difficult struggle that needs constant attention, re-inforcement, and will power.

Michael Gossop, who works at the Drug Dependence Clinical Research and Treatment Unit at Maudsley Hospital in London, argues that conven-tional discourses of addiction "construct an imaginary type with which the addict can identify."[42] The result is that the addict comes to believe in his or her own "total and irreversible slavery to drugs," and that "[i]f the addict believes that he is totally helpless before the power of heroin or whatever drug it might be, then he is indeed helpless."[43] We create a culture in which drugs are perceived as chemical slavery, and the addict then behaves as if this *really* is the case. Gossop feels that the horror stories we tell about with-drawal also keep people addicted to, rather than away from, drugs. Gossop suggests that "the idea that heroin withdrawal involves unbearable pain has proved to be a most convenient fiction for the media" as well as for ad-dicts.[44] Most opiate addicts then become "terrified of withdrawal" and will do anything rather than face the supposed pains of withdrawal.[45] For Gos-sop, "[t]he hyperbole of these accounts bears little resemblance to what might more realistically be compared to a dose of flu—certainly withdrawal is unpleasant and distressing, but it fails by some considerable distance to match up to the myth."[46]

Instead of considering the weaknesses of their own discourses and posi-tions, James and Johnson assert that the weaknesses of the traditional drug re-habilitation programs—which deploy the same logic as Mt. Zion and Glide—is not that the fundamental premises of the treatment centers are flawed, but that the premises are not being enforced strictly enough. For ex-ample, one problem for James and Johnson is that there is a "lack of a vari-ety of long-term treatment programs."[47] This is merely the ideological equivalent of the police raids on minority neighborhoods: the more police raids fail to change patterns of drug use, the more the police say they have to be stepped up if they are to be effective. The same logic is being extended to drug programs that, seeing the failure of their education programs, suggest, not that they be abandoned, but that they must extend the programs to even younger and younger groups. In addition to blaming the high relapse rate on a lack of funding, James and Johnson also assert that the high failure rate is due to the fact that crack cocaine is somehow a special case: "For treatment professionals, the high frequency of relapse is perhaps the single fact that sets crack cocaine addiction apart from other addictions."[48] The high rate of relapse is due apparently to the "wide availability of the drug" and its "cheap price."[49] In addition, the addicts, as always, are to blame: "[t]he majority of the addicts go back to the same drug-using environment they came from." Moreover, James and Johnson feel that "the high rate of relapse . . . is also due in part to the lack of attention given by the counselor and client to two factors: the role of money and sexuality in relapse."[50]

While this reminder is meant to be helpful in treating crack addicts, I would suggest that it has the opposite effect in that it simply creates two more foci around which the addict is now pathologized. Not content with asserting that the person has no control over cocaine, now we tell them that they have two more problems that they have no control over: money and sex. To begin with, James and Johnson have just asserted that crack use is widespread because of its "cheap price," and one page later they tell us that "crack cocaine transactions involve large amounts of cash."[51] While I find this confusing, I am even more puzzled by the way that even money is to be avoided as a possible trigger for relapse because "money is overwhelmingly the strongest memory trigger related to crack cocaine use."[52] So, in addition to struggling against drugs, addicts must now also struggle against the possibility that they may be tempted to lose control of money, which will somehow trigger a relapse. For James and Johnson, "treatment programs that provide addiction education without some form of established money management after treatment offer only the fantasy of recovery." In short, "[c]rack-addicted clients who handle paychecks, cash, money orders, or tax-refunds early in recovery will almost certainly relapse because of the physiological strength of money triggers."[53] In true Pavlovian fashion, addicts who encounter money will respond in ways that will lead them to relapse. James and Johnson suggest that "[i]ndividuals in early recovery who handle money will perspire, get an upset stomach, experience diarrhea, or get headaches because the money itself creates a visually induced memory of crack cocaine use. This memory in turn triggers physical cues that for the newly recovered addict *seem* almost impossible to resist."[54] What confuses me here is the mechanism of this trigger. They say that handling money will cause the addict to experience *physical* feelings such as headaches, diarrhea, and upset stomachs because the money creates a "visually induced *memory*" of crack use. Then, according to them, this memory in turn "triggers *physical* cues."[55] So the mechanism operates this way: money causes a physical reaction, which in turn produces a memory, which in turn produces a physical reaction. To me, this mechanism seems to be rather circular. If it is not circular, and it is really that money simply produces a memory that has a physical effect, why are the effects that James and Johnson list so obviously unpleasant?

Why doesn't the money induce a phantom rush, or induce pleasurable sensations if that is what the body *really* wants? Surely positive triggers would be more effective in getting the user to relapse. If the drug is some kind of evil demon why does it trigger feelings that would only remind the user of the unpleasant aspects of drug use?

In addition to having to avoid money, recovering addicts must also avoid sex because "so much crack cocaine use is done in highly charged sexual situations [that] sex becomes paired with cocaine use."[56] Even the usually positive benefits of closeness and intimacy are laced with danger for the recovering addict: "Intimacy with a sexual partner can induce strong memories of crack cocaine use experienced in a prior sexual situation and so jeopardize recovery."[57] Interestingly enough, James and Johnson tell us that addicts will "ignore the counselors input concerning money management or sexual behaviors."[58] Of course, at this juncture we are only allowed to conclude that the addicts are wrong to ignore this accurate advice, while we are left unable to ask whether the drug users have good reasons to avoid this advice. Unlike us, maybe they can see right through it. More importantly, I think they ignore it because they already have enough to deal with, and to be told that there are two extra landmines that they have to watch out for on the road to recovery can only be discouraging. These theories, like the addictions that they are supposed to treat, also begin an endless cycle of possibilities. Why could we not suggest that even masturbation should be seen as a kind of gateway drug for recovering addicts, which, by providing a reminder of past sexual encounters, could trigger a desire to smoke crack?

What is also curious about these warnings and danger zones that are to be avoided is that they only seem to apply to the recovering addict who is in the early stages of recovery. It is as if the addict in recovery has no skin and can be punctured by desire at the slightest whim, and, like someone recovering from a cold, must avoid contact with possible germs—in this case money and sex, as well as drugs. Once the recovering addict has passed the first hurdles, and their protective ego skin has regrown, then it seems that they can then safely masturbate, have sex, and cash a check with the full knowledge that they will be immune from a desire to smoke crack. Sadly, we do not even give the recovering addict this possibility of reaching a safe haven; they are always at risk—their skin, having been once breached by their drug addiction will now need *constant* maintenance: addicts can never recover in our schema, they can only remain in a permanent state of tentative recovery. As much as we say we want them to be free, our programs ensure that the specter of relapse follows them to the grave.

Having asked addicts to scale Mount Zion with the added burdens of money and sex triggers, is it any wonder that we see a 70 percent failure rate? Considering the obstacles that we place in their way it is amazing that there is even a 30 percent success rate. I would suggest that rather than making it hard for addicts by adding difficulties, historical burdens going back to 1700, or hidden triggers that lurk in the everyday nondrug world, we should make it easy on addicts. We should be removing hurdles, burdens, and the constantly receding summit of Mount Zion. Instead of looking for triggers that are just waiting to shoot them down, why not look for protection and safe places that would allow them to rest, relax, and feel that overcoming addiction is not an impossible feat, but simple and within easy reach? Rather than constructing the summit of Mount Zion as a possibility that will never arrive, why not allow them to find paths to healthy drug use or recovery by going *around* Mt. Zion? Instead of driving them to struggle up to the summit, why not admit that it is unnecessary or even a waste of time and energy to try to climb up Mount Zion?

We should also be paying attention to how we construct drug addiction as a "falling" or a "dropping." Addiction is always spatially downward—a freefall—whereas the cure is always constructed as a difficult movement upward. What if we reversed these spatial metaphors? What if the escalation of drug use was constructed as a struggle, and one that had to be fought for? What if addiction was spoken of in spatial terms that required the addict to actively climb *up* into drug use? We could then construct recovery not as an endless upward struggle with endless relapses and slippages, but as a trouble-free downward movement. Recovery could then be seen as a simple leap into the health of a drug-free space, with a safety net to catch them as they fall into being drug free. If our metaphors were reversed, I think we would start to find that the recovery terrain *would* shift and people would no longer be able to slip and slide into crime, drugs, and prostitution. Instead, people would be slipping and sliding into recovery all over the place, even if they stopped using for only a short time. Those who wanted to quit would then be surrounded by lots of trap doors through which they could choose to fall into health. In contrast, drug addicts would have to work very hard to ensure that they maintained their levels of addiction, which would require superhuman strength. These may seem like strange and irresponsible suggestions, but the only other alternative is to persist with the same mélange of positivist psychology and morality that is evidently no longer of use to any drug user or any drug program.

In their conclusion James and Johnson suggest that they had set out to look at African American addiction "objectively," but as they looked closer, what they saw was both "fascinating and frightening."[59] As with nearly every book on addiction, they assert in the conclusion that "[o]ur examination of African American alcohol and drug use prior to and during slavery convinced us that additional research is needed in this area."[60] This would involve investigating that perhaps "patterns of family alcoholism that started over one hundred years ago during slavery somehow play a generative role in the current epidemic of addiction."[61] This line of inquiry will not help addicts as they hope; all it will do is to extend the list of hurdles that already face the addict. In addition they also ask us to think about how "family patterns of alcoholism relate to current patterns of crack cocaine addiction."[62] Again, extending a history of *alcohol* addiction to current *crack* addiction is not helpful insofar as it just transposes the burdens of one substance onto another.

James and Johnson argue that "African American success in recovery from drug use may depend in part on the *strength of the link* between racism and addiction."[63] In short, I feel that given the current failure rates, strengthening the link is only going to reinforce the current failure rates—only by breaking the link can the situation be changed. While it is evident that "African Americans are disproportionately represented in the population of males incarcerated for drug sales," it is not because the link between racism and addiction is weak, it is because the two concepts *are* linked.[64] Strengthening the link between racism and addiction sounds pro–African American, but it means working within the current framework of burdens, triggers, struggles, recovery programs, and churches who will work with the police.[65] It also means perpetuating the ideology of self-control, and the narratives of self-empowerment and pride, which hold out the impossible promise of the cure, positions that no police force or D.A.R.E. program would disagree with.

If the positions that James and Johnson develop are the accepted answers to the questions posed by African American drug use, why is it that James and Johnson also recognize that the current frameworks are not working? For example, they discuss "the failures of our criminal justice system and drug treatment programs," as well as pointing out that "[i]ndividuals who were interviewed spoke of numerous drug treatment experiences with immediate relapses upon program completion."[66] In spite of such recognition they have no alternative space to turn to—like Reed, Maxine Waters, and Edwards—and thus must reassert the positions that they have already admitted are failing. I would suggest that the programs are failing not because they are underfunded or because they are not trying hard enough, but because they have accepted that their antidrug position is the only one possible and have chosen to simply persist in the ways that they are accustomed to, rather than run the risk of appearing anti–African American, or worse, out of a fear that any anti-antidrug position will be misread as prodrug.

While James and Johnson have admirable goals, their lack of alternative discourse with which to challenge the prevailing ideology about drug use means that they are left supporting the structure that is causing the conditions they wish to see removed. As Parker, Bakx, and Newcombe pointed out in relation to British Ecstasy users, once the meaning of the drug itself is redefined, then the theory that tries to explain its use as a form of deviance, a result of weak self-esteem, or peer/family rejection becomes neutralized and meaningless. Once our current dangerous narratives have been defused, other less harmful narratives can be written.

For Parker et al., one of the main obstacles to rewriting what drugs mean—in any race or community—is the persistence of the kind of "positivist psychology" that James and Johnson are using, which, in Parker's terms, is always "immensely durable."[67] The flaw with this kind of approach, and James and Johnson are representative of many texts that offer the "truth" of African American addiction, is that it only sees drug use as drug *abuse* and "sees drug taking as a sign of abnormality."[68] For Parker et al.,

> The North American literature in particular has taken this approach much further in attempting to identify "risk factors" which make young people susceptible to abusing drugs. . . . Having reviewed this literature in considerable detail, Davies and Farquhar conclude that psychology's search for risk and protection factors has not made a great deal of progress. This is because this type of psychology gets bogged down in the correlation-causation minefield where individuals are broken down into "disembodied variables" with "early and persistent behavior problems," "aggressive behavior," "disorders," "a family history of alcoholism," "academic failure," "low bonding to family," "hyperactivity" and so on being identifiers for those who "abuse" drugs.[69]

The real challenge that faces us is not drugs, but finding a way out of this kind of thinking. Only then will the war on drugs stop being a war on people of color, waged by whites *and* by people of color.

Iced

Ray Shell's recent novel *Iced,* about the life of a black crack addict, is described by the *San Francisco Examiner Chronicle* as "a chilling portrait of an addicted life . . . powerful and poetic."[70] The narrator, Cornelius, starts out with lots of academic and social potential, but after a series of tragic incidents, is unable to cope. He turns to crack, only to find that he is then powerless to stop, and ends up under lock and key "in this world for mentally deranged killers and rapists."[71] As with James and Johnson, at one point in the novel he realizes that his only hope is in control. Having laughed at the antidrug rhetoric of the squares throughout the novel, he now realizes, although it is too late for him, that they were right after all. As he takes crack, the usual slavery imagery reemerges: "I never knew that I was about to chain an eight ball around my neck that would enslave me to cocaine from that day to this . . . how things might have been different if I had simply said no;

but I didn't say no."[72] He tries many times to give it up, realizing that "I've got to develop a will/That's the only way I'm gonna live."[73]

The novel becomes powerful and true to us because it repeats the stories about black crack addicts that we all love to hear. According to Burroughs, this is exactly the kind of thinking that is dangerous and damaging. By repeating what Sedgwick calls "the propaganda of free will," the novel can only produce negative, not positive, results. The irony of *Iced* is that the truth of this portrait of addiction is measured by our inability to put the book down. The truth that *Iced* speaks is underlined by having a quote from Maya Angelou on the cover saying that Shell's novel is "[a] powerhouse . . . the book won't let me go. . . ." Thus the book's ability to draw us in and powerfully hold our imagination captive is proof of the truth that the book articulates: a book about how powerful crack is *has* to be telling us the truth because the book itself is so addictive. To suggest otherwise is to suggest that maybe this novel does not represent the truth of addiction but only rehearses one version of what addiction may look like.

Sadly, this limited framework is also redeployed in the social sciences. James Inciardi, toward the end of *Women and Crack Cocaine,* having described the various sexual acts that make up the sex-for-crack routine, outlines the plight of one prostitute named Leona. After doing all he could for her (he observed her gang raped in a crack house at age 14 while he was collecting his data, but was powerless to stop it), he sees her on the streets again. She is now 18 and "claimed to have her crack use 'under control'" (of course we really know that she does not). Leona mistakes him for a customer and eventually tells him that she is HIV positive, to which Inciardi adds, "[t]hat was the last time I saw her."[74] This sense that the addict always slips away from control, drifting off into the urban mass, like driftwood on an ocean of depravity, turns the addict into a highly charged erotic object. The note of longing and nostalgia inherent in the last line forces us to cry out for more control, more money, more police, more doctors, and more researchers, as the addict slides into the murky quicksand from which we can then rescue them. What is outrageous for Inciardi is not that Leona will die, but that he is powerless to stop it. Unlike the addict's supposed powerlessness, it is Inciardi's powerlessness that we are supposed to identify with and work to change. We ensure that addicts stay out of reach to justify the need for bureaucracies to establish more control over our lives. The solution to the drug problem, like the mythically elusive drug high, is only sought out, never attained. The solution, then, is more control, more surveillance, more money, and more informers, in the hope of attaining our goal, as well as the enjoyment of letting it slip through our fingers at the last minute.

If the circular logic of the antidrug rhetoric infects researchers, government officials, and authors like Ray Shell, it also infects movie producers. Julian Schnabel's recent movie *Basquiat* (1996) serves as a prime example of how our current positions prevent us from seeing addiction in any other way. In the early stages of the film the young black New York graffiti artist Jean-Michel Basquiat (portrayed by Jeffrey Wright) looks up at the sky as it transforms into a film of a white man surfing a huge wave over the New York skyline. Much later, when his heroin addiction has escalated out of control, he looks up again to see the same surfer, but this time the crest of the wave has passed and the surfer plunges from his board into an all-engulfing wave. If the allegory was not heavy enough, in the final stages of his heroin addiction a similar film clip is again inserted, but this time—having been metaphorically castrated by both the New York art world and heroin—the image is a female water skier, being recklessly dragged along by an unseen speedboat. The thrill of masculine surfing is now replaced by the passive skier being dragged along by something even more powerful than herself. As in *Iced*, this framework becomes the truth of addiction that we understand and want to hear repeated: your will has become enslaved and you can only mechanically follow on behind.

In the opening scenes of the film we see Basquiat in an art gallery as a child, holding hands with his mother, walking toward Picasso's *Guernica*. The film never quite recovers from this sense that heroin provides Basquiat with two things: a return to the mother and, secondly, to childhood, both of which are signified by Basquiat's constant desire to wear pajamas throughout the film; the sense being, of course, that sleep, synonymous with heroin, is also a return to innocence, childhood, and the mother. The mother/childhood thus becomes the place that Basquiat *really* desires, with heroin acting as a surrogate mother.

The anxiety with which Basquiat realizes too late that he has ignored his real mother during his rise to fame results in a scene where he attempts to get into the senior citizen's home where she now resides. The fact that he cries hysterically for his (now inaccessible) mother draws us to the association that it is the connection not only to "the (pusher) man" that is needed, but also to "the mother" and the sleep of the womb. The film makes it quite clear that we should understand that drug addiction is a retreat from the real world. Similarly, Basquiat must learn that both heroin and the New York art world are empty promises. Basquiat is also implicitly criticized in the film for having the usual arrogance that we like to place on the addict: he believes he can take on something as big and powerful as the New York Art Scene/heroin and survive. His inability to be a man and take control of his environment are signals of his introspective weakness—he is unable to face up to reality and in the end he is eaten alive by both the hype and the hypodermic needle.

By listening to his healthy basketball-playing friend—who strangely enough does a lot of drugs yet never seems to go either up or down—we come to know that Basquiat's failure is the failure to make healthy choices. His pal, by operating as the voice of (white) reason, places us outside of Basquiat's consciousness, allowing us the space from which to get a moral perspective on his behavior. The fact that the voice of white reason cannot save him is only proof not that white reason is weak as a cure, but that he is unable to hear its message. In contrast to Basquiat's weaknesses in the film, is Warhol's strength. Consequently, the movie mourns more over the death of the white (antidrug) entrepreneurial Warhol, than Basquiat himself. Warhol can be mourned because he stayed in control and was also (more or less) murdered by a woman who was herself constructed as being out of control. The narrative therefore establishes that addicts like Basquiat cannot be mourned—their combined hubris and arrogance/ignorance prevents it— but can only be pitied. By constructing this kind of truth of addiction the film upholds a belief in everything that we know to be true about drugs, addiction, and African American addicts: Drug addicts really desire to be children, they are weak, they lack a sense of self, and are unable to take responsibility for themselves or their actions. The film also produces the truth that drugs destroy friendships and relationships, make you turn against your family, will prevent you from succeeding in anything you try to do, even if you are genuinely talented. As a result of this truth, the film also suggests how we should respond: we should listen to the voice of white reason (i.e., "Just Say No") because if we do not, drugs will destroy us. In short, the only truth available is that doing drugs is stupid, and here, a fictionalized account of Basquiat's life and death is the "proof."

Mathea Falco

Another way of assessing the current shape of the drug debate is to examine a book like Mathea Falco's *The Making of a Drug-Free America*. The book came out of research (funded by David Hamburg, President of the Carnegie Corporation), that was designed to come up with drug solutions that showed "real promise."[75] Setting out to assess the damage in the war against drugs as well as establishing what is working and what is not working, Falco aims to establish practical guidelines for future action. However, Falco also suggests that drugs are "always on the horizon" and the drug problem "will never go away."[76] For Falco, the policy of enforcement and a federal budget of $11.9 billion has been "a dismal failure;" like James and Johnson, she recognizes that something else has to be done.[77] Realizing that nothing effective can be done against the supply of drugs she feels that we should go after changing the demand for drugs: "demand reduction" is the key.[78] Falco begins with certain assumptions regarding what works when it comes to drugs, outlining that "*[w]e know* prevention must begin early" and that these messages must also go into "families, neighborhoods, churches, businesses, the media," because "*[w]e know* that communities play a critically important role in combatting drugs. . . ."[79] Despite the surety of this kind of talk, Falco is faced with a dilemma: She has to show that there is a drug problem which requires intervention, and she has to show that her approaches are working successfully. The result of this dilemma is that we see strange patterns of drug use that magically come to support both sides of her dilemma. Within the space of two pages we hear that "[c]ocaine and heroin overdose cases . . . have also gone up. These figures suggest that the drug epidemic is far from over," followed later by a statement regarding the "recent declines in marijuana and cocaine use. . . ."[80] Similar paradoxes emerge over the role of communities. For Falco, given the failure of a repressive police policy, only a more insidious Foucauldian apparatus like the community is capable of combating the elusive drugs. Hence her praise is aimed at those communities who manage to drive out drugs: "some communities are fighting back, organizing themselves to drive out drugs."[81] However, these same communities can actually be a problem rather than a cure. Falco points out, for example, that there have been no new methadone clinics in New York since 1980, not because of police opposition or lack of funding, but due to "local community opposition."[82]

One of the clearest measures of the current position on drugs is to examine how children come into this debate. To begin with, it is clear that the real target in the war on drugs is children, not drugs. The rhetoric is always of how to "target younger children."[83] As with the recovering addict in James and Johnson's schema, the child is seen as being in a kind of larval stage with a very soft outer skin that drugs, for some reason, wish to penetrate. The function of an antidrug program is to provide the soft child with enough weapons to deflect an attack by drugs until such time as their skin has hardened and they can resist drugs on their own. According to Falco "[a] few years delay can provide time for the emotional growth that strengthens a child's ability to resist."[84]

Falco outlines the various approaches toward children in the 1970s, which centered on compensating the child for their "low self-esteem, poor communication skills, and [an] inability to make decisions," limitations that made a child vulnerable to drugs. In the 1980s this position was suddenly dropped and instead the common paradigm became one in which "[d]rug use begins not because children lack information or have personality problems, but because they are especially vulnerable in preteen years to social pressures."[85] Concerned that this approach sounds like a return to the failed approach of the seventies, Falco reassures us that this "social influences" approach is "very different from earlier efforts."[86] The goal in this case is "to help children understand the pressures they feel . . . and to teach them how to resist these pressures."[87] Again, as with the messages sent to African American adults, we feel that drugs must be *resisted*.

For Falco, another strategy involves "teaching adolescents to recognize how advertising tries to manipulate their behavior [which] helps them examine all packaged messages critically."[88] There are several difficulties here as well. To begin with, it assumes that adults are immune to a multimillion dollar advertising industry. But if children realize that adults lie on a mass-cultural scale, why should they trust adults who are supposedly providing them with a packaged message on drugs? Having said that the programs of the 1970s, which focused on self-esteem, did not work, Falco goes on to praise the work of a program called Life Skills Training (LST) that was developed in the 1970s by Dr. Gilbert J. Botrin of the Cornell Medical College in New York. Botrin's program teaches children "how to make decisions, solve problems and handle broader social relations so that they feel more confident."[89] Gloria Williams of LST says that "the idea is to help kids feel more confident so that they won't think they have to use drugs to fit in."[90] In spite of being modeled on the failed programs of the 1970s, LST "consistently reports positive results."[91] The same approach is adopted by the STAR program, which was started at USC in the 1980s. The acronym explains their position: Students Taught Awareness and Resistance. These programs, despite being intensive, always seem to lack staying power and the children seem to need constant "re-injections" of resistance. For example, in the STAR program "[a] five year booster program is taught the following year to reinforce their skills."[92] This gives the impression that the program really does offer a vaccine against drugs that wears off after a while and must be readministered. There are also "booster sessions for older children."[93] Confident that these programs' philosophies are correct, Falco feels that there is "powerful evidence that we're heading in the right direction."[94] Strangely enough, these programs seem to exist alongside children using drugs at younger ages. However, rather than thinking that maybe these programs are producing the drug use among younger children, the directors of these programs see it as evidence that they must push even deeper into younger age groups.

For a moment, let us imagine that we are one of the children that has gone through one of these programs that makes us think critically about all packaged messages. What if the packaged message that these groups are vaccinating children against drugs is false? Instead of racing to get to the child and insulate him or her before drugs can get there, what if these programs are actually infecting the child or opening the child up in some way that makes it easier for drugs to get to them. What if we stopped "targeting" children in this way? Falco would see it as a ridiculous idea, one that would leave children wide open to being swamped by drugs. But would this happen? Why?

Why would drugs want to swarm to young children more than, say, adults or housewives or ethnic minorities? Again, this model only works if we persist in thinking that children are some kind of drug magnet and that all that drugs want to do is race toward children whenever they get the slightest chance. If we think about it critically, drugs really have no interest in children, or any of us for that matter. Drugs cannot be interested in anything. It is *we* who have certain interests and *we* then displace those interests onto the drugs or children or minorities or women. As we can see, though, such ideas are deemed unacceptable. The more palatable solution is to persist with these programs, and, if possible, intensify them. As Susan Ayres, a teacher in Florida, says, "The younger we can start the better. . . ."[95] Falco, again, sounds very decided, "*We know* that prevention programs should begin as early as possible."[96] Falco points out that Head Start, another drug education program, "currently reaches less than a third of the nation's two million preschool-age children growing up in poverty. In 1990 Congress authorized extending Head Start to reach all eligible three-, four-, and five year olds by 1994. . . ."[97] In my critical frame of mind, questioning any packaged messages, I find this rather shocking: *three year olds* will be taught to "say no" to drugs? On the other hand, Falco finds herself shocked that this program is not going ahead effectively, and laments that "so far less than half of the additional $7.5 billion needed to make this a reality has been appropriated."[98]

All of these programs operate in essentially the same way, which is, as Dr. Susan Bridges points out, is "to bring coherence into [the children's] family life."[99] Again, this equation only works because we "know" that drugs produce chaos, so we respond with things that we "know" are stable. Would it not be easier to simply change what drugs mean rather than constantly battling to overcome the chaos that they supposedly endlessly create? To prove this point, having decriminalized heroin, the average age of heroin users in Holland has steadily gone *up* by one year for each year that heroin has been decriminalized.[100]

When it comes to drug dealers and the problems of black communities, we see a resurgence of the same issues that dominated the discussion of children and drugs. In Detroit's Pilgrim Village, Charlene Johnson operates the R.E.A.C.H (Reach Everyone and Administer Care and Help) program, which is currently trying to drive out drug dealers. Again, the weakness of the community is seen as a problem of self-esteem: "There are so many forces in the black community that destroy our self-esteem."[101] The same rhetoric is here shaping how drugs can and cannot be dealt with: If the black community, like the young child, is weak-willed or swayed by destructive peer pressure, then drugs can take hold. Many people will argue that this is true, though my concern is rooted in the way that this narrative appears so obviously true, and cannot be denied or questioned.

The understanding of drugs is also not separate from the issue of social control, as it is with children. T. Willard Fair of Operation P.O.P. (Push Out the Pusher) in the predominantly black area of Liberty City in Miami says that "[i]nner city residents who have seen the police as adversaries now learn to work with them in fighting dealers, the common enemy."[102] Obviously, in terms of controlling the black population, the police must be quite thankful for the dealers providing a focus for black anger. The difficulty when it comes to dealers is that no one community is prepared to locate a workable solution, but instead just wants the problem to move on. The idea behind the current community resistance to dealers is to make it as difficult for them to do business as possible. But here is another case of a solution causing the problem it is designed to eliminate. As Falco points out, "[f]aced with losing their customers and the possibility of arrest, dealers often move to safer areas. . . ."[103] So a problem is eliminated in one area while another community wakes up to find itself with a drug problem for no visible reason. The only solution is to repeat the pattern all over again. Falco feels that "[b]reaking up street markets is one of the most promising strategies for reducing crime and drug addiction."[104] Obviously, the opposite is happening, and the solution is causing the problem to spread to another area. Perhaps a more effective strategy would be to actually bring the dealers *into* the community. Make the dealer and the user a legitimate part of the neighborhood so that the question of drug administration could be dealt with openly by the whole community. In a White Paper published in England by Release in 1990, the same point was made: "A priority should be made to minimize the distance between drug users and helping or educational resources and to integrate drug use and drug users within mainstream social structures. This would increase the penetration of official health promotion messages and encourage social controls. Isolating drug users within a drug use subculture is likely to encourage extreme behaviour."[105] Even *The Economist*, as early as 1988, said the same thing: "[T]he best policy toward existing heroin users might be to bring them *within* the law. . . ."[106] Meanwhile, in the United States, these voices are silenced while we persist in *increasing* the distance between drugs and the mainstream, only to be surprised that this exacerbates any given drug problem. If we really wish to eliminate the drug subculture, it can only be done by providing another space for those people to move to. Given our current rhetoric of isolation and repression, we have given them no alternative but to remain where they are. In short, a policy of trying to wipe out a drug subculture has become the most effective way of *maintaining* it.

On the question of dealers, we see a return of the same metaphors that were used in conjunction with children. If the children required constant boosters against drugs, then the communities have to constantly keep a vigilant lookout against drug dealers. Getting rid of them once is not enough because, according to Audrey Brantley, "they are like weeds, they pop out everywhere. . . ."[107] Communities can band together, "driving out dealers and reclaiming their streets," but of course such victories are inevitably short lived as "dealers fight to regain their territory."[108] Once again, a constant battle is the only way for the war to proceed, and any victories must be closely guarded, and any terrain reclaimed must be constantly protected. Resisting drugs becomes a twenty-four-hour battle, with no hope of a final victory.

Naya Arbiter, director of Amity, a therapeutic community in Arizona, offers a glimmer of hope when she suggests that the problem is not drugs but people's perception of what drug addicts are. "So much of this war on drugs has been spent identifying and rejecting the enemy, deepening the division between us and them. . . . Once we make drug addicts into the enemy, society has a tough time taking them back in. Why would the public want to pay for more treatment if they're dealing with the enemy?"[109] We need to restructure the whole debate on drugs to the point that when we think of addicts we immediately think in terms of *we* rather than *them;* only then can the problem begin to be really solved. The terrain will only begin to shift when we see the drug problem as a health issue that affects the entire society, rather than a police issue that only affects "them."

Planet Crack

As with Rosenbaum's trip to planet heroin, so too the black drug universe continues to orbit discursively around planet crack. Although we seem to have passed through the explosion of crack culture that arose under the Reagan and Bush administrations, as recently as 1996, William H. James and Stephen Johnson can still assert that planet crack is "a world ruled by fear" in which the inhabitants "form a culture unto themselves with a separate sexual lifestyle, secrets, behaviors and language." The drug counselor has to then venture into this strange world if they are to have any success and learn to "understand the language" of these aliens.[110] James and Johnson point out that like some form of hypersensitive animal, "they" (crack users) "are very observant of human emotions, mood changes, behaviors, hidden intentions, deceptions and unspoken ideas."[111] While not really being human themselves, we must be amazed at the degree to which they "learn how to read human behavior."[112] However, we must also be careful because the inhabitants of planet crack can be dangerous because while they "have this sense of acute observation . . . they also have an out-of-proportion sense of uniqueness and specialness, a loss of control over most aspects of living, and a total lack of self-awareness and self-observation."[113] While this may sound true now, it is no different from those old arguments in the 1920s whereby drugs turned blacks into bulletproof machines: "Southern police departments (in the 1920s) switched to .38 revolvers, because they thought that cocaine made blacks impervious to standard issue .32 caliber bullets."[114] A story that seems idiotic now, but it was easily deployed against blacks on PCP, justifying the use of stun-guns to disable the superhuman drug user.

Not suprisingly, the force of the gravity on planet crack is also very high, and the narratives that we tell about the drug only seem to strengthen that gravity. Whereas the (white) English youth saw their own drug use as simply a form of stress-release leisure, African American drug use is relegated to the status of a serious illness that is inescapable: "Crack cocaine addiction must be understood as a chronic serious illness that, like diabetes, asthma, cancer, or a heart problem, requires ongoing support, education and care."[115] By pathologizing drug use in this way it is no wonder that we see such horrendous consequences. Note as well the use of the imperative: Crack use "must" be understood in this way, because if it is not, then we have no way to understand it. While saying that we "must" understand crack use in these ways, James and Johnson remind us of the failure rate of traditional approaches: "A generous estimate would have one crack-addicted person out of ten quitting on his or her own, one quitting because of a twelve-step recovery and treatment program, and the other eight out of ten continuing their addiction."[116] What is interesting is that in this statement 50 percent of the successes changed their drug use with absolutely no traditional intervention: If the drug and the conditions are so horrendous, how could this one person escape from planet crack on their own? What if this small percentage escaped precisely because they had no contact with the (failing) discourses of recovery that we say must be deployed? What if it was *because* this small percentage slipped through the net that actually made it easier for them to recover? What if it was their detachment from our unhealthy narratives of disease, pathology, and genetic sickness that actually provided them with a space in which to see their drug use in ways not covered by our limited and limiting narratives of "Just Say No"? It is obviously a very small "what if," but at this point we have no alternative but to try to break open the smallest possible openings in the hope that we can prevent James and Johnson from going in theoretical circles. More importantly, we also have to give those eight out of ten crack users who always relapse something to hold on to that may be more useful than telling them that their addiction has its roots in the 1700s.

James and Johnson suggest that for the African American community, crack addiction "is an addiction to the memories of the best experiences of the using the drug."[117] If this is true, then surely we should apply this truth to ourselves: Let us stop remembering what we know about drugs and start to let it all go and forget it. Only once our framework is forgotten can we begin to move forward and break free from our sick addiction to a system of thought that is obviously not working for drug users. If such a suggestion seems dangerous—in that once we forget all of our knowledge then thousands will drown in crack addiction—let us remind ourselves what Mike Davis said of the Los Angeles Police Department. Davis points out that the LAPD wants us to hold onto our cherished frameworks because it enables them to preserve a situation that gives them maximum power. According to Davis, the war on drugs is a war that "the LAPD secretly loves losing."[118] In a sense, the LAPD is no worse than any other institution that claims it wants to stop drug use; all that Davis is pointing to is that by their cynicism, the LAPD is simply more honest than drug recovery programs. It is easy to say that the LAPD secretly loves losing the drug war, but would it be acceptable to say that drug recovery programs and/or the church *also* secretly love losing their own war on drugs? In a sense everyone loves losing the war on drugs because by losing, we can keep on playing the power games that obviously give us pleasure.[119]

We tend to assume that the role of the police is somehow one of brute force and a continuation of racism by other means, and that clinics, even those with African American staff and concerns, are somehow working to heal the wounds that the police wish to see secretly exacerbated. But what would the terrain look like if for a moment we decided to make no separation between recovery programs and the LAPD? While it would be political to suggest that black rehabilitation programs are working in opposition to the LAPD, with a completely different set of politics, maybe we should recognize that, in Althusser's terms, they are in fact simply different arms of the same institution. The only difference is that the clinics are part of the Ideological State Apparatus while the LAPD is simply the Repressive State Apparatus, which physically enforces the same positions that clinics enforce ideologically and medically. This reading would explain why areas with high antidrug policing have no recovery programs. Mike Davis laments how Skid Row in downtown Los Angeles has "the largest single concentration of crack addicts—young and old—in the city, but not a single treatment facility."[120] He also outlines how Pasadena is fighting a crack-based gang in its Northwest ghetto, "including humiliating strip-searches in the field and drug-tenant eviction policy, without spending a single cent on drug rehabilitation."[121] While we could vent our outrage at this paucity of treatment programs, asserting that once again black people are being left to die, such anger would assume that the clinics are somehow not doing what the LAPD is doing. But once we accept that they are both playing the same game, we can see that if the LAPD has a hold over Skid Row it does not need a clinic to do the ideological work that it can handle with repression. Similarly, why would

Pasadena want clinics if it can achieve the same results with its police force? Replacing police with clinics would simply mean an ideological continuation of the same policy on drugs, not a change of policy.

One of the greatest problems of the African American community is AIDS, a problem that is directly related to intravenous drug use. To change the pattern of HIV infection the approach to drugs also has to shift. If clinics did begin to do something different that did really begin to threaten the status quo, then surely they would be harassed by the police and forced to shut down. In a sense, the current framework on addiction, because it does not do anything at all to change the rhetoric of the drug landscape, is precisely why the current clinics are kept open. By working within the boundaries of an accepted discourse, they are permitted free operation: Once they start to question the very roots of what they are doing per se, then (a) they would begin to make a real difference, and (b) they would be shut down as dangerous and unhealthy or prodrug. This is not merely my theoretical speculation. One good example of a group that is trying to question the parameters of the discourse is Clean Needles Now in Hollywood. Set up simply to hand out clean needles to addicts who are willing to hand in used ones, the centers are aiming only at harm reduction, which, as we saw in the last chapter, was something that Dr. John Marks did in Liverpool with great success.[122] However, as soon as they became established, the government moved in to shut them down. A recent article in the *Wall Street Journal* by David Murray suggested that giving addicts needles will actually "produce a public health tragedy" rather than prevent one. This view is summed up by his title "Clean Needles May Be Bad Medicine."[123] Rather than contemplating the benefits of the idea, Murray rounds up the usual list of scientific data to prove that "those who attended needle-exchange programs had a substantially higher risk of HIV infection than intravenous drug addicts who did not." I am not quite sure how that can be. Imagine attending a hospital in which doctors were not allowed to use clean needles, but had to use the same one all day. However, needle-exchange programs are seen not as health institutions, but as places where addicts can gather and promote the dangerous emergence of "new sharing networks," while the exchange becomes a "gathering place" for "isolated" addicts. Do not forget that we are also talking about an inner city (read: non-white) population here, so it is really no surprise that these programs cannot be allowed to succeed. Julie Bruneau and Martin T. Schecter, who authored the Montreal and Vancouver studies of needle exchanges, suggest that "these programs are in inner-city neighborhoods, [and therefore] they serve users who are at greatest risk of infection." While this would seem to me to indicate that such areas are therefore greatly in need of clean needles, they conclude the opposite: "Those who didn't accept free needles . . . were less likely to engage in the riskiest activities." So those who accept clean needles are somehow *more* at risk than those who insist on sharing? Bruneau adds to this by reporting how "addicts who were initially HIV-negative were more likely to become positive after participation in the needle exchange." Similarly the office of Barry McCaffrey (U.S. Drug Czar) put out a study that concluded, not surprisingly, that in Vancouver "2.5 million needles were given out last year, [and] the death rate from illegal drugs has skyrocketed."[124] The needle exchange is seen as somehow promoting drug use, so the government is working hard to stamp it out on those grounds. U.S. Senators John Ashcroft and Paul Coverdell are also pressuring the government to pull any funding that these exchanges receive. For these two (white) men, needle exchanges are seen predictably as "the moral equivalent to handing out heroin" and thus they must be banned, not to help addicts, but to "protect the nation," while also ensuring that "taxpayer's hard-earned dollars" are not used to buy "needles for drug addicts."[125] Significantly, when the Center for Disease Control and Prevention issued a report in 1994 stating its findings that needle exchanges "diminish transmission of the AIDS virus without increasing drug use," the Clinton administration refused to release the report.[126]

What can be done? To begin with, we need to shift our focus away from punitive measures to health measures. When twenty-two-year-old Dwight Gooden of the New York Mets was discovered to have been spending much of his earnings on cocaine, he was immediately rushed off to the $1,000-a-day Smithers Center at New York's Roosevelt Hospital. Instead of the current policy of alienation and imprisonment that would have been dished out to his poorer African American counterparts, he was instantly "taken back and embraced by the team."[127] As team management pointed out, "[t]he only thing that really mattered was his health."[128] We have to begin thinking of the rest of the drug using population in the same way: We should also embrace them, because all that matters is their health. If we take care of this, then the rest of the drug problems will be much easier to work with. Joseph McNamara has outlined some possible suggestions. Prior to the Harrison Narcotics Act of 1914, drug use was viewed as a medical and social issue and was not a violation of criminal law. The result was not widespread criminal drug use, nor did drug use totally disappear, but the problems associated with it did disappear: "There was no billion-dollar black market. No violent drug trade. No widespread official corruption. No widespread disrespect for drug laws. Drug users went to their doctors if they needed treatment."[129] By extension, as soon as Prohibition was instituted, all of these problems immediately returned. This easing up of the pressure on drugs is one possible direction that would also take the pressure off of the African American community, both internally and externally. In addition, this would lead to a position in which the morality of drug use could then begin to soften to the point that Daryl Gates's suggestion that "[c]asual drug users should be taken out and shot" will become a monument to the barbarity of the past.

Nietzsche has said that "[i]f one wants to get free from an unendurable pressure one needs hashish."[130] Taking this metaphorically, we need a hashish mentality to help us to relieve the unbearable pressure of the current situation. I feel that we need a kind of drugged thinking, which would also allow us to suspend judgement on what we think is right or wrong for a moment, in order to open up a space in which we can think clearly without the pressure of having to slot our ideas into the limiting pigeonholes of right/wrong. Instead of asserting what we know (i.e., have constructed) about drugs and race, I suggest that we begin to construct new combinations that fly in the face of our current logic. Only by constructing new positions on drugs that break with the old patterns do we stand a chance of finding our way out of the maze that we have built for ourselves.

It would be useful for us to imagine a time when, rather than being headline news, the drug problem has withered to a story that is too unimportant even to be mentioned by medical experts. A more contemporary reference point could be the comments of the English Advisory Council on the Misuse of Drugs in 1984: "While there has been a considerable amount of research into why people misuse drugs, no single cause or consistent pattern of multiple causes has been identified. *The majority are relatively stable individuals who have more in common with the general population than with any pathological sub-group.*"[131] Here is something unthinkable: not that drug users are a special case, but that they are normal and ordinary, and are closer to us than we could ever imagine. Such a position, rather than attacking the current logic, just makes it appear rather silly and embarrassingly unnecessary. Only when positions such as this have gained common acceptance will we truly have "won" the war on drugs. We should try to locate spaces such as this, spaces where our own current expert opinions and truths can be seen for what they really are: blindness parading itself as psychological truth, and barbarism dressed up as morality.

Postscript: Crack Fever

Immersed in the pleasure of our own positions, it is often hard to imagine how we could ever have a relationship with drugs other than our current one. However, a recent report in the *New York Times* points to the ways in which drug discourses do change and shift, changes that are unconnected to our policing, or our policies.[132] The title of the article is "A Drug Ran Its Course, Then Hid With Its Users." This "image-bite" offers us an immediate sense that crack has departed from certain trouble spots of New York, not because a victory was won in the war on drugs, but simply because the drug "ran its course."

The reporter, Timothy Egan, tells us of Mr. Rios, a former crack dealer who now sells Tommy Hilfiger clothing because he can make "more money" selling them than crack. Not only has Mr. Rios changed his marketing strategy, but he has also changed his own drug use. He is no longer using crack himself, and we are told that it was "not the many times he was arrested nor the year he spent in prison" that changed his mind. Instead, "[h]e simply grew tired of the drug." In the same way that the media also got bored with the crack narrative, so the article presents a similar pattern among its users. It would seem that no amount of law enforcement can do anything to stop crack use; eventually the drug users will just grow out of their habit. Ironically, Mr. Rios is still worried about his nicotine habit though: "I've got to quit these cigarettes . . ."

The reasons for the fading of crack use are left unclear, but several of the metaphors lend us a picture of how we are imagining this startling turnaround in the use of crack. What is clear is that "it was not the incarceration of a generation or the sixfold increase in the number of police assigned to narcotics which turned the tide in New York. . . ." Interestingly, we are also told that "every major American city plagued by the drug has matched New York's rise and decline in crack use, regardless of how drug enforcement responded." It would seem that all of our attempts at control were pointless, whether on a social level or on an individual level. A 1997 report indicated that when drug users stopped using crack, only 5 percent said that incarceration influenced their decision, while 19 percent said that they simply "grew tired of the drug life." How is it that a drug that we all agreed several years ago was the world's most addictive and powerful drug, is suddenly abandoned by its users, who simply grew tired of it? How could the most powerful drug suddenly become powerless? Suddenly crack has changed its role in our cultural narrative: no longer holding center stage as the villain par excellence, it is relegated to a bit part as a boring has-been.

The central explanation that the report presents is most telling: "The crack epidemic behaved much like a fever. It came on strong, appearing to rise without hesitation, and then broke. . . ." This is a startling cultural admission. Instead of saying that we must fight against crack we are now saying that we are powerless against the crack, and that it is okay to be powerless because if we just hold on, very soon the "fever" will break and things will return to normal. No one in their right mind would think of "struggling" against a "fever." It is as if the drug now has a natural cycle that it must run through and there is *nothing* that we can or should do to stop the "fever."

In contrast to our old story that the drug has the power to reduce everyone to a sex-for-crack fiend, the report also outlines how most people have a "natural" built-in ability to resist the drug, not because of some educational program, but simply because they decide, for themselves, that it is not something that they enjoy doing. So, for example, Egan tells us that one of the reasons for the decline in crack use is that there was "an entire generational revulsion against the drug." In contrast to the story in which one drug user sucks everyone around him or her into addiction, we hear one girl, whose mother was a "chronic" crack user, tell us that "[i]f you were raised in a house where somebody was a crack addict, you wanted to get as far away from that drug as possible." The story of crack's power to destroy whole families and neighborhoods in retrospect seems a narrative driven by panic. Thankfully, the experts were wrong: "Ten years ago, many experts feared that crack would be passed on from mothers to children. But the children did not follow the pattern." Nor is this miracle confined to New York: "National surveys of the general population show the same falling off in crack use among the young."

The shift in the perception of crack that we are seeing here is in sharp contrast to the stories in the eighties of crack's unlimited power: What we are telling ourselves now is much healthier and also far more empowering for both us and the users. We are hearing that people have the power to make up their own minds about any drug—no matter how powerful the media says it is—and that the drug itself can be constructed as fairly benign: It is not "wicked," it is simply a "fever" that will pass. By seeing crack through a narrative in which we take some of the importance and power away from the drug, we see how the results are to our benefit: "[A] little triangle of land near Bushwick, where crack dealers used to stage midnight fights with their pit bulls, is now a community garden." Jackie Robinson Park, which was once filled with crack dealers and users ten years ago "now looks like any slice of green in New York . . . mothers pushing strollers, children playing. . . ."

Nothing in the chemical make-up of crack has changed at all—the drug is still the same as it always was. The difference now is what *we* are making it mean. The degree to which these changing perceptions have an effect on the street is obviously profound; so much so that the police treat these current changes, we are told, as a "miracle." Crack, which we previously told ourselves had a superhuman grip on our communities and our bodies, appears to have decided to simply loosen that grip, not because it was forced to, because "[d]rug markets were in contraction well before the stepped-up police action," but simply because the fever "broke" and/or we got bored with using crack. The truth of this change is signaled by that remark that "even crack heads don't want to be crack heads anymore." Instead of panic, the report breathes calm; instead of impending doom, the tide is receding; instead of people being powerless in the face of the drug, lives are returning to normal. According to Egan, as early as 1989, the "fever had broken and the epidemic was beginning its slow decline." According to a study cited by

Egan, carried out by the National Institute of Justice, the "thousands of arrests 'appeared to have no major deterrent effect.'" Egan cites the work of Dr. Lyn Zimmer, professor of Sociology at Queens College, who tells us that "there is a natural cycle to these kinds of drug trends. Crack followed that." This is mirrored by an anthropologist, Dr. Curtis, who tells Egan that "the prophecy of [young men] becoming addicted and remorseless superpredators" was never fulfilled. Section headings such as "The Rebirth," "Neighborhoods Heal Themselves," and "Getting Better Amid Despair" allow us to realize that we are able to rewrite the meaning of any drug: All it takes is for us to choose a script in which drug users and we can be winners, rather than losers. Back in the 1980s Nancy Reagan claimed that "[d]rugs rip right through the moral fiber of our countries . . . ," but now it is quite plain to see that they are unable to do this at all.[133] The new metaphors make the old narratives unworkable: For example, it is unthinkable that a "fever" would have the destruction of a "moral fiber" as its goal. The old stories that we told ourselves with such vehemence have, like crack, lost their ability to charm us.

We should remember that the first front page report on crack also appeared in the *New York Times* on November 29, 1985, and by December 1, Jennifer McLogan on NBC spoke of crack as "the frightening wave of the future."[134] Having been scripted by us as a horror story, that is exactly what crack became. The decline of crack use in the 1990s is proof, not only that drugs are unable to do any lasting damage to the moral fiber of a culture, but that they have no interest in doing such a thing. More importantly, from this recent historical perspective, we can see that crack did not have to be scripted as a horror story after all. It is much healthier for us to write drugs into our cultural script as a "fever" that will "break," rather than as an out-of-control monster that gets stronger the harder we try to kill it. Besides, the "fever" metaphor is a lot easier on everyone, from addicts to police officers to children: easier than the "cockroach" metaphor, which makes everyone's position very exhausting. Hopefully, looking back on the 1990s, it should become clear that the solution to our drug problem has a simple cure, and that it resides in the way that we, as a culture, choose to speak about drugs. If we insist on scripting them as evil and dangerous, then we will have to deal with these effects in our culture. If, on the other hand we choose to see them, for example, as a benign "fever" that will follow a natural cycle, with no cause for alarm, then drugs become a very different thing, and we will see real changes in what drugs mean, not only in scholarly journals, the media, and the role of the police and government, but more importantly, in our own attitude toward drugs and drug users. As Jean Cocteau said, drugs mean nothing in themselves, and therefore "it is entirely up to us to make them well disposed."[135]

Notes

Preface

1. Walter Benjamin, *Reflections,* ed. Peter Demetz (Schocken Books: New York, 1978), p. 190.

Introduction

1. Jacques Derrida, *Of Grammatology,* trans. Gayatri Spivak (Baltimore and London: Johns Hopkins University Press, 1976), [hereafter *OG*], p. xxii.
2. Gilles Deleuze and Claire Parnet, *Dialogues* (New York: Columbia University Press, 1987), p. 10.
3. David Joselit, *Infinite Regress: Marcel Duchamp, 1910–1941* (Cambridge, MA: MIT Press, 1998), p. 185.
4. Michel Foucault, *Language, Counter-Memory and Practice: Selected Essays and Interviews* [hereafter *LCP*] (Ithaca, NY: Cornell University Press, 1980), p. 192.
5. Michel Foucault, *The Birth of the Clinic: An Archaeology of Medical Perception* (Vintage Books, Random House: New York, 1975), p. 3.
6. Gary Webb, *Dark Alliance: The CIA, The Contras and the Crack Cocaine Explosion* (New York: Seven Stories Press, 1998), p. x.
7. Jean Cocteau, *Opium: Diary of his Cure* (London: Peter Owen, 1990), p. 29.
8. Aleister Crowley, *The Diary of a Drug Fiend* (York Beach, ME: Samuel Weiser, 1970), p. 159.
9. For Bennet, see Michael Berube, *Public Access: Literary Theory and American Cultural Politics* (London and New York: Verso, 1994), p. x.
10. Eve Sedgwick, *Tendencies* (Durham, NC: Duke University Press, 1993), p. 133. For Sedgwick, the answer to the current "drug problem" will always be very difficult because we are trying to reconstruct an alternative language of addiction in a landscape that has been, as she says, "rubbled and defeatured by the twin hurricanes of Just Do It and Just Say No," p. 140. The third way out of this binary, according to Sedgwick, is to move toward thinking of "volition and compulsion differently . . . [and] resist simply repropelling the propaganda of a receding 'free will,'" p. 138. It is in this space that I aim to situate my own attempts to "think volition differently."

11. Marc Redfield, ed. *diacritics: a review of contemporary criticism* (Johns Hopkins University Press) vol. 27, no. 3 (Fall 1997): 5.

12. Ronald L. Akers, "Addiction: The Troublesome Concept," *Journal of Drug Issues* vol. 21, no. 4 (Fall 1991): 779 [hereafter Akers].

13. Akers, p. 779.

14. Akers, p. 780. David F. Allen and James Jekel, in *Crack: The Broken Promise* (New York : St. Martin's Press, 1991), p. 25, also resort to telling us of the "incomprehensible" nature of crack addiction.

15. Akers, p. 791.

16. Berube, p.138.

17. Berube, p. 146.

18. Redfield, p. 3.

19. Redfield, p. 6.

20. Lisa Farley, *Angel Dust: New Facts about PCP,* published by the Do It Now Foundation, 1999.

21. Jacques Derrida, "The Rhetoric of Drugs: An Interview" *Differences* vol. 5, no.1 (Spring 1993):11.

22. *LCP,* p. 154.

23. *OG,* p. xxiii.

24. Ibid., xxxi.

25. Ibid.

26. Ibid.

27. Ibid.

28. Cocteau, *Diary of his Cure,* p. 93.

29. *OG,* p. xxxi.

30. Ibid., p. xxx.

31. Ibid.

32. Ibid., p. 191.

33. Derrida, *Differences,* p. 15.

34. Cocteau, *Diary of his Cure,* p. 36.

35. William Burroughs, *Naked Lunch* (New York: Grove Press, 1990), p. 248.

36. Virginia Berridge and Griffith Edwards, *Opium and the People: Opiate Use in Nineteenth-Century England* (London and New York: Allen Lane/St. Martin's Press, 1981), p. 150.

37. Ibid.

38. Ibid.

39. Ibid., p. 162.

40. Ibid., p. 163.

41. Eve Sedgwick notes that this whole discourse of fear surrounding masturbation suddenly disappeared and that it probably "withered away from sheer transparent absurdity," (*Tendencies,* p. 112). One can only assume that the same thing will one day happen to the fears surrounding "drugs."

42. Berridge and Edwards, p. 150.

43. The disease theory surfaces in contemporary self-help books about drugs. For example, Deepak Chopra in *Overcoming Addictions* (Missouri: Three

Rivers Press, 1998) p. 59, reveals how "Exposure to drugs is comparable to being bitten by a mosquito carrying malaria. . . ."

44. Edward Levenstein, *Morbid Craving for Morphia* (1878), trans C. Harrer (New York: Arno Press, 1981), pp. 113–115.

45. Ibid., pp. 112–115.

46. Ibid., pp. 150–52.

47. Ibid., pp. 152.

48. Foucault, *History of Sexuality,* p. 36.

49. Ibid., p. 40.

50. Ibid., p. 103

51. Berridge and Edwards, p. 153.

52. Berridge and Edwards, p. 155. Susan Sontag charts a similar course for cancer. See *Illness as Metaphor* (New York :Vintage Books, 1978). For medical discussions of the period, see Woodwards, J. and Richards, D., ed., *Health Care and Popular Medicine in Nineteenth Century England: Essays in the Social History of Medicine* (New York: Holmes and Meier, 1977).

53. Berridge and Edwards, p. 155–156.

54. Ibid., p. 156.

55. Ibid., p. 157.

56. Ibid.

57. Do It Now Foundation, Tempe, Arizona, 1996.

58. Cocteau, *Diary of his Cure,* p. 29.

59. See news.bbc.co.uk, Thursday, April 22, 1999.

60. For an excellent discussion of these writers see Aleath Hayter's *Opium and The Romantic Imagination: Addiction and Creativity in De Quincey, Coleridge, Baudelaire and Others* (London: Crucible, 1988) or chapters two and three of Barry Milligan's *Pleasures and Pains: Opium and the Orient in Nineteenth CenturyBritish Culture* (Charlottesville and London: University Press of Virginia, 1995).

61. For more on the relationship between drug and alcohol discourses in the period see Harrison's *Drink and the Victorians: The Temperance Question in England, 1815–1872.* (Pittsburgh: University of Pittsburgh Press, 1971).

62. Susan Sontag, *Illness as Metaphor* (New York: Farrar, Strauss and Giroux, 1989), p. 13–14, suggests a parallel between the "war" on drugs and the "war" on AIDS, concluding that "metaphors . . . kill."

63. Michel Foucault, *Foucault/ Blanchot* (New York: Zone Books, 1987), p. 12.

64. Marcel Proust, *A Remembrance of Things Past: Vol. III* (London: Penguin Books, 1983), p.932.

65. In his introduction to a special edition of *diacritics* on addiction, Marc Redfield suggests that literature may be "perhaps our only chance—to think beyond the intoxicating absolutes of a society in denial," p. 6.

66. Similar analyses regarding female drug addiction can also be found in Cuskey. See also Ellinwood, Gerstein and Rovner, Prather and Fidell, Rosenbaum, Williams and Bates, and Mondanaro.

Chapter One

1. Catherine Peters, *The King of the Inventors: A Life of Wilkie Collins* (London: Secker and Warburg, 1991), p. 336.
2. Terry M. Parsinnen, *Secret Passions, Secret Remedies: Narcotic Drugs in British Society 1820–1930* (Philadelphia: Institute for the Study of Human Issues, 1983), p. 47.
3. Dolores Peters, "The British Medical Response to Opiate Addiction in the Nineteenth Century" *Journal of the History of Medicine* vol. 36, no. 4 (October 1981): 457.
4. Ibid., p. 457.
5. Ibid.
6. Ibid., p. 460
7. Ibid., p. 463.
8. Ibid.
9. Ibid., p. 464.
10. Ibid.
11. Irvine Welsh, *Trainspotting* (New York and London: Norton, 1993). The novel does manage to present a different view of addiction, particularly in the chapter sarcastically titled "Searching for the Inner Man," where the leading character critiques the jargon of addiction psychology, but this section is not included in the film.
12. In an interview, director Danny Boyle openly states that despite the surface hipness of the movie, "its message in the end is quite old-fashioned. Really. There's a warning there to anybody who's got any kind of open eyes at all. It's just done in a different way." Boyle goes on to prove his point by stating how at the Cannes Film Festival, Noel Gallagher, self-proclaimed bad boy of the British rock band Oasis, whom Boyle ironically characterizes as "hotel-smashing, cocaine sniffing"—was next to him, and in front of Gallagher was Virginia Bottomley, the Conservative Party's Minister of Culture. Bottomley's daughter had suggested that it would be "fun" for her mother to see the film, and, not surprisingly, she did like the film. This spectrum of youth culture hero to Tory minister is then wheeled out to explain the film's wide appeal, as well as supporting the sense that it articulates some kind of universal truth about drugs.
13. Nuel Pharr Davis, *The Life of Wilkie Collins* (Urbana: University of Illinois Press, 1956), p. 258.
14. See D. A. Miller's *The Novel and The Police* (Berkeley: University of California Press, 1988). p. 168, Davis pp. 258–9, 332.
15. See also Hayter p. 259.
16. Catherine Peters p. 304.
17. Ibid., p. 214.
18. Ibid., p. 336.
19. Cocteau, p. 93, 87.
20. Catherine Peters, p. 303.

21. If Collins did not recognize the text of *The Moonstone* as his own, then people with AIDS are paradoxically identified by their non-identity with their former healthy (pre-AIDS) selves. Here again the images of thin, dying people appear to substantiate the horror of what unwilled behavior leads to.

22. Peter Thoms, *The Windings of the Labyrinth: Quest and Structure in the Major Novels of Wilkie Collins* (Athens: Ohio University Press, 1992), pp. 156–58. While I am more interested in the preservation of non-meaning as opposed to its elimination, I find Thoms's theory that Jennings/the addict is a "model reader," p. 164, incredibly suggestive.

23. Wilkie Collins, *The Moonstone* (London: Penguin Books, 1992), p. 359 [hereafter *Moonstone*].

24. *Moonstone*, p. 359.

25. Ibid., p. 360.

26. Ibid., p. 267.

27. Ibid., p. 453.

28. Ibid., pp. 186–187

29. Ibid., p. 187. Mr. Candy becomes a parallel figure whose decadence joins hands with drugs and disease. Jennings visits the sick man and finds "nothing left of his former self, but the old tendency to vulgar smartness in his dress. The man was a wreck; but his clothes and his jewelry—in cruel mockery of the change in him were as gay and as gaudy as ever," p. 413. For a contemporary reading of illness and perversion see Martha Gever's article in Douglas Crimp, ed. *AIDS: Cultural Analysis / Cultural Criticism* (Massachusetts: MIT Press, 1988).

30. *Moonstone*, p. 187.

31. Ibid., pp. 371–372. Italics in original.

32. Ibid., p. 418.

33. Ibid.

34. Ibid., p. 417. The novel also makes clear the links between the "inscrutable" and detested Indians and Jennings.

35. Ibid., p. 372.

36. Ibid., p. 373.

37. Ibid.

38. Ibid., p. 371. Collins's description of Jennings is parallel to the image of the Shivering Sand: basically it "looks" like Jennings. See *Moonstone*, pp. 55–56.

39. Norman Page, ed. *Wilkie Collins: The Critical Heritage* (London and Boston: Routledge and Kegan Paul, 1974), p. 332. If Jennings can help them, it must be because the drug addict is always already part of the family. In this sense Lady Verinder is correct when she says that "This is not a matter in which any stranger can help us," p. 222. At some level she is aware that Jennings, like her very own laudanum drops, can "put [her] right in a minute or two," p. 253. Lady Verinder's bathroom cabinet contains opium, thus drugs are no stranger to this family. If we add to this the opium habits of Blake's relative, Colonel Herncastle, we begin to see that drugs have *always* been one of the family. It is surely significant that the opium that is used to

drug Blake, first by Candy and second by Jennings (which brings the diamond to light), comes in both cases from Lady Verinder's medicine cabinet.
As Jennings tells us, "I have only this moment found an opportunity of attending to the most important duty of all; the duty of looking in the family
medicine chest, for the laudanum which Mr. Candy used last year," p. 464.

40. *Moonstone*, p. 452.

41. Ibid., p. 471.

42. Ibid., p. 474.

43. Ibid., p. 476.

44. Ibid.

45. Ibid., p. 474.

46. Ibid.

47. The consanguinity of free will/addiction is also shown in the case of Colonel
Herncastle, who appears, as part of the family, to be the safely
domestic/pure/free willed subject of the British Colonel. However, he soon
turns out to have been, all along, part of the strange outside. At the beginning of the novel we hear how Colonel John Herncastle first brought the
moonstone into the family's possession and becomes "outlawed" because of
his involvement with the diamond and also because "the mystery of [his] life
got in [his] way," p. 64. Herncastle is shunned by all his friends at the clubs,
and women refuse his marriage proposals. His involvement with the diamond even results in his having a Jennings-like face, which, "handsome as it
was . . . looked possessed by the devil," p. 64. It is therefore no surprise to
discover that the Colonel "had been a notorious opium-eater for years past"
p. 69. Interestingly enough, when Collins rewrote the story for the theatre
in 1877 he left out "the opium, the Indians, Yorkshire, Ezra Jennings and
Rosanna Spearman." In short, he left out all the things that he had received
criticism for in 1868. See Sue Lonoff, *Wilkie Collins and His Victorian Readers: A Study in the Rhetoric of Authorship.* (New York: AMS Press Inc., 1982).
p. 266.

48. John Dent, *Anxiety and Its Treatment* (Stratford, London: Skeffington Press,
1955), p. 47.

49. *Moonstone*, p. 420.

50. Ibid., p. 438.

51. Ibid.

52. Ibid., p. 442.

53. Ibid., p. 468.

54. Ibid., p. 428.

55. Ibid.

56. Barry Milligan, *Pleasures and Pains,* p. 15.

57. Nuel Pharr Davis, p. 255.

58. See Hansard, 1556.

59. Ibid.

60. For background on the ways in which the 1868 Act restricted the sale of
drugs, see Berridge and Edwards, Chapter 10.

61. Antonin Artaud, *Selected Writings,* ed. Susan Sontag (Los Angeles and Berkeley: University of California Press, 1976), p. 101.

62. According to Terry M. Parssinen, *Secret Passions, Secret Remedies: Narcotic Drugs in British Society 1820–1930* (Philadelphia: I.S.H.I., 1983), p. 68ff, the 1868 act was, due to a legal loophole, rather ineffective. Whether this is the case or not, the "desire" to control drugs produced an ideological climate that enabled drugs to be "perceived" as a problem.

63. "Abuse of Narcotics," *The Times,* January 2, 1880, pp. 6–7.

64. Catherine Peters p. 473.

65. Cocteau, p. 64.

66. Ibid., p. 90.

67. Ibid., p. 123.

68. Ibid., p. 29.

69. Ibid., p. 68.

Chapter 2

1. Charles Baudelaire, *Artificial Paradise: On Hashish and Wine as Means of Expanding Individuality,* trans. Ellen Fox (New York: Herder and Herder, 1971).

2. See David Lenson, *On Drugs* (Minneapolis: University of Minnesota Press, 1995) p. 30.

3. Catherine Peters, p. 479.

4. William Burroughs, *Naked Lunch* (Grove: New York, 1990), p. 234.

5. Arthur Conan Doyle, *The Sign of the Four* (London: Penguin, 1987), p. 7.

6. Amy Scholder and Ira Silverberg, eds. *High Risk: An Anthology of Forbidden Writings* (Harmondsworth: Plume Books, Penguin, 1991), p. 73.

7. Doyle. p. 7.

8. Ibid.

9. Ibid.

10. Ibid.

11. Ibid.

12. Ibid., p. 8.

13. Ibid.

14. Ibid.

15. Ibid.

16. Ibid.

17. For the full story, see http://news.bbc.co.uk/hi/english/uk/newsid_303000.

18. Doyle, p. 8.

19. Ibid.

20. Ibid.

21. Ibid., p. 15.

22. Ibid., p. 14.

23. Ibid., p. 138.

24. Baudelaire, p. 56. My emphasis.

25. Ibid., p. 17.
26. Ibid., p. 23.
27. Ibid., p. 28.
28. Ibid., p. 23, 16.
29. Ibid., p. 16.
30. Ibid., p. 32
31. Ibid., p. 16.
32. Ibid., p. 6.
33. Ibid., p. 27.
34. Ibid.
35. Ibid., p. 26.
36. Ibid.
37. Ibid., p. 24.
38. Ibid.
39. Ibid., p. 26.
40. Ibid.
41. Ibid., p. 25.
42. Ibid., p. 25, 27.
43. Ibid., p. 82.
44. Ibid., p. 27.
45. Jacques-Jospeh Moreau, *Hashish and Mental Illness* (New York: Raven Press, 1973), p. xvi.
46. Ibid., p. xix.
47. Ibid., p. 2.
48. Moreau, p. 15. Berridge and Edwards outline the various ways in which addiction was increasingly structured as a cerebral disease. Many of the laws that permitted the incarceration of the first addicts were in fact laws designed to deal with the mentally ill. For example, as Berridge and Edwards point out, "Section 116 of the Lunacy Act had allowed a form of guardianship, too, which was on occasion applied to drug addicts," p. 167.
49. Ibid., p. 17.
50. Ibid.
51. Ibid.
52. Princess Diana, *The Times*, August 18, 1992 [hereafter Diana], p. 1.
53. Ibid., p. 1.
54. Ibid.
55. Ibid.
56. Ibid., p. 2.
57. Ibid.
58. Robert Louis Stevenson, *The Strange Case of Dr Jekyll and Mr. Hyde and Other Stories*, ed. Jenni Calder (Harmondsworth: Penguin, 1983), p. 69 [hereafter *Strange Case*].
59. Berridge and Edwards, pp. 155–156.
60. Diana, p. 2.
61. Ibid.

62. Ibid.
63. This notion is not confined to British royalty. A recent book from Harvard Medical School explores the same ideas in H. T. Blane and T. R. Kosten, eds., *Addiction and the Vulnerable Self: Modified Dynamic Group Therapy for Substance Abusers* (New York: The Guildford Press, 1990).
64. Sedgwick, *Tendencies,* pp. 130–142.
65. Douglas Crimp, ed. *AIDS: Cultural Analysis/ Cultural Criticism* (MA: MIT Press, 1988), p. 10.
66. Susan Sontag, *AIDS and Its Metaphors.* (New York: Farrar, Strauss and Giroux 1989). p. 18.
67. Recent critical readings of *Jekyll and Hyde* by Koestenbaum and Doane and Hodges offer some useful insights into the text, but I would like to look at their arguments as indicators of what can and cannot be said about drugs. Simply by saying that Hyde is the black, the homosexual, or the New Woman stops short of examining the origins of these discourses, or what it is that they must hide to assume control of the text. By eliminating the strangeness from the text and thereby uncovering the origins of Hyde's strangeness, the critics effectively police Hyde's behavior, indirectly fulfilling the surveillance mechanisms of a war on drugs whose function is to make Otherness both visible and quantifiable.
68. Stevenson, *Strange Case* p. 67 and p. 95.
69. Stevenson, *Strange Case* p. 49–50.
70. Stevenson, *Strange Case* p. 68. Eve Sedgwick, in *Tendencies,* argues that "In *The Picture of Dorian Gray* as in, for instance, *Dr. Jekyll and Mr. Hyde,* drug addiction is both a camouflage and an expression for the dynamics of same-sex desire and its prohibition: both books begin by looking like stories of erotic tensions between men, and end up as cautionary tales of solitary substance abusers," p. 172.
71. Stevenson, *Strange Case* p. 78, 40.
72. Ibid., p. 40.
73. Ibid., p. 70.
74. Ibid., p. 35.
75. Ibid., p. 34.
76. Ibid., p. 38.
77. Ibid., p. 72.
78. Ibid., p. 50.
79. Ibid., p. 95.
80. Ibid., p. 80.
81. Ibid., p. 81.
82. Ibid., p. 82.
83. Ibid., p. 56.
84. Ibid., p. 86.
85. Ibid.
86. Ibid., p. 44.
87. Ibid., p. 84.

88. Ibid., p. 83.

89. Stevenson, *Strange Case,* p. 83. In the same way that Blake laughs when he "sees himself," Jekyll/Hyde is accepting of his Other. Turning to Foucault, we see how, in the opening of *The Order of Things,* there is "a laughter that shatters all the familiar landmarks of cultural thought," p. xv. Blake's laugh, like Jekyll's acceptance, is also, I would argue, of this order.

90. Obviously we persist in seeing Hyde as the opposite of this, and the sense that Hyde is an *evil* side of the self persists in mass culture. Elaine Showalter, *Sexual Anarchy: Gender and Culture at the Fin de Siecle* (New York: Viking, 1990), points out that "[o]n the screen, the Jekyll-Hyde story has become the dark side film (*Something Wild, After Hours*), in which an innocent or upright young man meets a *femme fatale* who takes him to the dark side of himself: a violent, sadistic and sexually perverse man." It could be argued that culture has a vested interest in keeping these binaries in place for they provide a ready-made arena through which men and women can be (en)trapped, and drugs can be "understood."

91. Ibid., p. 83

92. Ibid.

93. Vladimir Nabokov, ed., *Robert Louis Stevenson: The Strange Case of Dr. Jekyll and Mr Hyde* (New York: Signet Classic, 1990), p. 10, suggests that "Hyde is Dr. Jekyll's parasite" but the novel reveals that Jekyll is equally parasitical on Hyde.

94. Stevenson, *Strange Case* p. 83.

95. Ibid.

96. Ibid., p. 84. Jekyll may confess that he has a problem, but Hyde never does, as he is too busy enjoying himself to think about confessing: an idea that would, in itself, seem very "strange" to Hyde's mind.

97. Ibid., p. 56.

98. Ibid., p. 85.

99. Ibid., p. 82.

100. Ibid., p. 96.

101. Ibid., p. 58.

102. Ibid., p. 79.

103. Ibid., p. 76.

104. Virginia Woolf, *To the Lighthouse* (London: The Hogarth Press, 1967), p. 21. For an excellent analysis of opium and empire in Woolf, see Jane Lilienfeld, *Reading Alcoholisms: Theorizing Character and Narrative in Selected Novels of Thomas Hardy, James Joyce and Virginia Woolf.* (New York: St. Martin's Press, 1999), p. 207ff.

105. Kim Wozencraft, *Rush* (Ivy Books: New York, 1990), p. 189. Gilles Deleuze and Felix Guattari, *A Thousand Plateaus: Capitalism and Schizophrenia* (Minneapolis: University of Minnesota Press, 1987), p. 285, also refer to the transparent and empty, "glassy body of the addict."

106. *OG,* p. 149.

107. This was a 1997 Partnership for a Drug-Free America slogan.

108. *OG*, p. 144, italics in original.
109. Ibid., p. 145.
110. Stevenson, *Strange Case,* p. 86.
111. Stevenson, *Strange Case,* p. 34.
112. Ibid., p. 62.
113. Ibid., p. 35.
114. *OG*, p. 145.
115. *OG*, p. 149.
116. Stevenson, *Strange Case,* p. 80.
117. *OG*, p. 153.
118. Stevenson, *Strange Case,* p. 80.
119. *OG*, p. 151.
120. The addict, as Derrida point out, produces nothing, withdrawing from the economy. The addict's mode of production as repetition has no use-value. See *Dissemination,* p. 135.
121. All quotations are from Jim Newton, "Smugglers Make Kennels with Cocaine," *Los Angeles Times,* October 28, 1992, A1.
122. *OG*, p. 154.
123. Ibid.
124. Stevenson, *Strange Case,* p. 86; *OG*, p. 155.
125. M. G. Schultz, "The 'Strange Case' of Robert Louis Stevenson" *Journal of the American Medical Association* vol. 216, no.1 (April 5, 1971): 94.
126. William Burroughs, *Naked Lunch* (Grove: New York, 1990), p. xv.

Chapter 3

1. *OG*, p. 142.
2. Sigmund Freud, *Cocaine Papers,* ed. Robert Byck (New York: Stonehill, 1974), p.41 [hereafter *CP*].
3. Schultz, p. 94.
4. *CP*, p. 154.
5. Ibid., p. 92.
6. E. M. Thornton, *The Freudian Fallacy* (Garden City, NY: Dial Press,1983), p. 2.
7. Thornton, p. 253.
8. *CP*, p. 35.
9. *CP*, p. 255.
10. Sigmund Freud, *Three Essays on The Theory of Sexuality* trans. James Strachey (New York: Basic Books, 1975), p. 16.
11. Kaja Silverman, *Male Subjectivity at the Margins* (New York and London: Routledge, 1992), p. 31.
12. Silverman, p. 32.
13. *CP*, p. 16.
14. *CP*, p. 18.
15. *CP*, p. 20.

16. *CP,* p. 21.
17. *CP,* p. 22.
18. *CP,* p. 25–26.
19. *CP,* p. 26.
20. Peter Gay, *The Bourgeois Experience, Victoria to Freud. Vol.1, Education of the Senses* (New York and Oxford: Oxford University Press, 1984), p. 741 [hereafter *The Bourgeois Experience*].
21. Ibid.
22. Ibid.
23. *CP,* p. xvii
24. *CP,* p. 743.
25. *CP,* p. 11.
26. Stevenson, *Strange Case,* p. 86.
27. *CP,* p. 11.
28. *CP,* p. 7.
29. *CP,* p. 10.
30. *CP,* p. 6.
31. Gay, *The Bourgeois Experience,* p. 43.
32. *CP,* pp. 64, 63.
33. *CP,* pp. 6, 40.
34. *CP,* pp. 10, 41.
35. *CP,* pp. 162, 42.
36. *CP,* pp. 99, 104.
37. Ibid., p. 104.
38. *CP,* pp. 67, 73.
39. *CP,* pp. 114–115.
40. *CP,* p. 50.
41. Ibid.
42. Ibid.
43. Ibid.
44. Ibid
45. Ibid.
46. Ibid.
47. Ibid. p. 49.
48. Ibid. p. 52.
49. Ibid. p. 57–58.
50. Ibid. p. 60–62.
51. Ibid. p. 60.
52. Ibid. p. 114.
53. Ibid.
54. Ibid. p. 165.
55. Ibid. p. 165.
56. Ibid. p. 60.
57. Ibid.
58. Ibid. p. 62.
59. Ibid.

60. Ibid.
61. Ibid. p. 63.
62. Ibid. p. 65.
63. Ibid. p. 66.
64. Ibid. p. 65–8.
65. Ibid. p. 68.
66. Ibid.
67. Ibid.
68. Ibid. p. 69.
69. Ibid. p. 70.
70. Ibid. p. 71.
71. Ibid.
72. Ibid. p. 73.
73. Ibid.
74. Ibid.
75. Freud closes *Uber Coca* by suggesting the "anesthetizing effect" of cocaine as a final possible use of the drug (*CP,* p. 73). In "The Dream of the Botanical Monograph" Freud will later castigate himself for not having been "thorough enough to pursue the matter further" (*CP,* p. 225).
76. *CP,* p. 107.
77. Ibid. p. 109.
78. Ibid. p. 171.
79. Ibid. p. 172.
80. Ibid. p. 176.
81. Ibid.
82. Ibid.
83. Ibid.
84. Ibid.
85. Ibid. p. 172.
86. Ibid. p. 173.
87. Ibid.
88. Ibid. p. 173–174.
89. Ibid. p. 174.
90. Ibid.
91. Ibid. p. 175.
92. Ibid. p. 174.
93. The second reason for discounting subcutaneous injections can be located in relation to Fleischl, who was a friend that Freud advised to take cocaine so as to cure him of his morphine addiction. Unfortunately, Fleischl decided, perhaps on Freud's advice, to inject the cocaine, and weakened by his addiction, eventually died in October 1891. Yet as Jones points out: "Years afterwards Freud asserted that he had never intended this, but only oral administration. There is, however, no evidence of any protest on his part at the time, and some months later he was himself advocating subcutaneous injections of large doses for just such cases as Fleischl's." See *CP,* p. 199.
94. *CP,* p. 198.

95. Gay, *The Bourgeois Experience* p. 45.

96. *CP,* p. 343.

97. *CP,* p. 343.

98. *CP,* p. 224. I do not have the space to pursue the relationship between drugs and writing, but I feel that a parallel needs to be explored between the dangerous supplement of the drug and the dangerous supplement of writing. For Derrida, "The "leaf": a significant metaphor, we should note, or rather one taken from the signifier face of things, since the leaf with its recto and verso first appears as a surface and support for writing. But by the same token, doesn't the unity of this leaf, of the system of this difference between signified and signifier, also point to the inseparability of sophistics and philosophy?" See *Dissemination,* p. 112.

99. *CP,* p. 229.

100. Ibid.

101. Ibid. p. 219. For an analysis of the place of trimethylamin in the dream, see Jeffrey Mehlman's "Trimethylamin: Notes on Freud's Specimen Dream" in *diacritics* (Spring 1976): 42–45.

102. *CP,* p. 368.

103. Avital Ronell, *Crack Wars: Literature Addiction Mania* (Lincoln, NE and London: University of Nebraska Press, 1992), pp. 52–53.

104. Gay, pp. 43, 45.

105. Ibid., p. 45.

106. *CP,* p. 7.

107. *CP,* p. 8.

108. Ibid.

109. *CP,* p. xxxiv.

110. Thornton, p. 253, 3.

111. Ibid., p. 3.

112. Ibid., p. 5, 6.

113. Gay, p. 749.

Chapter 4

1. William Burroughs, *Three Novels: The Soft Machine, Nova Express, The Wild Boys* (New York: Grove Press, 1988), p. 502.

2. Jim Parker, "The Junk Equation: Heroin" (Tempe, Arizona: DIN 105, September 1996).

3. William Burroughs, *Junky* (Harmondsworth: Penguin Books, 1987), p. xvi [hereafter *Junky*].

4. The pamphlet also presents us with the endorphin theory of addiction as the truth of why we get addicted. On this theory, Burroughs made the following comments in 1959: "Some of my learned colleagues (nameless assholes) have suggested that junk derives its euphoric effect from direct stimulation of the orgasm center. It seems more probable that junk suspends the whole

cycle of tension, discharge and rent." See William Burroughs, *Naked Lunch* (New York, Grove Press: 1990), p. 33.

5. John Marks, "The Drug Laws: A Case of Collective Psychosis," *Political Notes* no. 82. (London: Libertarian Alliance): 2 www.digiweb.com/igel-dard/LA/political/druglaws.txt

6. William Burroughs, *The Burroughs File* (San Francisco: City Lights Books, 1984), p. 97.

7. *NL*, p. xvi.

8. Burroughs, *Junky*, p. xvi.

9. *NL*, p. 8.

10. *The Burroughs File*, p. 62.

11. William Burroughs, *The Adding Machine: Collected Essays* (London: John Calder, 1985), p. 15 [hereafter *AM*].

12. *NL*, p. xi

13. *The Burroughs File*, p. 62.

14. *AM*, p. 16.

15. *AM*, p. 17.

16. *AM*, p. 18.

17. William Burroughs, *Naked Lunch* (New York: Grove Press, 1990), p. xix. [hereafter *NL*].

18. William Burroughs, *Ah Pook Was Here!* (London: Calder, 1979*)*, p. 25.

19. Barry Miles, *William Burroughs: El Hombre Invisible* (New York: Hyperion, 1993), p. 131.

20. Ibid.

21. Jimmie Reeves and Richard Campbell, *Cracked Coverage: Television News, The Anti-Cocaine Crusade and the Reagan Legacy* (Durham and London: Duke University Press, 1994), p. 63.

22. Scholder, p. 72.

23. Ibid., p. 73.

24. Ibid., p. 74.

25. Artaud, p. 99.

26. Ibid., p. 99, 101.

27. *Junky*, p. 142.

28. *NL*, xvi; Daniel Odier *The Job: Interviews with William Burroughs* (Harmondsworth: Penguin Books, 1989), p. 83.

29. *NL*, p. xviii.

30. William Burroughs, *Three Novels*, p. 208.

31. *NL*, p. xv.

32. Ibid., p. xxi.

33. Ibid.,

34. Ibid., p. 114. ellipses in original.

35. Ibid., p. 21.

36. Ibid., p. 18.

37. Ibid., p. 21.

38. Ibid., p. 84

39. Edward Halsey Foster, *Understanding the Beat*s (Columbia: University of South Carolina Press, 1992), p. 161.

40. Stevenson, *Strange Case* p. 86.

41. *NL*, p. 277.

42. Ibid., p. 124.

43. *NL*, pp. xvi, 152.

44. William Burroughs, *Cities of the Red Night* (New York: Holt, Rhinehart and Winston, 1981), p. 274 [hereafter *Cities*].

45. *NL*, p. 167.

46. *Cities,* p. 274.

47. Ibid., p. 274.

48. Foster, *Understanding the Beat*s, p. 171.

49. Foster, p. 172.

50. *NL*, p. 248.

51. Marek Kohn. *Dope Girls: The Birth of the British Drug Underground* (London: Lawrence and Wishart, 1992), p. 106.

52. Sheila Henderson, *Ecstasy: Case Unsolved* (London: Harper Collins, 1997), p. 65.

53. Ibid., p. 65.

54. Ibid.

55. Ibid.

56. Ibid.

57. Ibid., p. 67.

58. Ibid.

59. Ibid., p. 71.

60. Ibid., p. 72.

61. Ibid.

62. Ibid., p. 71.

63. Ibid., p. 116.

64. Ibid., p. 73.

65. Burroughs, *Ah Pook Was Here!*, p. 24.

66. Ibid.

67. Ibid., p. 25.

68. Ibid.

69. Ibid.

70. Deleuze, Gilles and Guattari, Felix, trans. Brian Massumi. *A Thousand Plateaus: Capitalism and Schizophrenia* (Minneapolis: University of Minnesota Press, 1987), p. 76.

71. *AM*, p. 116.

72. Ibid., p. 117.

73. Ibid.

74. Ibid., p. 14.

75. To this extent Burroughs's "cut-up" method would, quite literally, complete the "surgical" operation begun in *Naked Lunch*.

76. *NL*, p. 65.

77. Burroughs, *Three Novels*, p. 232.

78. *Junky*, p. 133.

79. Fitz Hugh Ludlow, *The Hashish Eater* (San Francisco: Level Press, 1975), p. 68.

80. Ludlow, p. 81.

81. *AM*, p. 123.

82. *NL*, pp. 148–149.

83. *Junky*, p. 7.

84. *NL*, p. 153.

85. Cocteau, p. 36.

86. William Burroughs and Brion Gysin, *The Exterminator* (The Auerhahn Press, 1960), p. 22.

87. Artaud, p. 102.

Chapter 5

1. Scholder and Silverberg, p. 63.

2. Similar analyses regarding female drug addiction can also be found in Cuskey. See also Ellinwood et al., Gerstein and Rovner, Prather and Fidell. Rosenbaum, Williams and Bates, and Mondanaro.

3. Marsha Rosenbaum, *Women on Heroin* (New Brunswick, NJ: Rutgers University Press, 1981), p. 7.

4. Ibid. p. 7.

5. Ibid.

6. Ibid.

7. Ibid., p. 13.

8. Ibid., p. 6.

9. Ibid., p. 11.

10. Ibid., p. 11. Krivanek also describes the process of heroin addiction as a "drift" (85), where the casual user "slips gradually" into addiction (86).

11. Ibid., p. 38.

12. Elizabeth Ettore, *Women and Substance Use* (New Brunswick, NJ: Rutgers University Press, 1992), p. 128.

13. Ibid., p. 131.

14. Ibid., p. 132.

15. Ibid., p. 134.

16. Ibid., p. 135–136.

17. Ibid., p. 138.

18. Slavoj Zizek, *Enjoy your Symptom* (London: Routledge, 1992), p. 133.

19. Zizek, p. 114.

20. Ettore, pp. 140.

21. Ettore, p. 142–143.

22. Ibid., p. 147.

23. Ibid., p. 148.

24. Ibid., p. 155.

25. Ibid., p. 151–152.
26. Ibid., p. 156, my emphasis.
27. Michel Foucault would probably refer to Ettore's narratives surrounding drug addiction as a "reverse discourse." As James Kincaid explains, such a discourse may " . . . [look] like an oppositional discourse, a minority or persecuted group speaking out for itself, but in fact is simply a tactical element operating within the same field of force, in the same vocabulary, using the same categories by which it was once attacked or disqualified." See James R. Kincaid, *Child-Loving: The Erotic Child and Victorian Culture* (New York and London: Routledge, 1992), p. 21.
28. A recent phenomenon is the resistance to DARE by several parent groups who are objecting to the damaging propaganda being conducted in the name of education. See Leslie Stackel, "Programming Fascism: The Drug War on Our Children" *High Times* (June 1994): 18–34.
29. Dava L. Weinstein, ed. *Lesbians and Gay Men: Chemical Dependency Treatment Issues* (New York: Haworth Press, 1992), p. 5.
30. Ibid., p. 5.
31. Ibid., p. 7.
32. Ibid.
33. Ibid., p. 8.
34. Ibid., p. 10.
35. Ibid., p. 12.
36. Ibid., p. 13.
37. Ibid., p. 14.
38. Ibid., p. 14.
39. Ibid., p. 18.
40. Mike Gray, *Drug Crazy* (New York: Random Press, 1998), p. 154.
41. Avril Taylor, *Women Drug Users: An Ethnography of a Female Injecting Community* (Oxford: Clarendon Press, 1993), p. 128.
42. See. for example, James Inciardi, *Women and Crack Cocaine* (New York: Macmillan, 1993).
43. Rosenbaum, p. 76.
44. Gray, p. 154.
45. Ibid., p. 162.
46. Ibid., p. 154.
47. Avril Taylor, *Women Drug Users,* p. 9.
48. Ibid., p. 9.
49. Ibid., p. 9.
50. Ibid., p. 31.
51. Ibid., p. 40.
52. Ibid., p. 45.
53. Ibid.
54. Ibid.
55. See, for example, Chein, I. et al, *Narcotics, Delinquency and Social Policy: The Road to H* (London: Tavistock, 1964), and Cloward, R. and Ohlin, L., *Delinquency and Opportunity* (New York: Free Press, 1960).

56. Avril Taylor, p. 52.
57. Ibid., p. 59.
58. Ibid.
59. Ibid.
60. Ibid., p. 60.
61. Ibid., p. 62.
62. Ibid.
63. Ibid., p. 64.
64. Ibid., p. 65.
65. Ibid., p. 75.
66. Ibid., p. 77.
67. Ibid., pp. 79–80.
68. Ibid., p. 80.
69. Ibid., p. 61.
70. Ibid., p. 84.
71. Ibid., p. 82.
72. Ibid., p. 84.
73. Ibid., pp. 86, 84.
74. Ibid., pp. 85–86.
75. Ibid., p. 93.
76. Ibid., p. 24.
77. Ibid., p. 99.
78. Ibid.
79. Ibid., p. 100.
80. Ibid.
81. Ibid.
82. Ibid., p. 109.
83. Ibid., p. 117.
84. "In the US the situation has reached the point whereby addicted pregnant women are being punished for delivery of controlled substances to a minor: i.e., their own foetus. While nominally based on trafficking and child abuse laws, in essence it punishes women for their status as addicts." See P.A. O'Hare, et al., *The Reduction of Drug-Related Harm* (New York and London: Routledge, 1992), p. 106. In 1962 the California court "struck down a California law that made the mere status of being an addict a crime punishable by a prison sentence." The court pointed out that "We forget the Eighth Amendment if we allow sickness to be made a crime and sick people to be punished for being sick . . ." However: the punishment of pregnant mothers in essence "punish women for their status as addicts." The criminalization of mothers has a negative and not a positive effect on society: it drives mothers away from health care establishments who could help them to have a healthy pregnancy, not toward them. It also "turns caring physicians into medical cops," as well as being "blatantly racist in its application" and "by blaming victims, the government gets itself conveniently off the hook . . . by [p]ointing the finger at "bad mommies," p.106.
85. Ibid., p. 118.

86. Ibid., p. 122.

87. Ibid.

88. Ibid., p. 123

89. Ibid., p. 125. On this point Avril Taylor also suggests J. C. Marsh and D. D. Simpson, "Sex Differences in Opiod Addiction Careers," *American Journal of Drug and Alcohol Abuse* vol. 4, no. 12 (1986): 309–29.

90. O'Hare., p. 126.

91. Ibid., p. 129.

92. Ibid., p. 150.

93. Anna Kavan, *My Madness: The Selected Writings of Anna Kavan,* ed. Brian Aldiss (London: Picador, 1990), p. vii.

94. *My Madness,* p. 171.

95. Ibid., p. 67.

96. Ibid., p. 68.

97. Ibid.

98. Ibid., p. 72.

99. Ibid., p. 166.

100. Ibid., p. 143.

101. Ibid., p. 104.

102. Ibid., p. 115.

103. Ibid., p. 86.

104. Ibid. p. 87.

105. Ibid., p. 115.

106. Ibid., pp. 121, 123–129.

107. Ibid., p. 169.

108. Ibid., p. 194. In Deleuzian terms the house of sleep would be a rhizome: "A haecceity has neither beginning nor end, origin nor destination; it is always in the middle. It is not made of points, only of lines." See Deleuze, *A Thousand Plateaus,* p. 263.

109. Ibid. p. 194.

110. Ibid., p. 194. Kavan utilizes the house of sleep in the same way that Derrida utilizes the undecidable of the pharmakon: "The 'essence' of the pharmakon lies in the way in which having no stable essence, no 'proper' characteristics, it is not, in any sense(metaphysical, physical, chemical, alchemical) of the word, a substance. It keeps itself forever in reserve even though it has no fundamental profundity nor ultimate locality. We will watch it infinitely promise itself and endlessly vanish through concealed doorways that shine like mirrors and open onto a labyrinth. It is also this store of deep background that we are calling the pharmacy." See *Dissemination,* pp. 125–128.

111. *My Madness,* p. 194.

112. Ibid., p. 195.

113. Ibid.

114. Ibid., p. 171.

115. Ibid., p. 195.

116. Ibid., p. 193. In Zizek's discussion of architecture in Kafka he points out how there is always a "surplus of inside in relation to outside." See *The Zizek Reader* ed. by Elizabeth and Edmond Wright (Oxford: Blackwell publishers, 1999), p. 20. For Zizek, this surplus is precisely an "excess" space of fantasy. In Kavan, I think we can see the same desire to gain access to this excess surplus space and bring it into contact with the Symbolic as a way of rewriting and increasing the range of available positions for herself as a drug user.

117. *My Madness,* p. 196.

118. Ibid., p. 197.

119. In 1947, when *Sleep Has His House* was first published in America, the *New York Times* critic Alice Morris (July 20), suggested that "there are difficulties in the book. The swift and lucid character of the prose . . . never entirely dispels the sense of ambiguity of meaning glimpsed and snatched away." The work is thus weakened by being "too often indirect." See Alice Morris, "Anna Kavan" in the *New York Times Book Review,* July 20, 1947. Over 40 years later, Jenny Turner repeats this position when she says that we may find Kavan's work "insubstantial and a bit boring" and that the texts are "strange things, obeying no unities or decorum." See *New Statesman and Society,* April 20, 1990, p. 37. If Morris felt that Kavan's work refuses to dispel "a sense of ambiguity," Vivian Gornick, in "The Great Depression of Anna Kavan" *Village Voice* (XXVI No. 49, December 2—8, 1981): 49–51, 113 indicates that the reader is somehow poisoned by Kavan's text and made sick, as she concludes her analysis of Kavan by asserting that "the art is not healing." By offering us a way out of the drug problem, Kavan's ideas become perceived as strange, and paradoxically, are read as sickening.

120. *My Madness,* pp. 139, 151.

121. Ibid., p. 151.

122. Crowley, p. 158.

123. Ibid., p. 364.

124. *My Madness,* p. 134.

Chapter 6

1. Reeves and Campbell, *Cracked Coverage,* p. 38, and Bertram, Eva, et al., *Drug War Politics: The Price of Denial* (Berkeley: University of California Press, 1996), p. 127.

2. Mike Davis, *City of Quartz: Excavating the Future in Los Angeles* (London and New York: Verso, 1990), p. 268 [hereafter *CQ*].

3. Marek Kohn, *Dope Girls,* p. 10.

4. *CQ,* pp. 284, 286.

5. O'Hare, p. 73.

6. See *The Boston Globe,* December 3, 1995.

7. O'Hare, p. 73.

8. *CQ,* p. 290.

9. Ibid., p. 291.

10. Ibid., p. 292.
11. The British Police recently took this approach in their slogans: "Crack Down On Drugs" and "A crack down on drugs is a crackdown on crime."
12. *CQ*, p. 292.
13. Ibid., p. 292. As Mike Davis notes, Edwards is now a professor of sociology at UC Berkeley and "a highly paid consultant to professional sports," p. 292.
14. Ibid.
15. William H. James and Stephen L. Johnson, *Doin' Drugs: Patterns of African American Addiction* (Austin: University of Texas Press, 1996), p. ix [hereafter *DD*].
16. Ibid., p. ix.
17. Ibid., p. x.
18. Ettore, p. 141.
19. *DD*, p. x.
20. See Stanton Peele, ed., *Visions of Addiction: Major Contemporary Perspectives on Addiction and Alcoholism* (Toronto: Lexington Books, D. C. Heath and Company, 1988).
21. *DD*, p. xi.
22. Ibid., p. xi.
23. The U.S. prison population is close to one million, while "Fifty percent of those prisoners are Black men who constitute only 3 per cent of the country's population." See also Seigel in O'Hare, p. 105.
24. *DD*, p.1.
25. Ibid.
26. Ibid., p. 2.
27. Ibid., p. 10.
28. Ibid., p. 66.
29. Ibid., p. xi.
30. Ibid.
31. Ibid., p. 13.
32. Ibid., p. 67.
33. Ibid., pp. 75, 88.
34. Ibid., p. 111.
35. Ibid., p. 134.
36. Ibid., p. 138.
37. Ibid.
38. Ibid., p. 139.
39. Ibid., p. 140.
40. Ibid., pp. 141, 150.
41. Ibid., p. 106.
42. Michael Gossop, *Living with Drugs* (Cambridge: Cambridge University Press, 1993), p. 170.
43. Ibid., p. 171, 173. The same idea has been put forward in the United States by Richard Stephens, who argues that addicts are really addicted to the fiction of The Addict. My concern with this analysis is that it still depends on

a need to pull away from artifice and fictions, and move toward a "real" and therefore healthy subjectivity.

44. Ibid., p. 172.
45. Ibid., p. 173.
46. Ibid., p. 172.
47. *DD,* p. 106.
48. Ibid.
49. Ibid.
50. Ibid.
51. Ibid., pp. 106–107.
52. Ibid., p. 107.
53. Ibid.
54. Ibid.
55. Ibid.
56. Ibid.
57. Ibid.
58. Ibid.
59. Ibid., p. 147.
60. Ibid.
61. Ibid.
62. Ibid.
63. Ibid., p. 148.
64. Ibid.
65. Ibid., p. 139.
66. Ibid., p. 98.
67. H. Parker; K. Bakx, and R. Newcombe, *Living with Heroin* (Milton Keynes, Open University Press, 1988), p. 18.
68. Ibid., p. 18.
69. Ibid., p. 19.
70. Ray Shell, *Iced* (New York: Penguin, 1993).
71. Shell, p. 270.
72. Ibid., p. 139.
73. Ibid., p. 93.
74. Ibid., p. 156.
75. Mathea Falco, *The Making of a Drug Free America: Programs That Work* (New York: Times Books, 1992), p. ix.
76. Ibid., pp. 5, 6.
77. Ibid., pp. 6, 7.
78. Ibid., p. 13.
79. Ibid., p. 12, my emphasis.
80. Ibid., p. 11, 12.
81. Ibid., p. 12.
82. Ibid., p. 27.
83. Ibid., p. 35.
84. Ibid., p. 32.

85. Ibid., pp. 34–35.
86. Ibid., pp. 35.
87. Ibid.
88. Ibid., p. 36.
89. Ibid.
90. Ibid., p. 37.
91. Ibid.
92. Ibid., p. 39.
93. Ibid., p. 45.
94. Ibid.
95. Ibid., p. 63.
96. Ibid., p. 69.
97. Ibid.
98. Ibid., p. 69.
99. Ibid., p. 65.
100. See Govert Frank Van de Wijingaart, *Competing Perspectives on Drug Use: The Dutch Experience* (Amsterdam: Swets and Zeitlinger, 1991).
101. Ibid., p. 79.
102. Ibid., p. 80.
103. Ibid., p. 86.
104. Ibid.
105. Mike Ashton, *Release: A White Paper Release on Reform of the Drug Laws* (London: Release Publications) vol. 16, no. vii. 1992): 17.
106. Wijingaart, p. 122, my emphasis.
107. Falco, p. 89.
108. Ibid., pp. 76, 89.
109. Ibid., p. 109.
110. *DD,* p. 110.
111. Ibid.
112. Ibid.
113. Ibid.
114. Falco, p. 20.
115. *DD,* p. 117.
116. Ibid., p. 116.
117. *DD,* p. 106–7.
118. *CQ,* p. 267.
119. Youthful undercover cops, in fact, infiltrate high schools, enticing students to sell them drugs. Howarth (ACLU attorney) particularly denounces "the exploitation of peer pressure to create narcotic offenses, in many cases the undercover police (male and female) exploit sexuality and attractiveness. . . . The program is a complete fraud . . . [but is still] a cheap source of the felony arrests that make the Chief look heroic in the media." See *CQ,* p. 287. Thanks to such programs, the figures "reveal" that "juvenile crime in Los Angeles County is increasing at 12 per cent per annually." See *CQ,* p. 287.
120. *CQ,* p. 314.

121. Ibid., p. 314.

122. For more examples of the success of needle exchanges, see chapter 2 of Van de Wijingaart.

123. See David Murray, "Clean Needles May be Bad Medicine," *Wall Street Journal*, April 22, 1998. For a reproduction of the article see *www.junkscience.com/news2/needles.htm*

124. Ibid.

125. See *www.senate.gov/~ashcroft/4–29–98b.htm*

126. Bertram et al, *Drug War Politics,* p. 123.

127. O' Hare, p. 72.

128. Ibid.

129. Jennifer Frey, "In Coming Back, Gooden Comes Clean," *The Washington Post,* May 26, 1996: D6.

130. Friedrich Nietzsche, *Ecce Homo* (London: Penguin Books, 1992), p. 61.

131. Mike Ashton, *Release,* p. 12.

132. Timothy Egan, "A Drug Ran Its Course, Then Hid with Its Users," *New York Times,* September 19, 1999. All references are to pp. 1, 27.

133. Reeves and Campbell, p. 203.

134. Ibid., p. 162.

135. Cocteau, p. 29.

Bibliography

"Abuse of Narcotics." *The Times* January 2, 1880; pp. 6–7.

Adams, J. W. *Psychoanalysis of Drug Dependence: The Understanding and Treatment of a Particular Form of Pathological Narcissism.* New York: Grune and Stratton, 1978.

Akers, Ronald L. "Addiction: The Troublesome Concept." *Journal of Drug Issues* 21: 4 (Fall 1991): 779–92.

Allen, David F., and James F Jekel. *Crack: The Broken Promise.* New York: St. Martin's Press, 1991.

Artaud, Antonin., *Selected Writings.* ed. Susan Sontag. Los Angeles and Berkeley: University of California Press, 1976.

Ashton, Mike. *Release: A White Paper Release on Reform of the Drug Laws.* London: Release Publications. Vol. 16, no. vii, 1992.

Baudelaire, Charles. *Artificial Paradise: On Hashish and Wine as Means of Expanding Individuality* trans. Ellen Fox. New York: Herder and Herder, 1971.

Benjamin, Walter. *Reflections: Essays, Aphorisms, Autobiographical Writings.* trans. Edmund Jephcott. New York: Schocken Books, 1978.

Bennett, William J. et al. *Body Count: Moral Poverty and How to Win America's War against Crime and Drugs.* New York: Simon and Schuster, 1996.

Berridge, V. and Edwards, G. *Opium and the People: Opiate Use in Nineteenth-Century England.* London and New York: Allen Lane/St. Martin's Press, 1981.

Berridge, Virginia. "The Making of the Rolleston Report, 1908–1926." *Journal of Drug Issues* 4: 1 (Winter 1980): 7–28.

Bertram, Eva; Blachman, Morris; Sharpe, Kenneth and Andreas, Peter. *Drug War Politics: The Price of Denial.* Berkeley: University of California Press, 1996.

Berube, Michael. *Public Access: Literary Theory and American Cultural Politics.* London and New York: Verso, 1994.

Blane, H. T. and T. R. Kosten, eds. *Addiction and the Vulnerable Self: Modified Dynamic Group Therapy for Substance Abusers.* New York: The Guildford Press, 1990.

Brennan, Teresa. *The Interpretation of the Flesh: Freud and Femininity.* New York: Routledge, 1992.

Burroughs, William Seward. *Exterminator!* Harmondsworth: Penguin Books, 1979.

———. *Ah Pook was Here!* London: Calder, 1979.

———. *Cities of the Red Night* New York: Holt, Rhinehart and Winston, 1981.

———. *Naked Lunch.* New York: Grove Press, 1990.

———. *Junky*. Harmondsworth: Penguin Books, 1987.

———. *Interzone*. Harmondsworth: Penguin Books, 1987.

———. *Three Novels: The Soft Machine/Nova Express/The Wild Boys*. New York: Grove Press, 1988.

———. *The Burroughs File*. San Francisco: City Lights Books, 1984.

———. *The Adding Machine: Collected Essays*. London: John Calder, 1985.

Burroughs, William and Allen Ginsberg. *The Yage Letters*. San Francisco: City Lights Books, 1975.

Burroughs, William and Brion Gysin. *The Exterminator*. San Francisco The Auerhahn Press, 1960.

Burroughs, William and Brion Gysin. *The Third Mind*. New York: Seaver Books, 1978.

Callard, David. *The Case of Anna Kavan*. London: Peter Owen Publishers, 1992.

Canguilhem, Georges. *The Normal and The Pathological*. New York: Zone Books, 1991.

Chopra, Deepak. *Overcoming Addictions: The Spiritual Solution*. Missouri: Three Rivers Press, 1998.

Clarke, William. M. *The Secret Life of Wilkie Collins*. London: Allison and Busby, 1988.

Clément, Catherine. tr. Nicole Ball. *The Weary Sons of Freud*. London and New York: Verso, 1987.

Cocteau, Jean. *Opium: Journal of a Cure*. Peter Owen: London, 1990.

Collin, Francoise. "Coupes/coupures." In *Le Colloque de Tanger*, ed. Gerard-Georges Lemaire. Paris: Christian Bourgeois, 1976, 63–72.

Collins, Wilkie. *The Moonstone*. London: Penguin, 1992.

Courtwright, David T. *Dark Paradise: Opiate Addiction in America Before 1940*. Cambridge, MA: Harvard University Press, 1982.

Crimp, Douglas. ed. *AIDS: Cultural Analysis / Cultural Criticism*. Cambridge, MA: MIT Press, 1988.

Crosland, Magaret. *Beyond the Lighthouse: English Women Novelists in the Twentieth Century*. New York: Taplinger, 1981.

Crowley, Aleister. *The Diary of a Drug Fiend*. Maine: Samuel Weiser, Inc. 1970.

Csath, Geza. *Opium and Other Tales*. New York: Penguin, 1983.

Cuskey, Walter. "Female Addiction: A Review of the Literature." *Focus on Women* 3: 1 (1982): 3–33.

David-Mènard, Monique. *Hysteria from Freud to Lacan*, tr. Catherine Porter. Ithaca, NY and London: Cornell University Press, 1989.

Davies, Earle. *The Flint and the Flame: The Artistry of Charles Dickens*. Columbia: University of Missouri Press, 1963.

Davis, Mike. *City of Quartz: Excavating the Future in Los Angeles*. London and New York: Verso, 1990.

Davis, Nuel Pharr. *The Life of Wilkie Collins*. Urbana: University of Illinois Press, 1956.

Decker, Hannah S. *Freud, Dora and Vienna, 1900*. New York: The Free Press, 1991.

Deleuze, Gilles, and Felix Guattari. *A Thousand Plateaus: Capitalism and Schizophrenia*. Tr. Brian Massumi. Minneapolis: University of Minnesota Press, 1987.

————. *Kafka: Towards a Minor Literature. Theory and History of Literature.* Vol. 30, trans. Dana Polan Minneapolis: University of Minnesota Press, 1986.

Deleuze, Gilles and Claire Parnet. *Dialogues.* New York: Columbia University Press, 1987.

Dent, John Yerbury. *Anxiety and Its Treatment.* Stratford Press, London: Skeffington, 1955.

Derrida, Jacques. *Dissemination.* Tr. Barbara Johnson, Chicago: University of Chicago Press, 1981.

————. *Of Grammatology.* Trans. Gayatri Spivak. Baltimore and London: Johns Hopkins University Press, 1976.

————. "Rhetorique de la Drogue." *Autrement* 106 (1989): 197–214.

————. "The Rhetoric of Drugs: An Interview." *Differences* 5:1 (Spring 1993): 1–25.

de Wijingaart, Govert Frank Van. *Competing Perspectives on Drug Use: The Dutch Experience.* Amsterdam: Swets and Zeitlinger, 1991.

Doane, Janice and Devon Hodges. "Demonic Disturbances of Sexual Identity: The Strange Case of Dr. Jekyll and Mr./s Hyde." *Novel* 23 (Fall 1989): 63–74.

Dorr, Priscilla Diaz. *Anna Kavan: A Critical Introduction.* Unpublished Dissertation, University of Tulsa, 1988.

Doyle, Arthur Conan. *The Sign of the Four.* London: Penguin, 1987.

Ehrenreich, Barbara, and Deirdre English. *Complaints and Disorders: The Sexual Politics of Sickness.* New York: Feminist Press, 1973.

Ellinwood, E. H., Smith, W. G., and Vaillant, G. E. "Narcotic Addiction in Males and Females: A Comparison." *International Journal of the Addictions* 1 (1966): 33–38.

Ettore, Elizabeth. *Women and Substance Use.* New Brunswick, NJ: Rutgers University Press, 1992.

Falco, Mathea. *The Making of a Drug Free America: Programs That Work.* New York: Times Books, 1992.

Farley, Lisa. *Angel Dust: New Facts about PCP,* Do It Now Foundation, 1999.

Ferguson, Delancy and Marshall Waingrow, eds. *RLS: Stevenson's Letters to Charles Baxter.* London: Kennikat Press, 1973.

Foster, Edward Halsey. *Understanding the Beats.* Columbia: University of South Carolina Press, 1992.

Foucault, Michel. *Foucault/ Blanchot* New York: Zone Books, 1987.

————. *Language, Counter-Memory and Practice: Selected Essays and Interviews.* Ithaca, NY: Cornell University Press, 1980.

————. *The Birth of the Clinic: An Archaeology of Medical Perception.* New York: Vintage Books, Random House, 1975.

————. *The Order of Things: An Archaeology of the Human Sciences.* New York: Vintage Books, Random House, 1973.

————. *The History of Sexuality. Volume One: An Introduction.* New York: Vintage Books, 1978.

Frey, Jennifer. "In Coming Back, Gooden Comes Clean." *The Washington Post,* May 26, 1996: D6.

Freud, Sigmund. *Cocaine Papers.* Ed. Robert Byck. New York: Stonehill, 1974.

———. *Civilization and Its Discontents,* trans. James Strachey. New York: Norton, 1989.

———. ed. James Strachey. *Collected Papers: Volume Five.* New York: Basic Books, 1959.

———. ed. by Anna Freud. *The Origins of Psychoanalysis: Letters to Wilhelm Fleiss, Drafts and Notes: 1887–1902.* New York: Basic Books, 1954.

———. *Three Essays on The Theory of Sexuality.* Trans. James Strachey. New York: Basic Books, 1975.

———. *Standard Edition of the Complete Psychological Works.* London: Hogarth Press, 1962.

———. *Dora: An Analysis of a Case of Hysteria.* Ed. Phillip Reiff. New York: Collier Books, 1963.

———. *An Autobiographical Study.* Trans. James Strachey, London: Hogarth, 1935.

———. "On Narcissism: An Introduction." *The Standard Edition of the Complete Psychological Works of Sigmund Freud.* Tr. J. Strachey. London: Hogarth Press, 1957.

Gay, Peter. *The Bourgeois Experience, Victoria to Freud. Vol. 1, Education of the Senses.* New York and Oxford: Oxford University Press, 1984.

———. *Freud: A Life for Our Time.* New York: Norton, 1988.

Gertsein, D., L. L. Judd, and S. A. Rovner. "Career Dynamics of Female Heroin Addicts." *American Journal of Drug and Alcohol Abuse* 6 (1977): 1–23.

Gever, Martha. "Pictures of Sickness: Stuart Marshall's *Bright Eyes*" in *AIDS: Cultural Analysis/ Cultural Criticism.* Douglas Crimp, ed. Massachusetts: MIT Press, 1988.

Gill, Kerry. "Princess Speaks Up for Addicts." *The Times* (London) August 18, 1992: A1

Ginsberg, Allen. *Collected Poems, 1947–1980.* New York: Harper and Row, 1984.

Gomberg, E. "Historical and Political Perspectives: Women and Drug Use." *Social Issues* 38: 2 (1982): 9–23.

Goodman, Michael Barry. *Contemporary Literary Censorship: The Case History of Burroughs's Naked Lunch.* Metuchen, NJ and London: Scarecrow Press, 1981.

Gornick, Vivian. "The Great Depression of Anna Kavan." *Village Voice* 26: 49 (December 2–8, 1981): 49–51, 113.

Gossop, Michael. *Living with Drugs.* Cambridge: Cambridge University Press, 1993.

Gray, Mike. *Drug Crazy.* New York: Random House, 1998.

Grunberg, Serge. "A la recherche d'un corps": *Langage et silence dans l'oeuvre de William S. Burroughs.* Paris: Editions du Seuil, 1979.

Haley, Bruce. *The Healthy Body and Victorian Culture.* Cambridge, MA: Harvard University Press, 1978.

Hansard: Parliamentary Debates 192, June 15, 1868. col. 1554–56.

Harding, G. "Patterns of Heroin Use: What do we know?" *British Journal of Addiction* 83 (1988): 1247–1254.

Harrison, Brian. *Drink and The Victorians: The Temperance Question in England, 1815–1872.* Pittsburgh, PA: University of Pittsburgh Press, 1971.

Hayter, Alethea. *Opium and The Romantic Imagination: Addiction and Creativity in De Quincey, Coleridge, Baudelaire and Others.* London: Crucible, 1988.

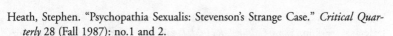

Heath, Stephen. "Psychopathia Sexualis: Stevenson's Strange Case." *Critical Quarterly* 28 (Fall 1987): no.1 and 2.

Henderson, Sheila. *Ecstasy: Case Unsolved.* London: HarperCollins, 1997.

Hennessy, James Pope. *Robert Louis Stevenson.* New York: Simon and Schuster, 1974.

Hollender, Marc H. "Conversion Hysteria: A Post-Freudian Reinterpretation of 19th Century Psychosocial Data." *Archives of General Psychiatry* 26 (1972): 31–34.

Inciardi, James. *Women and Crack Cocaine.* New York: Macmillan, 1993.

James, W. H., and S. L. Johnson. *Doin' Drugs: Patterns of African American Addiction.* Austin: University of Texas Press, 1996.

Jordavana, Ludmilla. *Sexual Visions: Images of Gender in Science and Medicine between the Eighteenth and Twentieth Centuries.* Madison: University of Wisconsin Press, 1989.

Joselit, David. *Infinite Regress: Marcel Duchamp 1910–1941.* Cambridge, MA: MIT Press, 1998.

Kandall, Stephen. *Substance and Shadow: Women and Addiction in the United States.* Cambridge, MA: Harvard University Press, 1996.

Kavan, Anna. *My Madness: The Selected Writings of Anna Kavan,* ed. Brian Aldiss. London: Picador, 1990.

———. *Julia and the Bazooka and Other Stories.* Ed. Rhys Davies. New York: Alfred Knopf, 1975.

Kincaid, James R. *Child-Loving: The Erotic Child and Victorian Culture.* New York and London: Routledge, 1992.

Kofman, Sarah. *The Enigma of Woman: Women in Freud's Writing.* Trans. Catherine Porter, Ithaca and London: Cornell University Press, 1985.

———. *Freud and Fiction.* Tr. Sarah Wykes. Boston: Northeastern University Press, 1991.

Koestenbaum, Wayne. "The Shadow Under the Bed: Dr. Jekyll, Mr. Hyde, and the Labouchere Amendment." *Critical Matrix* 1 (Spring 1988): 31–55.

Kohn, Marek. *Dope Girls: The Birth of the British Drug Underground.* London: Lawrence and Wishart, 1992.

Koller, Karl. "Personal Reminiscences of the First Use of Cocaine as a Local Anasthetic in Eye Surgery." *Anasthesia and Analgesia* (January-February 1928): 10–11.

Krivanek, Jara. *Addictions.* Sydney: Allen and Unwin, 1988.

Lenson, David. *On Drugs.* Minneapolis: University of Minnesota Press, 1995.

Levenstein, Edward. Trans C. Harrer. *Morbid Craving for Morphia* (1878). New York: Arno Press, 1981.

Levine, H. G. "The Discovery of Addiction: Changing Concepts of Habitual Drunkenness in America." *Journal of Studies in Alcohol* 39 (1979): 143–74.

Lilienfeld, Jane, *Reading Alcoholisms: Theorizing Character and Narrative in Selected Novels of Thomas Hardy, James Joyce and Virginia Woolf.* New York: St. Martin's Press, 1999.

Longmate, Norman. *The Waterdrinkers: A History of Temperance.* London: Hamish-Hamilton, 1968.

Lonoff, Sue. *Wilkie Collins and His Victorian Readers: A Study in the Rhetoric of Authorship.* New York: AMS Press, 1982.

Ludlow, Fitz Hugh. *The Hashish Eater.* San Francisco: Level Press, 1975.

Lydenberg, Robin. *Word Cultures: Radical Theory and Practice in William S. Burroughs's Fiction.* Urbana: University of Illinois Press, 1987.

Mackay, Magaret. *The Violent Friend: The Story of Mrs Robert Louis Stevenson.* New York: Doubleday, 1968.

Maixner, Paul. *Robert Louis Stevenson: The Critical Heritage.* London: Routledge and Kegan Paul, 1981.

Marks, John. "The Drug Laws: A Case of Collective Psychosis." *Political Notes* 82. London: Libertarian Alliance. Online: www.digiweb.com/igeldard/LA/political/druglaws.txt

Marsh, K. L., and D. D. Simpson. "Sex Differences in Opioid Addiction Careers." *American Journal of Drug and Alcohol Abuse* 12: 4 (1986): 309–329.

Marx, Karl. *Critique of Hegel's Philosophy of Right.* Trans Annett Jolin and Joseph O'Malley. Cambridge: Cambridge University Press, 1970.

McKenna, Andrew J. *Violence and Difference: Girard, Derrida and Deconstruction.* Chicago: University of Illinois Press, 1992.

Miles, Barry. *Ginsberg: A Biography.* New York: Harper Perennial, 1989.

———. *William Burroughs: El Hombre Invisible.* New York: Hyperion, 1993.

Miller, D. A. *The Novel and the Police.* Berkeley: University of California Press, 1988.

———. "Cage aux folles: Sensation and Gender in Wilkie Collins's *The Woman in White.*" In Elaine Showalter, ed. *Speaking of Gender.* New York: Routledge and Kegan Paul, 1989.

Milligan, Barry. *Pleasures and Pains: Opium and the Orient in Nineteenth-Century British Culture.* Charlottesville and London: University Press of Virginia, 1995.

Mitchell, Juliet. *Psychoanalysis and Feminism: Freud, Reich, Laing and Women.* New York: Vintage, 1974.

Mondanaro, J. *Chemically Dependent Women: Assessment and Treatment.* Lexington, MA: Lexington Books, 1989.

Moreau, Jacques-Joseph. *Hashish and Mental Illness.* New York: Raven Press, 1973.

Morgan, Ted. *Literary Outlaw: The Life and Times of William Burroughs.* New York: Avon Books, 1988.

Morris, Alice. "Anna Kavan" in the *New York Times Book Review,* July 20, 1947: 12.

Mottram, Eric. *William Burroughs: The Algebra of Need.* London: Marion Boyars, 1977.

Murphy, P. N., R. P. Bentall, and R. G. Owens, "The Experience of Opioid Abstinence: The Relevance of Motivation and History." *British Journal of Addiction* 84 (1989): 673–679.

Murray, David. "Clean Needles May be Bad Medicine." *Wall Street Journal,* April 22, 1998. Online: www.junkscience.com/news2/needles.htm.

Nabokov, Vladimir. ed. *Robert Louis Stevenson: The Strange Case of Dr. Jekyll and Mr Hyde* New York: Signet Classic, 1990.

Nadel, Ira Bruce. "Science and *The Moonstone.*" *Dickens Studies Annual: Essays on Victorian Fiction* 11 (1983): 239–59.

Nenadic, Stana. "Illegitimacy, Insanity and Insolvency: Wilkie Collins and the Victorian Nightmares." In Arthur Marwick, ed. *The Arts, Literature, and Society.* London: Routledge and Kegan Paul, 1990, pp.133–62.

Newton, Jim. *The Los Angeles Times,* "Smugglers Makes Kennels with Cocaine." October 28, 1992. A1.

Nietzsche, Friedrich. *A Nietzsche Reader.* trans R. Hollingdale. Harmondsworth: Penguin, 1986.

———. *Thus Spake Zarathustra: A Book for Everyone and For No One.* Trans. R. J. Hollingdale. London: Penguin Books, 1969.

———. *Ecce Homo.* Trans R. Hollingdale. London: Penguin Books, 1992.

Noble, Andrew, ed. *Robert Louis Stevenson.* London: Vision Press, 1983.

Odier, Daniel. *The Job: Interviews with William Burroughs.* Harmondsworth: Penguin Books, 1989.

O'Hare, P. A., R. Newcombe, A. Matthews, E. C. Buning and E. Drucker. *The Reduction of Drug-Related Harm.* New York and London: Routledge, 1992.

O'Neill, Phillip. *Wilkie Collins: Women, Property and Propriety.* Metuchen, NJ: Barnes and Noble Books, 1988.

Osbourne, Lloyd. *An Intimate Portrait of R. L. S.* New York: Charles Scribner and Sons, 1924.

Page, Norman. ed. *Wilkie Collins: The Critical Heritage.* London and Boston: Routledge and Kegan Paul, 1974.

Palmer, Cynthia and Michael Horowitz, eds. *Shaman Woman, Mainline Lady: Women's Writing on the Drug Experience.* New York: Quill, 1982.

Parker, Jim. "The Junk Equation: Heroin." Tempe, Arizona: DIN 105, September 1996.

Parker, H., K. Bakx, and R. Newcombe. *Living with Heroin.* Milton Keynes: Open University Press, 1988.

Parsinnen, Terry M. *Secret Passions, Secret Remedies: Narcotic Drugs in British Society, 1820–1930.* Philadelphia: Institute for the Study of Human Issues, 1983.

Peele, Stanton. ed. *Visions of Addiction: Major Contemporary Perspectives on Addiction and Alcoholism.* Toronto: Lexington Books, D. C. Heath and Company, 1988.

Peters, Catherine. *The King of Inventors: A Life of Wilkie Collins.* London: Secker and Warburg, 1991.

Peters, Dolores. "The British Medical Response to Opiate Addiction in the Nineteenth Century." *Journal of the History of Medicine* 36: 4 (October 1981): 457.

Poog, Jurgen. "A Burroughs Primer." Trans. Regina Weinreich. *Review of Contemporary Fiction* 4: 1 (1984): 135–140.

Prather, J., and L. Fidell. "Drug Use and Abuse among Women: An Overview." *International Journal of the Addictions* 13 (1978): 863–885.

Proust, Marcel. *Remembrance of Things Past.* Trans. Terence Kilmartin. London: Penguin Books, 1983.

Redfield, Marc. ed. "Addictions." *diacritics: a review of contemporary criticism* (Johns Hopkins University) 27: 3 (Fall 1997).

Reeves, Jimmie and Richard Campbell. *Cracked Coverage: Television News, The Anti-Cocaine Crusade and the Reagan Legacy.* Durham, NC and London: Duke University Press, 1994.

Riceour, Paul. *Freud and Philosophy: An Essay in Interpretation.* Trans. Denis Savage. New Haven and London: Yale University Press, 1970.

Robinson, Kenneth. *Wilkie Collins: A Biography.* Westport, CT: Greenwood Press, 1951.

Roe, Sue. "Anna Kavan: My Madness." *Times Literary Supplement,* May 11, 1990, 496 (1).

Ronell, Avital. *Crack Wars: Literature Addiction Mania.* Lincoln, NE and London: University of Nebraska Press, 1992.

Rosenbaum, Marsha. *Women on Heroin.* New Brunswick, NJ: Rutgers University Press, 1981.

Scholder, Amy and Ira Silverberg, eds. *High Risk: An Anthology of Forbidden Writings.* Harmondsworth: Plume Books, Penguin, 1991.

Schultz, M. G. "The 'Strange Case' of Robert Louis Stevenson." *Journal of the American Medical Association* 216: 1 (April 5, 1971): 90–94.

Sedgwick, Eve Kosofsky. *Between Men: English Literature and Male Homosocial Desire.* New York: University of Columbia Press, 1985.

———. *Epistemology of the Closet.* Berkeley: University of California Press, 1990.

———. *Tendencies.* Durham, NC: Duke University Press,1993.

Shell, Ray. *Iced.* New York: Penguin Books, 1993.

Showalter, Elaine. *Sexual Anarchy: Gender and Culture at the Fin de Siecle.* New York: Viking, 1990.

Skerl, Jennie and Robin Lydenberg, eds. *William Burroughs At The Front: Critical Reception, 1959–1989.* Carbondale and Edwardsville: Southern Illinois University Press, 1991.

Silverman, Kaja. *Male Subjectivity at the Margins.* New York and London: Routledge, 1992.

Sontag, Susan. *AIDS and Its Metaphors.* New York: Farrar, Strauss and Giroux, 1989.

Stackel, Leslie. "Programming Fascism: The Drug War on Our Children." *High Times* (June 1994): 18–34.

Stephens. Richard C. *The Street Addict Role: A Theory of Heroin Addiction.* New York: State University of New York Press, 1991.

Stevenson, R. L. *The Strange Case of Dr Jekyll and Mr. Hyde and Other Stories.* Ed. Jenni Calder Harmondsworth: Penguin English Library, 1983.

———. *The Essays of Robert Louis Stevenson.* New York: Coward-McCann, 1950.

Stimson, Gerry, and Edna Oppenheimer. *Heroin Addiction: Treatment and Control in Britain.* London and New York: Tavistock Publications, 1982.

Taylor, Avril. *Women Drug Users: An Ethnography of a Female Injecting Community.* Oxford: Clarendon Press, 1993.

Taylor, Mark C., ed. *Deconstruction in Context: Literature and Philosophy.* Chicago and London: University of Chicago Press, 1986.

Thoms, Peter. *The Windings of the Labyrinth: Quest and Structure in the Major Novels of Wilkie Collins.* Athens: Ohio University Press, 1992.

Thornton, E. M. *The Freudian Fallacy.* Garden City, NY: Dial Press, 1983.

Trocchi, Alexander. *Cain's Book.* New York: Grove Press, 1990.

Tucker, Martin. Review of *Cain's Book* in *New York Herald Tribune Book Reviews.* May 22, 1960: 6.

Turner, Jenny. Review of Anna Kavan: My Madness in *New Statesman and Society* 3: 97 (April 20, 1990): 37.

Tytell, John. *Naked Angels: The Lives and Literature of the Beat Generation*. New York: McGraw-Hill, 1973.

Veeder, William, and Gordon Hirsch, eds. *Dr Jekyll and Mr. Hyde After One Hundred Years*. Chicago and London: University of Chicago Press, 1988.

Waterston, Alisse. *Street Addicts in the Political Economy*. Philadelphia: Temple University Press, 1993.

Webb, Gary. *Dark Alliance: The CIA, The Contras and the Crack Cocaine Explosion*. New York: Seven Stories Press, 1998.

Weinstein, Dava, ed. *Lesbians and Gay Men: Chemical Dependency Treatment Issues*. New York: Haworth Press, 1992.

Welsh, Irvine. *Trainspotting*. London and New York: Norton, 1993.

Williams, J. E. and Bates, W. M. "Some Characteristics of Female Narcotic Addicts." *International Journal of the Addictions* 5 (1970): 245–52.

Winter, William. *Old Friends: Being Literary Recollections of Other Days*. New York: Moffat, Yard, and Company, 1909.

Woodwards, J. and D. Richards, ed. *Health Care and Popular Medicine in Nineteenth Century England: Essays in the Social History of Medicine*. New York: Holmes and Meier, 1977.

Woolf, Virginia. *To The Lighthouse*. London: Hogarth Press, 1967.

Zizek, Slavoj. *Enjoy Your Symptom*. London: Routledge, 1992.

———. *The Zizek Reader*. Ed. Elizabeth Wright and Edmond Wright. Oxford: Blackwell Publishers, 1999.

Index